SEATOLLER
History of a Hamlet
2: Miners, Mountaineers
and Motorists

Steve Uglow

In memory of Edith Jackson (née Kelly) 1911-1982
of 4 New Cottages, Seatoller

*To save something from the time
where we will never be again*
                              (Annie Ernaux)

BOOKCASE

Steve Uglow was born in North Devon. He has taught law in California, London and at Kent Law School in Canterbury, researching and writing on criminal justice. He and his wife, the biographer and historian Jenny Uglow, moved to Borrowdale in 2014. Research into the history of his Seatoller cottage led to a broader interest in the history of the valley, especially the development of local tourism.

Copyright: Steve Uglow
First edition 2024
ISBN 978-1-912181-70-4
Published by Bookcase, 19 Castle St., Carlisle, CA3 8SY
01228 544560   bookscumbria@aol.com
Printed by The Amadeus Press.

Preface

I have lived in Seatoller for ten years. When I arrived in the cottage, Graham, the previous owner, had left a file with old manuals on the working of the Hotpoint washing machine and whom to contact when the TV reception, a cable from a mast on High Doat, went skew-whiff. On the front of the file, it read "Edith's Cottage".

I'd spent some years exploring Uglow family history, accustomed to using online registers and censuses, so 'who was Edith?' was a challenge. She was Edith Alice Kelly, born at Warton with Lindeth, north Lancashire. In 1929, aged eighteen, she married a twenty-year-old quarryman, William Jackson, born in Idaho, USA (a later story). In November 1947 (I was six days old and in a North Devon hospital), William was killed in an accident at the Honister mine. Edith, living in 4 New Cottages, was widowed with four children. This was, thankfully, an uncommon incident at Honister and Edith did not fold under the pressure, helped both by the close quarry community, her neighbours and by the fledgling welfare state reforms being introduced at exactly that time. Her story brought home to me both the difficulties of ordinary working lives and how frequently those lives went unrecorded, especially in the countryside. Historians paint broad brush pictures, but the granular detail of the daily world of individuals is all too often missing.

Perhaps at that point the project of writing a village history was born. I knew that, to an extent, those lives and their land were documented by the church and the state. The Crosthwaite parish registers of births, marriages and deaths meant that families could be traced over centuries. Much can be gleaned from land registers and from the censuses. The wonderful Cumbria Archive Service has the wills of many Seatoller people and from the 19th century, the British Newspaper Archive provided information that gave us more than names and dates of birth. Many stories emerged about the village, the farm, the guesthouse, the miners and their families. But there are few primary sources – Seatoller people did not write diaries nor leave chests of letters.

The story of Seatoller begins with the last Ice Age when a stream of ice from Honister joined the main glacier, forming a shelf, above any flood waters and sheltered from prevailing winds. It has always been cut off from the east, south and west. And the trip north to Keswick even today requires navigation past potholes, floods, the occasional tree or fallen rock. For most of the last millennium, Borrowdale has been a secret valley, originally managed by the church and then by a monarchy, merely interested in what minerals could be extracted. In the seventeenth and eighteenth centuries, landlords, especially for Seatoller, were notable for their absence (but manorial court records are very limited). The families were Cumberland statesmen, independent and proud of it.

This first volume initially explores the early history of Seatoller from the Norse settlers to the Stuarts. Inevitably we know more about the landowners, be they monks or monarchs, than we do about the families who lived in the hamlet and worked the fields. But from the seventeenth century, the families who lived at the farm or in Yew Tree Cottage come more sharply into focus, with key family events recorded by the parish and with wills delineating not just their belongings but also their relationships. The second volume concentrates on the Fishers at Seatoller House and the mining communities.

The families, whether farmers, miners or hotel keepers (or sometimes all three) were intertwined. But there is something exceptional about the valley – as a township, the physical boundaries of the thirteenth century manor remain those of the twenty first century parish council, from Manesty on the west shore of Derwentwater, Lodore on the east, extending through the Jaws to the villages. The shapes of the fields, the routes of the roads have lasted over centuries as have many of the farms and other buildings. There remains a strong sense of identity, especially in the upper valley. The story of the Borrowdale cuckoo (another for later) has a grain of truth. Borrowdale folk remain a race and a law unto themselves.

Steve Uglow
Seatoller
March 2024

Notes appear at the end of each chapter. There are usually self-explanatory but there are two abbreviations which occur regularly:

CRO refers to Cumbria Record Office, officially Cumbria Archives. It is followed by the name of the archive centre (eg Carlisle) and the file reference number. The staff at the centres will always help you navigate the inevitable obscurities and point you in directions that you may not have thought of.

CW refers to the Transactions of the Cumberland and Westmorland Antiquarian and Archaeological Society. These are in three series – CW1 refers to the 19th century series, CW2 refers to the 20th century series and CW3 to the 21st century series. In the true spirit of the world wide web, these are freely available online at cumbriapast.com with a searchable index.

Acknowledgements

First and foremost, this book would not have seen the light of day without the help of my friends and neighbours in Borrowdale, especially Dan and Ruby Simpson at Seatoller Farm, Prentice and others at the Honister Slate Mine, the Beresfords, Brian Kearvell-White. There have been many conversations with valley folk such as Carole Hawley and Billy Bland which have provided both facts and insights into valley life.

Trish and Nigel Jackson, Sarah Bradley and The Lakes Hunts of Seatoller House have been wonderfully helpful, allowing me to poke around the rooms, take away the guest books and ask endless questions. Nigel in particular has found several important documents for me. At Grasmere, Jeff Cowton and Beccy Turner of Wordsworth Trust found a small trove of letters for me. Others, such Richard Stockwell, Douglas Hope, Diana Matthews, Deborah Roberts David Ratledge, Joanne Heather and Harriet Harris, have provided photos and patiently answered queries. The staff at the Cumbria Archive Service in both Carlisle and Whitehaven have been unfailingly helpful.

Nowadays there is a hidden, anonymous army of workers, responsible for digitising newspapers, wills, passenger lists on ships and all manners of public records at the British Newspaper Archive, at Ancestry or FindMyPast. It is unglamorous, unseen and probably poorly rewarded but they have made accessible huge amounts of material that are invaluable to local historians.

The people of Cumberland have a widespread sense of and love for the county's history, whether this is shown through Facebook groups such as Old Keswick, its family history society or, more academically, the Cumberland and Westmorland

Antiquarian and Archaeological Society. Their Transactions Series cover is a wonderful source and in the true spirit of the original world wide web, these are freely available online at cumbriapast.com with a searchable index.

In many places, I have relied on (and owe a debt of gratitude to) researchers and authors who have focused on Keswick and the Borrowdale valley, whether these are Victorian antiquarians such as J Fisher Crosthwaite or more recent writers such as Susan Johnson, Ian Tyler or Phillipa Harrison.

Bookcase of Carlisle and Steve Matthews have an enviable track record in publishing about Cumbrian history and culture. I doubt any other county is so well served. I am delighted now to be part of this.

Finally, I am the luckiest of men as I have a wife who is both an editor and a historian. For years over coffee, Jenny has listened to a latest discovery about Seatoller houses and their people. She invariably had a percipient comment (or several). She then read the entire manuscript. The final product owes everything to her enthusiasm about the project, her professional judgment, and her clear-eyed critique.

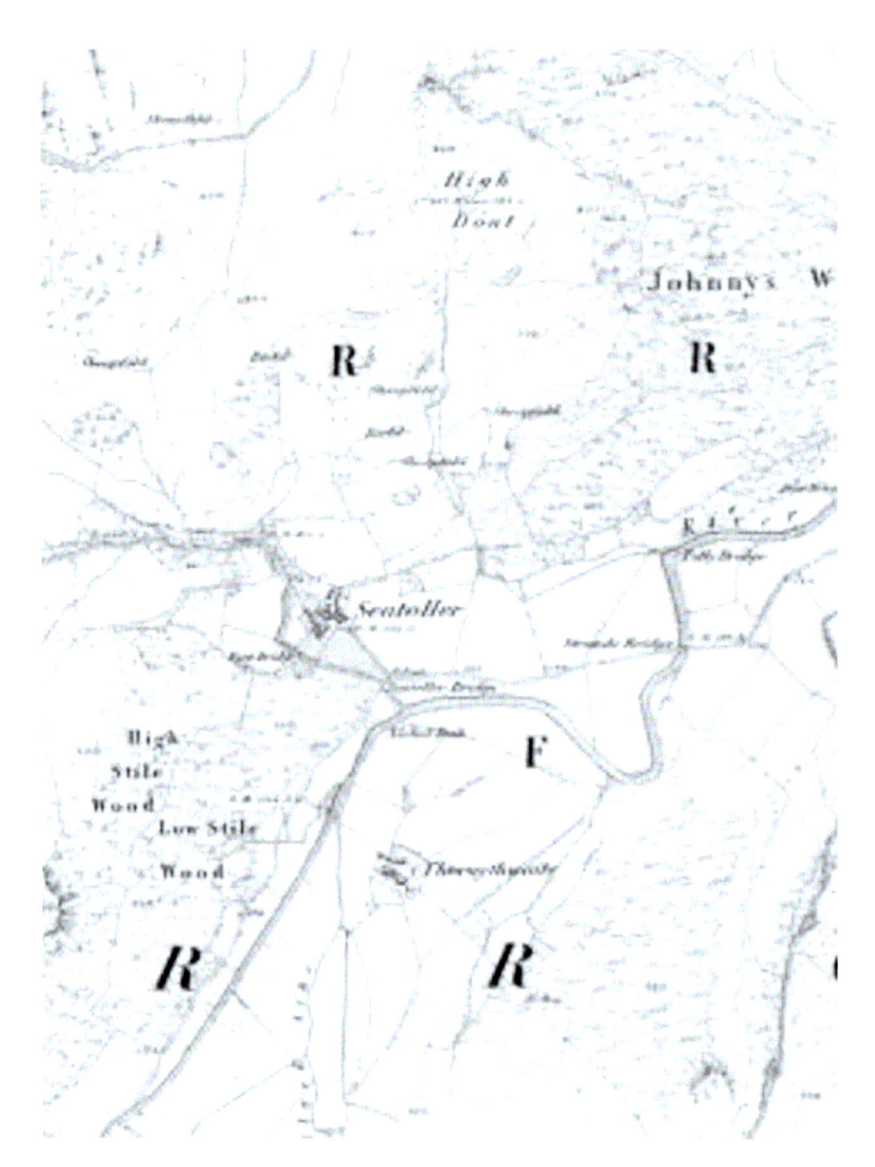

Seatoller as it appears on the First Edition of the 6 inch Ordnance Survey map of 1862-67

Contents

Preface	iii
Acknowledgements	vi
Contents	ix
8: The Fishers and Seatoller House	5
9: Abraham Fisher (1807-1864)	61
10: Seatoller House: The Guest House Owners after Abraham Fisher	101
11: New Cottages and Top Row	181
12: Mountain View and Glaramara	247
Epilogue – Seatoller in modern times	303
Select Bibliography	314
Index	321

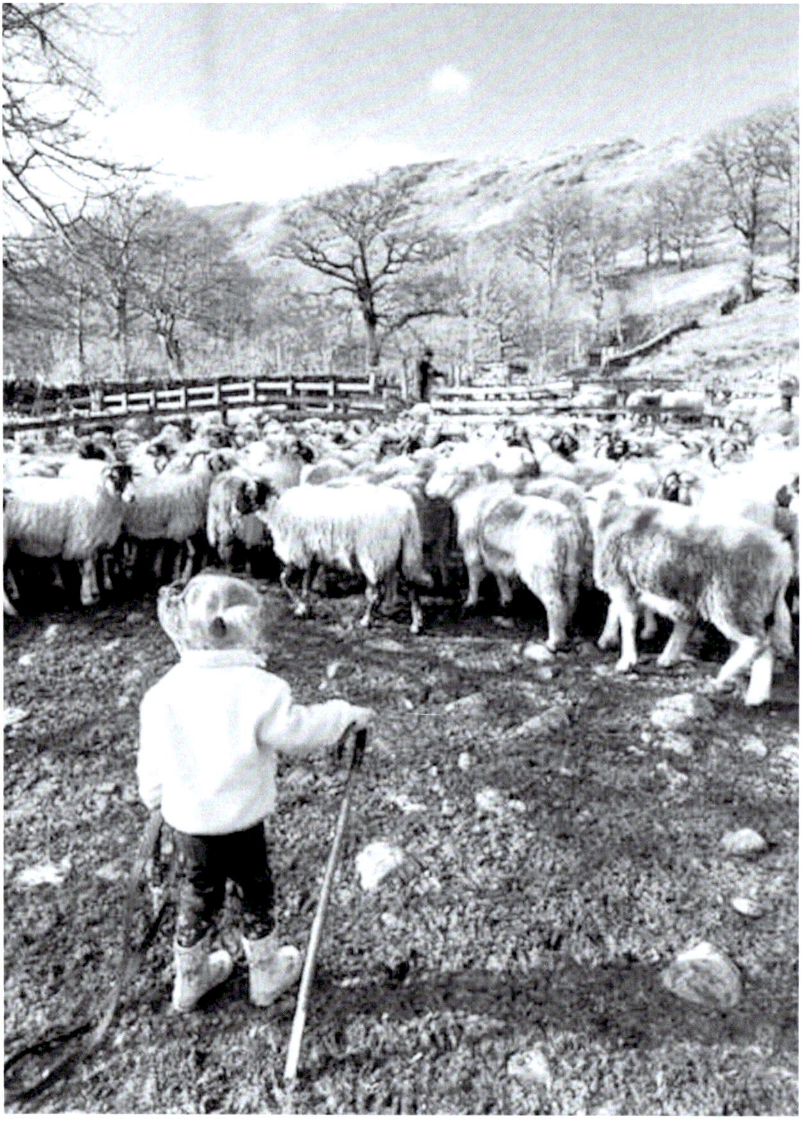

8: The Fishers and Seatoller House

Abraham Fisher died on 20th October 1864 at Seatoller House. He was the last of the Seatoller Fishers,

...one of the oldest families in the county. By far the largest proprietor in Borrowdale and everyone noticed the comfortable looking homestead.[1]

In 1864, the *'comfortable looking homestead'* was two hundred and forty years old, built by Abraham's ancestors in 1624. The house and Little Close, the field immediately below it, covered two acres and nineteen perches on the 1842 Tithe Map. It was a tenement that had been in the possession of the Fisher family since the middle of the 16th century. Establishing which family were the owners in 1624 is inevitably speculative – in the 1590s, there may have been six John Fishers of various ages in Seatoller. Finding a path through the genealogical maze is never likely to produce certainty.

The Fishers were not just in Seatoller but were well-established across the northwest Lakes. One local historian has suggested that the neighbouring upper Newlands valley 'belonged' to the Fishers.[2] The family are also to be found at Grange, Snabb and Gillbank in Newlands, Watendlath and Naddle.[3] The loyalty oath in the 1642 Protestation Return underlines this,

Particularly striking is the pattern in Borrowdale, where the 55 oath-takers included 13 Birketts and 11 Fishers. Most of

the Fishers were in the hamlet of Grange, while the bulk of the Birketts were nearby at Watendlath and further up the valley at Rosthwaite and Seatoller.[4]

The Seatoller story was not just a linear tale of eldest son to eldest son but often involved those collateral branches, especially cousins in Grange and Newlands.

At the start of the 17th century, there were three Fisher families in Seatoller, although the Great Deed in 1614 mentioned just two: John Fisher the younger and Thomas Fisher.

John (1570-1633) and Margaret Walker

In the reign of Elizabeth, Robert Fisher and his wife, Elizabeth, had a son, John. He married young, perhaps just sixteen and over the next twenty-four years, he and Margaret Walker would have ten children, all born in Seatoller. However, at least four died in infancy and there is little trace of the others.

Thomas Fisher (1565-1623) and Margaret Wakthwaite

Another Tudor Fisher was Anthony. He and his wife, Janet, had a son, Thomas. He left the valley to work in Newlands but returned and in 1591 married Margaret Wakthwaite. In 1614, Thomas bought his land from Whitmore and Verdon by the Great Deed. The couple had two children, both born in Seatoller, John in 1593, and Isabel in 1600.

Isabel married a fiddler from St Bees, Roger Dickinson and they settled in Seatoller where they had five children. A fellow musician, John Nicholson, a piper, was living nearby at Thorneythwaite. The fiddle gradually replaced the pipes as instrument of choice but in the Crosthwaite parish registers, a dozen men (either bridegrooms or fathers) were identified as pipers between 1562-1670 whereas Roger Dickinson was the

Fig 1: North Lancashire fiddlers leading the villagers to a celebratory feast after the harvest (18th century)

only fiddler.

One regular job may have been to play at the chapel of ease on Sundays. There would have been no piano or organ and it would have been up to the curate or reader to lead the singing. Later famous Cumbrian fiddlers played in church – William Irwin (1822-1889) was born in Keswick and learned his trade from Gillespie, a North Cumbrian fiddler. He worked in Langdale at the Gunpowder Company but played in Langdale's Holy Trinity Church with two other fiddlers and a cellist. He composed *Mrs Greenup's Reel* for his wife.

Traditional music was strong in Cumberland - *Wat's that, that growes in t'wood, sings in t'toon, An' earns its maister many a croon?* went a Cumbrian riddle. The answer was a fiddle.[5] Whether music constituted a full-time job to feed the family in the 17th century may be questioned – sources are sparse until 200 years later. While some musicians in Cumberland were able to make a living at it, perhaps by teaching music and dancing, that seems unlikely in Borrowdale.

There was no 'big house' or nobility in the valley to

subsidise musicians and yet fiddling and dance was embedded in rural culture (Fig 1). A North Lancashire schoolmaster described it,

They have a merry night as they call it, against which each family of the better sort contributes, some time before, its quota of malt, which is brewed into ale, of which, and a plentiful entertainment provided at the joint expense of the masters of families, the whole village are partakers.
The old people after supper smoak their pipes, and with great pleasure and delight behold the younger spending the evening in singing, dancing etc[6]

In Borrowdale, festivities largely followed the farming year – and taken place in barns, as the chapel was the only communal meeting place: sheep clipping, kurn suppers (harvest festivals), with Christmas Eve to Twelfth Night being the high point of the annual festivities. Dancing was a furious affair for both women and men,

Local poets describe this fury of energy, as at the 'Worton Wedding' where Tamar in her stocking feet banged out 'Wully in his clogs' and again in Mark Lonsdale's 'Th' Upshot' where it is recorded that Tom Little, the dancing master, took the floor, and while dancing a 'famish' jig, gave such a spang that the loft boards broke and he 'stuck a-straddle cocked o' the hallan'.[7]

One engagement was '*hunsupping*' at Christmas from a song '*The King's Hunt is up*' dating from Henry VIII. Musicians went around to every house in the early hours of December 25th, playing the tune for each person in the house, who had to appear at their window to acknowledge the compliment. Perhaps it was at the Christmas shindig at Grange when matters got a little out of hand because ten months later, little Isabel was christened in

Keswick, the daughter of Roger and a Janet Wilkinson.

There were also Shrovetide revels and May Day and weddings. After a clipping, the evening music and dancing comprised an important part of the day's – Dickinson and Nicholson may well have been shearing all day. Broadside ballads such as the Lass of Cumberland would have been popular[8]

> *I am a lass o' th' North Countrey,*
> *And I was born and bred a-whome ;*
> *Many a lad has courted me,*
> *And swore that they to woo me come.*
> *But to bed to me, to bed to me,*
> *The lad that gangs to bed with me,*
> *A jovial plowman must he be,*
> *The lad that comes to bed to me.*

Ballads were handed down orally from generation to generation and published collections of songs were rare. The same might be said of folk dances although John Playford in 1651 produced *The English Dancing Master, or Plaine and Easie rules for the dancing of Country Dances, with the tunes to each*. Some 17th century wills (John Fisher's will in 1671 was an example) mention Bibles and other books and (just maybe) these 'other books' were not religious tracts but *Plaine and Easie rules for dancing*.

Dickinson and Nicholson would have played a mix of older indigenous forms such as jigs, a lively, festive kind of dance involving a lot of time hopping, kicking, and shuffling your feet. In reels, the dancers perform travelling figures alternating with "setting" steps danced in one place. Hornpipes were danced in hard shoes and northern popular tunes were *Dance to thy Daddy* and the *Lads of Alnwick*.

Did the farmers pay them to entertain the workers? Entertainment for the valley folk must have been DIY – travelling groups of actors performing 'jiggs' or 'drolls' (short, comic dramas) had been around since Chaucer but, while there is evidence that there were performances at Keswick in mid-late eighteenth century and at big houses such as Townend, Troutbeck, such groups would have seen the valley as too far, too difficult and not worth the effort! Roger and Isabel lived in Seatoller until the 1640s but then disappear from the record. Isabel's brother, John, also leaves no mark.

John Fisher (1580 –1633) and Elizabeth Hudson
The third family of Fishers in Seatoller was the descendants of William Fisher. This branch endured down the generations and in the early 17th century saw them make an indelible mark on the village when they built Seatoller House. William's son, John (c 1550 - ?1622), spanned the Tudor and Stuart periods. In 1577 he had married Elizabeth Hudson, from neighbouring Thorneythwaite. The couple had eight children, five of whom survived into adulthood. Their eldest daughter, Frances born in 1583, married Anthony Braithwaite, son of a Seatoller resident, William, and they were sold or gifted a Seatoller tenement in 1615.

John and Elizabeth's eldest son was John, born in 1580. In 1614 the Great Deed referred to '*John Fisher the younger*'. This would not be the father, born around 1550, who was undoubtedly senior and, if still alive, would be in his sixties. He may well have left the village as the Great Deed referred to two other John Fishers, one as a tenant at Grange and another at Hollows. Either of these could be John the elder.

In 1614, there were also two other John Fishers in Seatoller. John, born 1570 and the husband of Margaret Walker, was the son of Robert Fisher but, as the son of a Robert, he would not need identifying as 'junior' and his own son, also John, was too young for these transactions. The other John was the son of Thomas Fisher and Margaret Wakthwaite, born in 1693, but again would not need identifying as 'junior' and furthermore was too young.

The likeliest scenario was that it was William and his descendants who had been living on the tenement on which Seatoller House would be built and that it was William's grandson, John, who bought it from Whitmore and Verdon. John had married Elizabeth on 15th July in 1610, possibly the trigger for his father to move to Grange or Hollows. No surname for Elizabeth was given in the parish record but she came from Seathwaite, possibly Elizabeth Dickinson, born 1577, or Elizabeth Birkett, born 1585. Between 1611 and 1630 they had six children. The village must have had a lively feel in the decades leading up to the Commonwealth – as well as Fisher children, there were large families of Birketts, Braithwaites and later, Dickinsons.

Not only does John buy the freehold but within a few years, he starts to rebuild. It was the right time. The old farmhouse was physically a ramshackle affair but there was considerable uncertainty about the security of their tenure. Had John built a new house in 1610, there would have been protracted negotiations with (and payments to) the royal bailiffs. After 1614, John Fisher could build with more assurance as the Great Deed had confirmed his title to the land. That confidence grew after 1625 when the Court of Star Chamber made it clear that the residual rights of the Crown were limited.

Change of Scenery
John set about demolishing a cruck-based longhouse around 1624. What did it replace? Brunskill has described the vernacular buildings of the Lake Counties as ...*rough huts of turf and rubble*

*Fig 2: A 17th century Ravenglass farmhouse
(Lake District National Park)*

Fig 3: A Rosthwaite cottage circa 1768 (Wordsworth Trust). The road leads to Keswick and the slightly darker silhouette of Castle Crag is in the middle distance.

walls with turfed or heather-thatched roofs.[9] Wattle and daubed timber framed houses were restricted to urban settings. However, by the mid-18th century, stone-built houses on two storeys appeared across Cumberland replacing the old longhouses.

Initially the house would have looked rough and ready. At Ravenglass is a 17th century farmhouse (Fig 2) which shows some of its original stone wall underneath the modern rendering. By the door is a place to mount and dismount. The chimney is also ancient.

The modern Ravenglass guttering is in need of repair! Guttering dates back to the Romans, to manage the rainflow and to gather fresh water. While the thatch of the medieval huts jutted out well beyond the walls, taking rainwater away, this was more

Fig 4: Approach to Seatoller with Seatoller House 'well built of stone, the blue slate roofs, and white dashed walls'.

difficult for slate roofs. Some lead was mined in Borrowdale and Newlands and more at Alston in Westmorland but lead guttering was for grander houses. Built-in eaves or box gutters were an alternative but an 18th century print (Fig 3) shows that a small cottage in Rosthwaite did without altogether. Across the county, these new buildings changed the landscape. A 1794 survey of Cumberland farming, while criticising much of Cumberland farming practices, had praise for its architecture,

...the farmhouses are remarkably well built of stone, the blue slate roofs, and white dashed walls, give them a look of neatness, and of comfortable dwellings, that is peculiarly pleasing... The houses, have for the most part, a kitchen and a parlour in front, a toofall,[10] back-kitchen and milk-house

behind, with four or five lodging-rooms above; the front contains five middle-sized sash windows, two below stairs, and three above[11]

Further south in England, the 'Great Rebuilding' had taken place during the seventy years between 1570 and 1640 when improved economic conditions led to thousands of houses being rebuilt. But in the north, these *'remarkably well-built farmhouses'* were more likely to be 18th century in origin. The emergence of these new buildings, reflecting a willingness to invest in land and property, suggests a greater affluence based on the wool trade and an increase in confidence, reflecting a greater sense of security: politically after the bloodless revolution of 1688, legally knowing that the courts will protect tenure and physically with the decrease in border raiding after the union of the crowns in 1603 and the creation of the United Kingdom in 1707.

This makes Seatoller somewhat unusual, as its stone-built houses were perhaps seventy years earlier than similar development elsewhere in the Lakes - Seatoller House, the farm, some farm buildings and the Yew Tree Cottage[12] all date from the early part of the 17th century. The purchase of their land in 1614 gave them a sense of security but that confidence was founded on a written contract – all too easily torn up by self-appointed lords of the manor such as the Isel Lawsons. But in 1625, this sense that they, the tenants, had a right to their land was strengthened when the court of Star Chamber in London upheld the rights of inheritance and alienation for Kendal's (and Cumberland's) customary tenants.[13] The death that year of James I did not end the issue as Charles I raised the matter but in 1639, the judges again ruled '*...the descent of the Crown of England upon your majesty's father did neither alter nor determine the customary estates of inheritance in the counties of Cumberland,*

Northumberland, Durham and Westmorland... '[14] Such definitive rulings encouraged the small valley farmers to see the value of solidarity and co-operation against the aristocracy, to identify as yeomen and to invest in their property and to build.

As these events unfolded in Kendal and London, the Seatoller smallholders contemplated new builds - alongside the Fishers in Seatoller were the Jopsons and the Birketts. Robert Jopson had married Alice Wilson in 1621 and moved from Seathwaite to Seatoller where they had seven children. Robert Birkett was named in the Great Deed and lived at the farm. He had married late to Isabel with children, John born in 1614 and Jane in 1616. John Fisher and his wife Elizabeth had six children between 1611 and 1630.

These three couples, all with young children, were secure in their newly established legal status, free from the constraints of the royal bailiff and with no obvious lord of the manor. There was nobody who would prevent the new builds.

The Tudor Fishers had lived in single-storey medieval longhouses roofed with timbers covered in reeds, bracken, heather or turf. Rocks and stone were plentiful and there may have been low, stone walls to which were attached roof timbers. These would have been crucks: long, generally naturally curved, timber members that leant inwards and formed the ridge of the roof, connected by longitudinal beams (purlins). Dissatisfaction with the comfort and amenities of the average longhouse would have been muted when there was no obvious alternative. But the farmers regularly visited Keswick which, in the late 16th century, had been transformed. The gold rush of Elizabethan England brought the Augsburg miners to Cumberland (and a German son-in-law for William Fisher). It also fuelled a building spree in the town. One example was the old copper store on the site of the Moot Hall – the walls were twenty-four feet high, compatible

Fig 5: External wall to Johnny Wood barn with remains of floor joists (photo Steve Uglow)

with a two-storey building – and it had a stone flagged floor, a prominent chimney stack and fifty-three square feet of glass in the first-floor windows.[15] The farmers would have seen at first-hand what could be achieved and witnessed and learnt from the craft skills that were on display.

There was a plentiful supply of irregular boulders all over the fellside for the external walls of these new valley houses. These walls are now hidden under rendering but in the west end of of Johnny Wood, there is a well-preserved wall, the ruin of a

Fig 6: Corner boulders on Johnny Wood barn (photo Steve Uglow)

bank barn, described by the National Trust as post medieval.[16] Fig 5 show how the walls of these houses were constructed.

When the rendering on the south end of Seatoller House was removed around 2015, it revealed a rough slate/cobblestone wall, with some large boulders, very similar to this. The larger boulders (Fig 6) formed the corners.

The Borrowdale yeomen and the shepherds had spent centuries building and maintaining miles of drystone walling across the valley. As Fig 7 shows, those skills are still in demand

Fig 7: Modern dry-stone walling (photo James Rebanks)

in the 21st century.

The structural strength of an enclosing stone wall meant that the old medieval crucks could be re-used (as was done in Keswick). These crucks were substantial, strong enough to support the heavy roofing slates. They were shortened and raised higher and higher up the walls until they began to resemble conventional roof trusses.[17]

Other farm buildings, byres for housing cattle in winter,

Fig 8: Seatoller Farm barn where the 17th century gable end is clearly visible as are the original corner blocks (photo Steve Uglow)

stables and storage areas were constructed at the same time. The gable end of the Seatoller farm barn (Fig 8) still shows the original 17th century wall, now enclosed in a 19th century enlargement, as well as the large corner boulders.

Fig 9: Slatestone wall   *Fig 10: Cobble wall*

Domestic building was likely to have been more considered and maybe some of the external walls would have used slate. Slatestone walls are characteristic of the heart of the Lake District (Fig 9). The Honister slates are olive green and extremely hard – the modern cheap B&Q electric drill makes little progress. Walls built with this were,

...commonly laid 'watershot', i.e. with a distinct tilt towards the outer face, a technique which certainly helped to direct any water driven into the wall back out of harm's way but which also helped to give a fair face to the wall, the stones splitting naturally at an obtuse angle between bed and face. Slatestone walls often appear to have been laid 'dry' i.e. without mortar or any other bedding, relying on skilful selection of interlocking pieces of stone for stability and plastered inner surfaces to keep out draughts...[18]

The walls were thick with some packing of the interior with small flakes. A variant of the slatestone wall may have had cobbles, small boulders cleared from the fields. Split, they gave extra body to the wall but required a bedding of clay or some other form of mortar. The walls would then be plastered inside and rendered outside with the '*white dash*' providing that traditional Cumberland look.

The roof consisted of heavy roofing slates from local quarries.[19] On the Seatoller buildings, these would have been crude and irregular. They were chipped to give a rounded upper end and pegged to rough laths, laid in diminishing courses with the wider ones towards the eaves and narrower ones at the ridge. The ridge itself would have been slate, cut to give interlocking ears known as '*wrestler slates*'.[20] Using slate rather than thatch also meant that there could also be a change of pitch – instead of 45° of thatched roofs, the slate roof is closer to 30°.

Who were the builders? The Fishers, along with the Birketts and Jopsons, would need to complete the building using their own resources as wallers, masons and carpenters. The Crosthwaite parish registers has an index of trades of the happy fathers and bridegrooms and of those buried. Surprisingly, between 1570-1670, just one person was recorded as a carpenter. There were some smiths but no builders or masons.

The clearest evidence of age of these buildings is from Yew Tree Cottage, now backing onto Seatoller House. This has the date 1628 (but this was put there in the 1990s) above its door. It was the home of Robert Jopson (1594-1657) who lived there with his wife, Alice Wilson and was a substantial, two-storey, detached dwelling similar in size to Seatoller House.[21] The front of Yew Tree has remained remarkably unchanged. Between the two houses

Fig 11: The well in Seatoller House

Fig 12: Sitting Room Cupboard detail

was a well (Fig 11), still visible in Seatoller House's storeroom

There is no conclusive evidence as to when Seatoller House was built but internally the architectural evidence, such as the beams and cupboards in the sitting room (Fig 12) suggests that the building was well-established by the mid 17th century.

Unlike Yew Tree, Seatoller House has undergone many changes. One scenario is that it was originally built as (or soon divided into) two cottages – between the two middle chimneys in photograph (Fig 13). As we shall see, there was a Fisher widow who referred in her will to the land as 'Lowhouses' and to her 'two houses'. In 2015, rendering was removed from the wall under the second chimney from the left. It revealed a rough slate/cobblestone wall, with some large boulders, very similar to 17th century construction and suggesting that the entire middle section was constructed at that date.

The first alteration was when, early in its life, the

Fig 13: Hearth beam, now in Seatoller House office

Fig 14: Seatoller House – the older part of the building is in the middle

Fig 15: Seatoller House front with southern extension baetween the chimneys on the left

house was extended to the north (on the righthand side Fig 14) when the '*hallan*' was incorporated into the house. The '*hallan*' was a cross passage entry which ran behind the original hearth and firehouse. There was a door at each end into the house.[22] The doorway from the present front door into the passage may have been one external door while the threshold-like stone on the outside of the office may have been the other.

At an early stage, the hallan was incorporated into the main body of the house and a bedroom added above it. The hallan became the kitchen with its fire and chimney and is now the office. The hearth beam can be seen there (Fig 13) and outside there is the additional chimney stack. Later the kitchen moved again to the site of the present dining room where the simple stone mantelshelf is typical of the period 1790-1820.

The second major alteration came much later when further rooms added at the south end under the chimney at the far left of the photograph in Fig 15 – dating from around the 1820s.

There was a staircase and large pane sash windows on the ground floor and multi-pane ones of the first floor. When was this done? Grey[23] suggests that these improvements were made by John Fisher after the death of his brother, Isaac, in 1819, and the subsequent inheritance. In the 20th century, after it had become a guesthouse, there were practicalities to be dealt with – extending the kitchen and the dining room with a glazed passageway between these and the sitting rooms. There was also a need for storage rooms, a drying room for walkers' boots and clothing, as well as the installation of hot water and toilets. All have changed the original house.

Seatoller was not the only village undergoing a face-lift. Across Borrowdale, the farmhouses at Longthwaite, Thorneythwaite and High House at Seathwaite also date from that time. High House is now a bunkhouse for the climbing club,

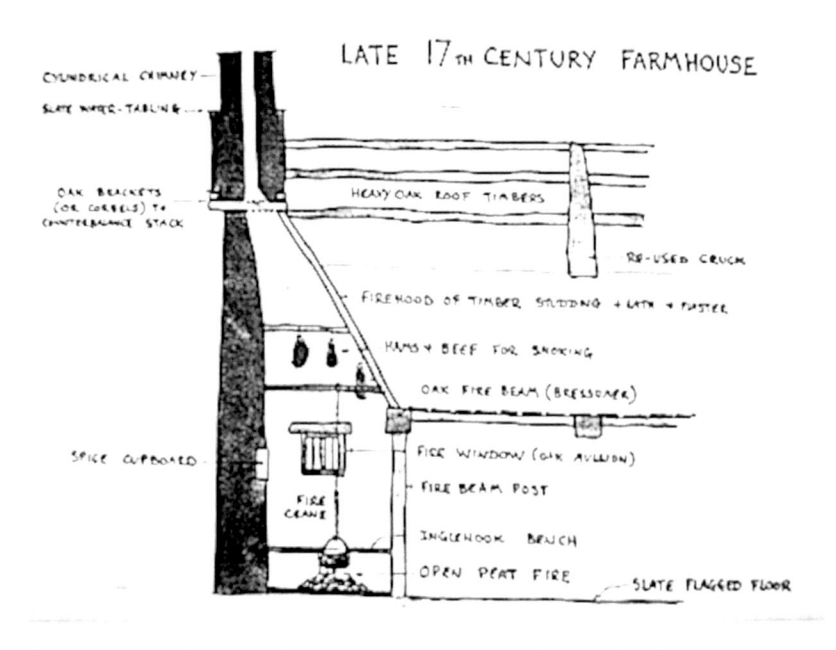

Fig 16: A firehouse - drawn by Andy Lowe, former Built Environment Conservation Advisor with the Lake District NPA

K Fellfarers. Seatoller House started life as a small dwelling house, with just two rooms, like High House.[24]

There was one main room, often known as the firehouse. A typical firehouse (Fig 16[25]) was heated by a hearth or gable fireplace, off which opened another, smaller, room. There was an upper storey or loft. Inside, the ground floor would have had a large living area around the hearth. This was set against a gable wall, forming an inglenook. Above was a hooded chimney, made of studs lined with wattle, clay daub and plaster which led into a stone chimney stack.

This was the only fire and the 'firehouse' was the room where cooking, eating, domestic tasks and daily life took place. At the hearth end of the firehouse was a cross passage or hallan.

Fig 17: A restored 17th century hearth (Diane Matthews)

Entrance into the living room was through this. The fire itself would have been peat, possibly burning continuously, with a smoke hood.

In the modern Seatoller House, there is a massive ceiling beam in front of the main fireplace in the library. The scorching evident on it suggests that this beam may have supported the front of the smoke-hood, forming the inglenook fireplace. The left-hand side of the beam rests on a thicker section of wall, the 'heck' dividing the room from the passage. On the other side, there was a small window in the front wall to give some light to proceedings.[26] The remains of this window can be seen at the back of the cupboard, as can the remains of the original hearth wall. There was also a small recess storing salt or other spices which is still visible.

The hearths of these 17th century farmhouses were fuelled by peat. Each one of the families who bought their tenement in 1614 had the right of turbary, to dig peat from common land. This right passed to their heirs or to those who bought the land.

Common of turbary (the right to dig peat for fuel on the manorial waste) was ubiquitous in Lakeland manors and was controlled by the manor court. In the 17th and 18th centuries the courts attempted to conserve supplies of peat by insisting that peat could only be used in houses in the manor where it was dug; by restricting the amount of peat each commoner could dig to a limited number of "dayworks" each year; and by fixing a date between late April and late May (often 1st May) before which peat-cutting was illegal. The usual calendar for obtaining peat in Cumbria involved peat-cutting in May, after which the peats were stacked to dry on the moss until they were brought into the farmstead after hay-making in July.

Where would the farmers in Seatoller have got their peat?

A hint of the activity is also provided by the place-name of Peat Howe next to Longthwaite Farm. Further evidence exists as linear scars in the ground, which have been identified on Seathwaite Common and on the high ground overlooking Honister Pass to the north. After being dug up the peat was piled onto wooden sledges and taken down the fellside by horse, or more frequently, by a single man pulling and guiding its descent. ... The tracks down the fellside created by this operation exhibit a distinctive zig-zag pattern that can still clearly be seen today. Further evidence of this activity is represented by the discovery of a peat hut ... Such huts were used for the storing and drying of cut peat and were usually located on the fellside about halfway between the peat cutting areas and the settlements[27]

A peat cutting hut has been identified at Lingy End at Stonethwaite. There were peat bogs at Watendlath and Armboth Fell and scars left by peat cutting can be seen in Langstrath, Dock Tarn, Stonethwaite and south of Launchy Tarn between Sea-toller and Newlands. A century later, Hutchinson would suggest,

> *The procuring of fuel is among their greatest hardships. In most parts of the world this article is sought, either in pits, or on the surface of the earth. Here the inhabitants are obliged to procure it from the tops of mountains, which abounding with mossy grounds...*[28]

***

At the other side of the firehouse was a screen which separated the room from a pantry and a parlour. The latter was the bedroom for the owners - the bed was constructed with a wooden frame, with supports made of rope or leather. The mattresses were typically filled with straw or down, held together by cheap fabric. The ropes needed to be tightened on a regular basis due to the sagging of the mattress. These two ground floor rooms probably represent the initial size of the house. They would have windows, initially without glass but with oiled paper – although glass was used in Keswick in 1570.[29]

The rooms upstairs were reached by a wooden ladder. These were lofts, used for storage and sleeping areas for children and servants. Over the course of time, side walls were built and the loft would be divided into separate bedrooms. From around 1700, the ladder was replaced by a curved or dogleg staircase (Fig 18).

In the 20th century, after it had become a guesthouse, there were practicalities to be dealt with – extending the kitchen and the dining room with a glazed passageway between these and the sitting rooms. There was also a need for storage rooms, a drying room for walkers' boots and clothing, as well as the installation of hot water and toilets. All have changed the original house.

John Fisher (1611-1671) and Elizabeth Langstrath (1616-1695)
This John was the son of John Fisher the younger, named in the Great Deed. Elizabeth was the youngest child of John Langstrath and Agnes née Wilson of Watendlath and she had four older brothers. The marriage was in November 1639. These early Fishers were not rich. On his death in 1671, John's inventory (Fig 19) itemises some brass and pewter, pots and pans, wooden vessels, chests, tables, bed frames and the like. There were no luxury items, unless one counts the bible and other books. But did he read them? He could not write and made his mark at the bottom of his will alongside a seal. The inventory showed property worth some £73 but John's debts amounted to some £37. His net worth amounted to some £6000 in 2023 prices.

Similarly, when John's widow, Elizabeth, died in 1695, the only chattels she mentions were the cupboard fixed to the wall, the table in her dwelling house and the great brass pot. These wills reinforce the feeling that life in Seatoller House in the 17th century was a spartan affair. There were solid stone walls and a warm, well-stocked

Fig 18: A dog-leg staircase in a 17th century Ravenglass farmhouse (Lake District National Park)

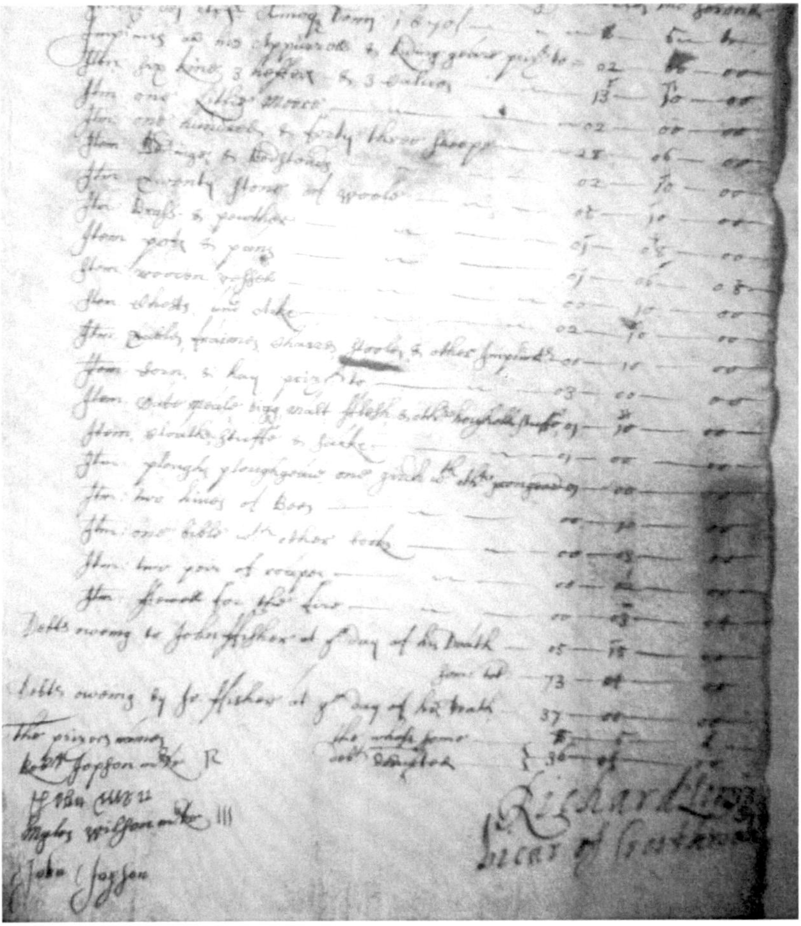

Fig 19: Inventory for John Fisher (1611-1671)

kitchen, if a little smoky. But the chairs were wooden, the walls bare and the bed hard. Social life revolved around the church and the seasonal festivities.

John and Elizabeth had a single child, also Elizabeth. Her mother left 5s to her, a paltry amount but this child was not even

31

mentioned by her father in his will in 1671. Elizabeth junior would have been well into middle age by the time of her mother's death. Why did she not inherit?

One notable aspect of the Tudor and Stuart Seatoller wills is that none of them mention the land and the houses. Instead, the early wills all focus on chattels and livestock. The title to the land passed silently to the heir. Seatoller House would have been inherited by the eldest son but there were no sons. In this case, in Cumberland, the eldest daughter inherited[30] and so should have Elizabeth junior. One possibility was that she had married a widower, Richard Hynde of Manesty in 1686 and moved away – their young son, John, died in infancy in 1688. But that would have no impact on Elizabeth's rights and there was no sign of any Hynde family in Seatoller. Another possibility was that Elizabeth was in some way disabled and did not have the capacity to own land or run a farm. However, her mother made no provision for her care in her will, although Elizabeth's will revealed a strong family network of Langstraths, Wilsons and Fishers. Taking care of Elizabeth would take care of itself.

The next matriarch to live in Seatoller House would be very specific in her will as to who got which house!

John Fisher (1679-1722) and Sarah Bank (?1685-1738)

As John Fisher and Elizabeth née Langstrath had no heirs, the house descended to the heirs of Henry Fisher from Stonethwaite. Henry was the brother of John and, like him, born in Seatoller. He had married Eleanor Youdale and moved to Stonethwaite, the stronghold of the Youdale family. Henry had died as had his son, John, but Henry's grandson, another John (1679-1722), inherited the house in 1695 when his aunt died, although he was only sixteen.

John lived in Seatoller from at least 1706. Whereas old John

Fig 20: The brideswain

Fisher was established church, Henry's branch of the family were dissenters. St Andrew's had been consecrated in 1687 but in 1706, John petitioned that his house be registered as place of worship under the Toleration Act 1689. Their minister was William Archer.[31] Despite this, John and his wife Sarah Bank had married by Anglican rites in Crosthwaite church on 15th March 1706 (1705 in old money[32]). This compromise made it more likely that he leaned towards the Presbyterian or Congregationalist.

Their marriage is commemorated in the library in Seatoller House where the initials JSF and the date 1705 are carved on the old partition cupboard. A piece of fitted furniture such as this was traditionally made for newlyweds, known as a brides-wain (Fig 20 - so called because it followed the bride in a wain or cart from the church to the house).

Sarah Bank was probably the daughter of Thomas and Ann Bank from Grange. Although there were no Crosthwaite baptisms recorded for John and Sarah, they had four children. In 1722, John was killed when the wooden bridge he was on collapsed.[33] There was no will and Sarah had to apply for letters of administration for John's estate at the bishop's court in Carlisle. In this application, she named Mary, Sarah, Hannah and Joseph as the lawful children of John and herself.

John was forty-three years old at his death. The family was well-off – were Henry's Stonethwaite family wealthier than the Seatoller Fishers? The inventory of his goods (excluding the land) had a total value of £369, ten times that of his great-uncle on his death fifty years earlier. That affluence was founded on the wool trade. The inventory showed that he was a considerable farmer with a flock of more than three hundred sheep, plus cattle and a mare. There was hay and corn and a good quantity of wool. The house was well-furnished with chests, arks, tables, cupboards, boards and chairs. And £2 5s worth of books suggests a small library and literacy.

Clearly, life had become more comfortable. The brideswain cupboard suggests that the house was no longer a simple firehouse, with crude partitions, simple furniture and a ladder leading to an upper floor. Instead, rooms have been furnished with some oak panelling to keep out drafts, some chairs had replaced stools and became far more comfortable. Upholstered (padded and covered) chairs were found in wealthy people's homes. In the mid-17th century chests of drawers became common. Grandfather clocks also became popular. Later in the century, the bookcase was introduced. There were more comfortable beds. Maybe there was glass in the windows and some carpeting on the floor, supplementing the rush mats.

They could also afford domestic help. The servants appear briefly on the parish records but leave no wills but there were young women such as Jane Wilson, in 1732, perhaps her sister Sarah Wilson in 1733 and Bridget Tubman in 1739, all of whom were living in Seatoller when they married.

After John's death, Sarah continued to live at the house with her four children and when she died, her will treated the land, house and all the chattels as her own. Although customary land would normally go according to the rules of primogeniture, with personal property, widows of intestate men enjoyed equivalent benefits as widows of men who had made wills.[34] In 1722, Joseph, the youngest child and only son, was still a baby. If a court had been asked, she was merely a trustee for Joseph and the other children. There were also three girls - the two younger girls, Hannah and Sarah, would marry and move away. Mary was the oldest. She too would marry – yet another John Fisher, this time from the Newlands valley – but moved back to Seatoller by the time of the death of her mother.[35]

Joseph (1721-1744)

Joseph was seventeen when his mother, Sarah died in 1738.[36] Her will treated the land, house and all the chattels as her own. She was helpfully specific and left Joseph the *'messuages,*[37] *houses and freehold estates called and known by the name of Lowhouses in Seatoller...'*. Naming it Lowhouses suggests that it was a single block. Perhaps the *'low'* distinguishes it from Yew Tree Cottage which was wholly separate and is a little higher up the hill. Later in her will, she talks of *'both'* of her houses. This is some evidence that the house was divided into two separate cottages.

Along with the house, Joseph inherited all the household goods that were '*nailfast*' or permanently attached (but including some specified chests and tables). There was also the flock of '*heafgoing*' sheep. Joseph had to pay his sister Hannah, £100 and his sister, Sarah, £30, when he became 21. Sarah was by then the wife of Joseph Harris in Grange. Hannah would marry John Bank in Grange a few years after her mother died.

Joseph himself died young in 1744 aged twenty-three.[38] His sister, now Hannah Banks of Riggside, received £200 of '*lawful money of Great Britain*' and her husband, John, a watch – clearly the family finances were still in a healthy state. His other sister, Sarah Harris, had died in childbirth in 1742 – the baby, also Sarah, died five months later. Her only surviving child, Joseph Harris, was left £30 when he reached twenty-one and his father £1.

The charitable side of the Fishers emerged with the poor of Borrowdale each being given 6d – with the population of the valley being just a few hundred, even if twenty per cent were treated as poor, this would be small change. £10 would cover 240 poor residents. More instrumentally, 3d was to be given to those indigents who turned up at the church for his funeral.

The bulk of his property was the two messuages bequeathed to him to by his mother. These were left to his loving sister, Mary, who also acted as executrix.

Mary Fisher (1707-1772) and John Fisher (1714 –1771): When John Fisher fell off the bridge in 1722, his only son, Joseph, was a baby. His oldest child, Mary, was in her teens. Mother Sarah, with four small children, was unlikely to have taken on the management of the farm and livestock, perhaps calling on help from the Grange side of the Fisher clan. Some evidence for this is that, nine years after John's death, his eldest daughter, Mary, married a cousin, John Fisher, from Grange on

23rd December 1731. Where did the newlyweds, mother Sarah and brother Joseph live? Babies soon arrived and perhaps Joseph and his mother lived in the northern, slightly larger, cottage and Mary and John in the adjoining cottage to the south. Or, of course, vice versa...

Mary's mother, Sarah, died in 1738[39] and made Mary, now in her thirties, the executrix of her estate as her brother Joseph was still in his teens. Mary also inherited all the wool lying in the two cottages, although five stones of wool were reserved for Hannah. All the ready cash and outstanding bills and bonds also went to Mary, although she had to find £40 for her sister, Sarah Harris. Hannah and Mary shared the movables that were not nailed down and took half the books.

Mary and John took responsibility for running the farm, even after Joseph turned twenty-one, as his early death suggested that he was not robust. In 1746 there is an account book of a Robert Grave in which Grave notes down a conversation between John Fisher and Thomas Wren (- 1750) of Seatoller Farm. The pair were in a dispute over some issue regarding Johnny Wood between Seatoller and Rosthwaite, perhaps grazing rights for livestock or gathering wood?[40]

After 1744, did Mary and John now turn the cottages back into a single unit? That would have been a sensible move as, over two decades, the couple had nine children: Sarah 1732, John 1736, Dinah 1737 (died in infancy), Joseph 1738 (died in infancy), Joseph 1739, Timothy 1742, Caleb 1744, Joshua 1746 and possibly Mary 1758 (died in infancy). The parish register records that they were all born in Seatoller.

Mary and John eventually moved back to Grange where Mary's sister, Hannah Banks, lived at Riggside. It was also the home of John's sister, Rebecca Banks. Mary and John both died in Grange, John in December 1771 and Mary just three weeks

37

later in January. Their marriage had meant that this branch of the Fishers had substantial landholdings in Grange and in Seatoller. The bequests in John's will suggest that just three of their children had survived. The eldest, Sarah, had married Chapel farmer, John Jopson, and was given a legacy of £100. John split the land between his two surviving sons.

John made his wife, Mary, his executrix and residuary legatee. He left his houses and lands in Grange, as well as his flock of sheep, to son Caleb (1744-1820). In his twenties, Caleb had been an assistant agent at the Seathwaite Wad mine[41] but in 1769 Thomas Gray described him as that *"hospitable young farmer"*.[42] He would serve as Crosthwaite churchwarden in 1784 but perhaps he was quite jovial - a century later, John Fisher Crosthwaite talked of Caleb '*of facetious memory*'.

Joseph, Caleb's elder brother, was living at Seatoller but was not mentioned in John's will. The Seatoller land was, of course, their mother Mary's property. But John made small bequests of 10s to three of Joseph's children, Timothy, Joseph and Dinah.

When Mary died so soon after John and intestate, it was Caleb that picked up the pieces. Brother Joseph died eighteen months later – perhaps he was already in ill-health? Caleb travelled by himself to Carlisle in September 1772 in order to be appointed administrator of his mother's estate.

Joseph (1739-1774) and Mary Fisher (1737-1823)
On 13th January 1759 in Crosthwaite church, Joseph married Mary Fisher, the daughter of Joseph and Sarah from Low Snab in Newlands. Her brothers, Stephen and John, were witnesses.[43] When did the couple move into Seatoller House? This was probably soon after the wedding as Joseph's parents, John and Mary, moved to Grange and appear well-settled there by the time of their death in 1771. Joseph and Mary had five children, John

1759, Timothy 1761, Joseph 1764, Dinah 1770 and Isaac 1772.

Farming was no longer just subsistence and the Fisher fortunes had been founded on sheep. Wool was no longer just for domestic use but was supplied to the Keswick looms. By the middle of the 18th century, there was plenty of other commercial activity. There were the packhorse routes through Stonethwaite to Langdale or from Sty Head to Wasdale and the coast. And everywhere around Borrowdale, there were mines and quarries – at Newlands and Dalehead, at the Seathwaite wad mine and the slate mine at Honister. There must have been some disruption to life from the wagon traffic to and from Seathwaite although Honister was less of a problem as the slates were taken through Buttermere. Seathwaite had the added problem of robbers who scavenged for wad on the hillside or made frontal assaults on the mine itself.[44] Tyler suggests that there was an upside: this injection of small-scale industry and the consequent rise in population led to the farming community using fields for arable to supply the thriving villages of Rosthwaite and Stonethwaite.[45]

The wad mine raised other issues. For decades, the freeholders on Seatoller Common had felt that their rights in the mining activities had been ignored. In December 1769, there was a meeting in Keswick of freeholders with the mine company run by John Bankes (1692-1772). Joseph Fisher and John Braithwaite of Seatoller attended. Things moved slowly but by 1775, the threat of litigation led the Bankes' lawyer to suggest that the freeholders sell their rights to Bankes. It appears that this happened and that the '...*local people felt that they had finally got some kind of compensation for the years of trespass*'.[46]

Joseph died in his thirties in 1774 when the children were still young. His eldest son, John, inherited the land and his stock of sheep, with the provision that it would go to Timothy, were John to die before reaching twenty-one. This was a sensible

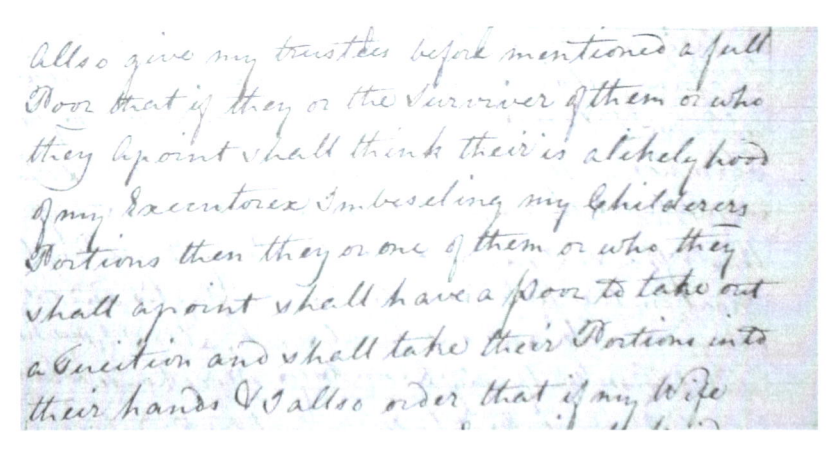

Fig 21: Excerpt from Joseph Fisher's will (1774) suggesting that Mary might embezzle the children's portions.

condition, as several Seatoller House yeomen had died young or childless. All the other children would all receive £150, either from John or from the executrix, when they reached twenty.[47]

Mary was appointed executrix but Joseph's relationship with his wife seems fraught. She could choose any house for her own except the *'one we now live in'*, presumably Seatoller House which would go to John. Mary should act with advice from Samuel Norman from Buttermere and from Joseph's brother, Caleb, from Grange. These were to act as trustees in the children's interests. One intriguing passage (Fig 21) talked of a likelihood of the executrix embezzling (*imbeciling*) the children's portions and the need for Caleb and Samuel to step in.

Furthermore, while Mary was to have the income from his real and personal estate until the children were of age, if she were to marry again, then no sheep were to be drawn from the flock without Samuel and Caleb's consent. There was a certain lack of trust.

And in 1778 Mary did marry again, this time to John Birkett, a Rosthwaite yeoman. She died in 1823 aged eighty-six and, in her will, she named all her children – including Mary Wilson (née Birkett) from her second marriage. Mary had married a Rosthwaite farmer, John Wilson and their youngest daughter, Sarah Wilson, would marry Thomas Simpson, who built Hazel Bank.[48]

Mary's will had an 'everything must go' quality. Mary Wilson inherited a substantial proportion of her mother's movables: the corner cupboard, the clock, the large Bible, the feather bed bedstead, hangings, the square table, teaspoons etc. However, her mother did not mention any of her Wilson grandchildren, except granddaughter, Betty, who got a three footed table, a tin oven and the mortar and pestle. John Wilson was named as an executor alongside his wife. Mary was also the residual legatee along with her half-siblings, sister Dinah and brother, Isaac. However, Isaac had died four years previously and so the bequest to him of the best wainscot and a chest must have gone back into the pot.

The oldest son, John (1759-1835), had already inherited Seatoller House and received a closet, a bedstead, two grates and crooks, wood, peat and a prayer book. His wife, Agnes, was left one of Mary's gowns. Granddaughter Mary had the china cups and tea pot. Young John got the large tea box.

Of the other Fisher children, Timothy (1761 -) and Joseph (1764 -) had both married and both had left the valley (Timothy was a Glasgow manufacturer) but both died before their mother. Their children were left £5 each.

At the time of her death, Mary was living with her youngest daughter Dinah and her children, Daniel and Grace. Dinah, had married Joseph Gibson (- 1810) at Powter Howe, Thornthwaite. They had four daughters and a son but over two weeks in March 1807, three of Dinah's daughters died. Just Daniel and Grace

41

survived. Dinah received a chest, a carpet and some milk cattle while Grace was given a small chest of drawers and the silver tea tongs.

Although named as an executor, Mary's son, Isaac (1772-1819), had died four years earlier. He was an important figure in the history of Borrowdale and Seatoller House. Christened at St Kentigern's church in Crosthwaite parish on 2nd December 1772, he was the youngest of Joseph and Mary's five children. Isaac was only two years old when his father died in his thirties in 1774. Isaac would receive £150 when he reached twenty but in 1786, when he was just fourteen, he was apprenticed to a silversmith in London in 1786. The connections by which this came about are a mystery, but Kent's directory shows that in 1807, Isaac Fisher was a goldsmith and jeweller based in Cockspur Street, in the parish of St Martin in the Fields, London and that was his base until his death. He became very successful as a gold and silversmith, probably having served his time with an established craftsman and then setting up on his own, from c.1793. He does not appear in the Goldsmiths' Library records as an apprentice and his maker's mark does not appear in the registers.

Isaac went into partnership with William Jones and Frank Braithwaite. Frank (1784 - 1862) was the son of John who farmed at Birkett Mire in St John's in the Vale. Frank was also apprenticed at fourteen to the goldsmith, Thomas Parker. Their trade card was engraved with the royal arms and a gothic pinnacle. Braithwaite and Jones continued trading after Isaac's death with John Fisher as a sleeping partner – the partnership was eventually dissolved in 1829.[49]

Isaac became rich. It seems unlikely that he made his money solely as a retailing goldsmith – his partner, Frank Braithwaite, left just a small estate at his death. Perhaps the French Wars had

Fig 23: Greta Hall

Fig 22: Robert Southey (1774-1843)

provided other business opportunities. By June 1817, aged 46, Isaac was sufficiently affluent to begin the purchase of Greta Hall in Keswick (Fig 23), a signature building in the town, where the poet Samuel Taylor Coleridge (1772-1834) had lived and where Robert Southey (Fig 22), the poet laureate, was the tenant. However, Southey was not pleased with this disturbance,

> *My house was purchased by a silversmith in Cockspur Street, a native of Borrodale here; – an injunction against the sale was obtained in favour of the widow of a former owner; the*

43

matter is in Chancery; the actual Landlord is in Carlisle jail, & I am paying rent to a mortgagee. Disturbed in possession of the house I cannot be for twelve years to come; & as long as there is any litigation I am in no danger of being annoyed by cutting up the grounds. Unless some such annoyance should drive me away, in all likelihood I shall be settled here for life. [50]

Legal complications arising from the previous landlord's debts halted the purchase. This attempt to regain a personal foothold in his home parish shows how Isaac never lost touch with his roots. Among his silverwork was the presentation epergne made c.1813 for Dr Joshua Dixon (1743-1825)[51] physician of Whitehaven, which was decorated with a representation of the Good Samaritan, in token of Isaac's generous use of Dixon's own medical expertise. It was a connection that endured – in 1861, Isaac's nephew, Abraham, made a generous donation to Whitehaven Hospital for their fever ward.[52]

Isaac was also a steward for the Cumberland Society in London for many years. Possessing that charitable instinct that seemed to be in the Fisher DNA, he was actively involved in raising money to help destitute married women stay in their own '*habitations*'. That sense of social injustice might also have got him involved in radical politics in the turbulent Westminster election of 1818-1819 that followed the suicide of Sir Samuel Romilly (1757-1818).

Isaac died young in 1819, aged 47, probably in Cockspur Street. In his will he left substantial bequests to his surviving siblings and to his nephews and nieces, especially brother Joseph's daughter, Mary, who was living with him in London. He also ensured that his servants were properly dressed at the funeral:

> *And I direct that such persons as are in my service at the time of my decease shall be provided with a proper suit of mourning according to their respective situations and the expenses thereof be defrayed out of the remainder of my estate.*

But the bulk of his considerable fortune (estimated at £50,000 in 1819 prices) went to his Seatoller brother, John. The Fisher family used it to buy up substantial landholdings in the Borrowdale valley. However, when the last direct heir, Abraham, died childless in 1864, the estate was broken up and sold.

John (1759-1835) and Agnes Dowthwaite (1767-1847)

In October 1834, Edward Baines visited Seatoller '*in its perfection of beauty*', introducing himself to John Fisher '*the principal statesman of Borrowdale*'. Edward Baines (1800-1890) was the son of a Leeds MP and proprietor of the *Leeds Mercury*. Soon after his tour of Cumberland, Baines took over the editorship when his father was elected to parliament. He later became an MP himself. He was a liberal reformist and supporter of working-class adult education.[53]

The pair had friends in common and Fisher pressed him to stay to dinner at the '*good old-fashioned hour of half-past twelve*'. They were joined by the children of a Buttermere clergyman who had come over on their ponies. After dinner, a young Fisher son took him to the wad mines (but there was no comment on the working conditions at which he visited the following day). Baines then climbed Great Gable before he went back to Seatoller for tea – at seven o'clock.

> *Seatoller unquestionably furnishes the finest bread and sweetest honey I ever ate:and I am sure I took enough of both with my tea to form an opinion. The honey is of that kind called*

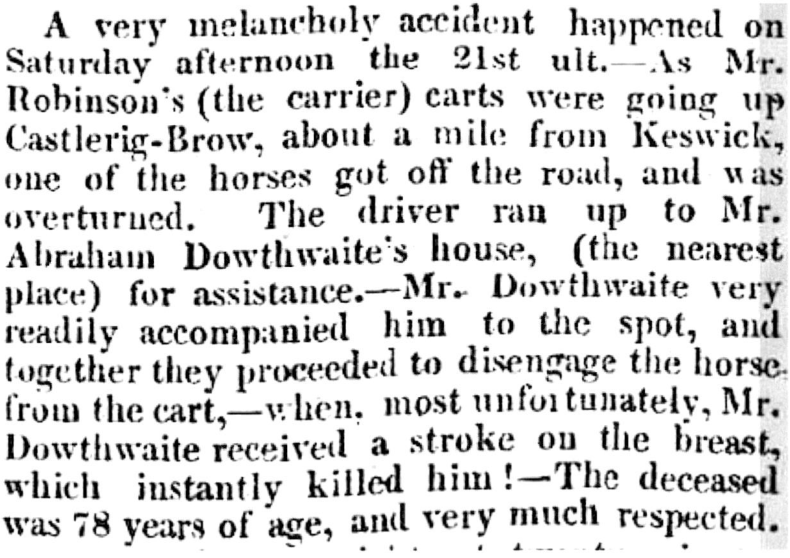

A very melancholy accident happened on Saturday afternoon the 21st ult.—As Mr. Robinson's (the carrier) carts were going up Castlerig-Brow, about a mile from Keswick, one of the horses got off the road, and was overturned. The driver ran up to Mr. Abraham Dowthwaite's house, (the nearest place) for assistance.—Mr. Dowthwaite very readily accompanied him to the spot, and together they proceeded to disengage the horse from the cart,—when, most unfortunately, Mr. Dowthwaite received a stroke on the breast, which instantly killed him!—The deceased was 78 years of age, and very much respected.

Fig 24: Lancaster Gazette 5th July 1817

heath honey, the bees which produce it feeding much on the heath-flowers: it is if a darker colour and a much finer flavour than the honey produced by bees which feed on garden flowers[54]

When his father, Joseph, died in 1774, John was still a teenager. His mother, Mary, presumably managed the house and farm. It must have been Mary who benefited when the Seatoller Fell freeholders sold their rights over the wad mine to John Bankes.[55] Mary continued to live from time to time in Seatoller. She was active and involved in decisions around the farm and not necessarily agreeing with her husband – Joseph sought to oversee her behaviour from beyond the grave by appointing trustees to look after the children's interests. But her own will showed that she was mindful of those children and grandchildren.

She was a woman of appetites with, by the time of her death, an accumulation of personal property and, of course, two husbands. It was probable that she and John Birkett lived in Rosthwaite until his death in 1802 but that she then moved back to Seatoller - although with daughter Dinah at the time of her death in Powter Howe, her will speaks of her as a widow '*of Seatoller*'.

You wonder how a woman of such spirit got on with her daughter-in-law? She acknowledged her by leaving one of her gowns to Agnes in her will. This was Agnes Dowthwaite who married Mary's son, John, on 22nd February 1791 in Crosthwaite church. Agnes was probably from Keswick, the daughter of Abraham and his first wife, Elizabeth Park. Abraham would be killed by a kick from a horse, a '*very melancholy accident*' (Fig 24).

John and Agnes had several children, among them were Mary (1793 -), Joseph (1796-1839), (John 1799–1814), Isaac (1803-1824) who died of typhus in London and Abraham (1807-1864) who would become a valley patriarch. However, they all died childless.

On 3rd September 1819, John travelled to London to prove Isaac's will, alongside his fellow executors, London friends of Isaac's. Also in that year, William Green's Guide[56] identifies five houses in the valley – one occupied by "*that worthy yeoman, Mr John Fisher, brother of Mr Isaac Fisher, silversmith of London and nephew of Mr Caleb Fisher of Grange...*"

The family fortunes took a decidedly upward shift:

The fortunes of the dalesmen have been increased from time to time by second and younger sons going out and succeeding in business in the metropolis. In the year 1786 Isaac Fisher, son of Mr. Joseph Fisher of Seatoller, was apprenticed to a silversmith in London, and the witness to his indentures was William Birkett, a banker's clerk, who went from Borrowdale,

Fig 25: The barn converted into a garage (1950s). The gate into Seatoller House is on the left. The Barn is now a two storey house

and was the person who first suggested the Clearing House System for private bankers, which is now also in use by all Joint Stock Banks, and by the Railway Clearing House, for which he received a retiring pension from the London Private Bankers. Mr. Isaac Fisher died at the early age of forty-five, in the year 1819... He amassed a considerable fortune, which he left to his brother, Mr. John Fisher of Seatoller, and an adequate competency to his sister, Mrs. Gibson of Pouter Howe, and others of his relations. The former bought many valuable estates in Borrowdale, and others in this neighbourhood, leaving his youngest surviving son, Mr. Abraham Fisher, a large landed proprietor.[57]

The fortune was considerable. Under Isaac's will, in 1819, the 12-year-old nephew Abraham inherited £4000, equivalent to £250,000 each in 2020 – and this was a minor bequest. The bulk went to brother John. A major project was to extend the house - further rooms were added on the south side, dating from around 1820-1850. There were improvements outside as well. In the 18th century, when the Fishers were still farmers, there was a barn just across the track –It was probably John who turned the building into the stables and coach house, referred to in the adverts when the Marshall estate was put up for auction.[58] In the 20th century, one part became a garage and another a National Trust information centre (Fig 25).

Perhaps one of John's first acts was to buy Seatoller Farm. Thomas Gaskarth was then the owner and was leasing the farm and its lands to Henry Bragg. Bragg was described as a farmer in Seatoller in his will in 1814.[59] Perhaps John Fisher bought the farm at this point or later in 1826 when Henry's widow, Sarah,[60] still '*of Seatoller*', died. By 1840, the Fishers owned the land, with a tenant, Thomas Wren (1796-1858). He may well have moved in after his marriage to Sarah Birkett (1794 -1872) in 1824.

John Fisher also bought Seathwaite farm in upper Borrowdale. Another farm, Thorneythwaite, came into the family through a different route. Thorneythwaite had been in the Birkett family ever since the Great Deed and by the Land Tax Redemption records in 1798, it was owned by Mary Birkett.

By the mid-18th century, the Birkett family no longer farmed at Thorneythwaite. Instead, it was leased to the Jopson family from Chapel. By the 1830s, the tenancy was held by John (1763-1831) and Daniel Jopson (1746-1833). They appear to be unmarried and were possibly half-brothers.

John was drowned, returning from Rosthwaite (Fig 26) –

Mr. John Jopson, of Thornythwaite, in Borrowdale, was unfortunately drowned about a mile from his own dwelling on Wednesday week. He had left Rosthwaite at ten o'clock at night, and is supposed to have fallen into the river when on his way home. His body was found on Thursday morning.

Fig 26: Cumberland Pacquet 15th February 1831

perhaps a social evening at the Miners' Arms? There were several wad miners and their families living at Thorneythwaite around this time. However, John was apparently alone. Over the years, there were several press reports of such accidents – on a dark winter night, the path by the river with its rocks and roots could be dangerous, particularly after a few pints.

Two years later, Daniel also died, again suddenly but at an '*advanced age*'. Consequently, Thorneythwaite reverted to Mary Birkett, John's mother and the widow of John Birkett (1725-) of Rosthwaite whom she had married in 1778. On Mary's death in 1823, it became the property of her son, John Fisher.[61] John installed Henry Dawson (1814-1893), grandson of Henry Bragg, to look after the farm. In the 1841 census, the wad miners had stayed on as lodgers – Dawson himself married Mary, the eldest daughter of John Dixon, manager at the black lead mine.[62]

John Fisher's acquisitions ranged beyond the valley. In 1820, Gate How estate in Hartsop, Patterdale was put up for sale and the advert suggested that particulars might be had from Mr Fisher in Seatoller.[63] John apparently became the owner because in 1865, at the auction of Abraham Fisher's properties, Gate How was bought by H C Marshall for £850.

Another major acquisition was Lyzzick Hall, owned by John Banks of Keswick. Banks had been killed in August 1829[64] when thrown from a gig near Bassenthwaite. The estate, divided into three farms (Lyzzick, Dancing Gate and Annatrigg), was put up for auction on 8th October 1830 at the Royal Oak in Keswick[65] and was bought by John. The tenant at the Hall at that time was Joseph Flintoft (1796-1860), a sculptor and fern collector, who made an extraordinary and detailed model of the Lakes, which took him six years to complete. It is in the Keswick Museum. It covers 1200 square miles of all the mountains, valleys, rivers, roads, mines, lakes, and tarns.

By 1841, the Flintoft family had moved and the Fishers leased the Hall to John Monkhouse (1799-1865), until his death. Monkhouse was the holder of the perpetual curacy of Newlands.

Joseph (1796-1839)

John Fisher died on 24th May 1835, 'awfully sudden' aged 75. He was,

'a gentleman respected and beloved by all who had the pleasure of knowing him and whose loss will be severely felt by the poor and indigent of his neighbourhood who had long and largely partaken of his bounty'.[66]

On the death of his father, John, Joseph ran the estate for four years and died unmarried. He had carried on adding to the estate, buying Thorneythwaite and Seathwaite Farms in 1836.[67] By 1842, the work of the Tithe Commissioners shows that, except for a couple of fields, all the land around Seatoller, Thorneythwaite and Seathwaite belonged to the Fishers.

The family's property included thirty-five plots, in all about two hundred and fifty acres, mainly around Seatoller and Thorneythwaite, including Seatoller House and Seatoller Farm, occupied by Thomas Wren. They also owned Thorneythwaite Farm and another house in Stonethwaite.

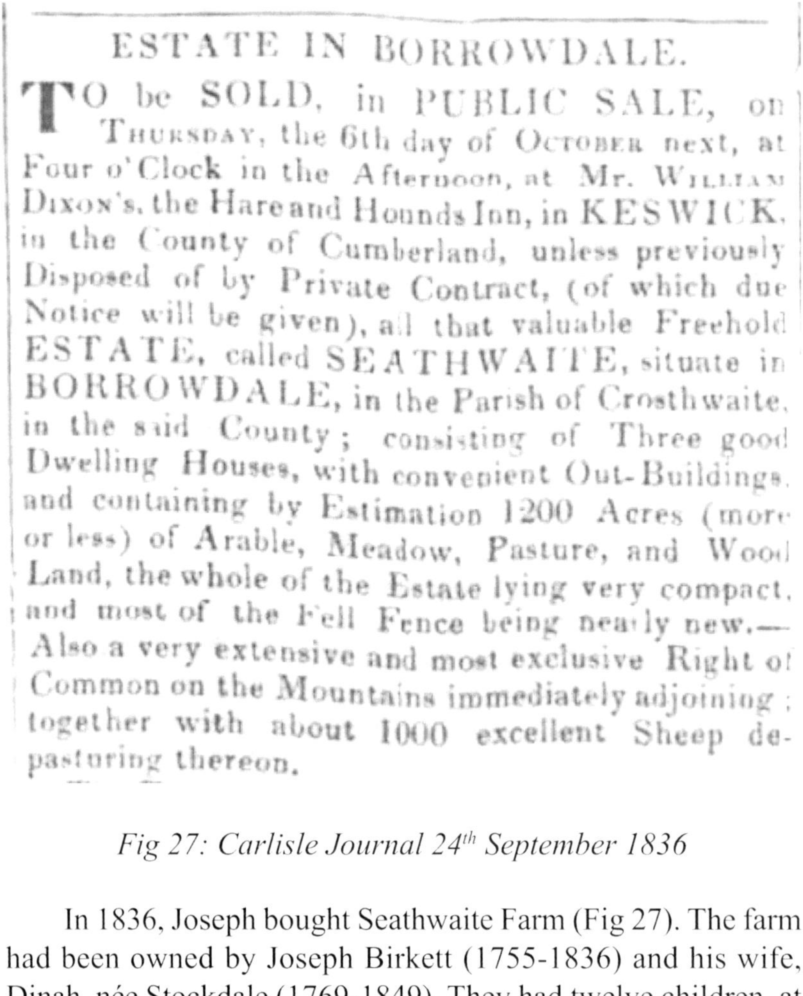

> ESTATE IN BORROWDALE.
>
> **TO** be SOLD, in PUBLIC SALE, on Thursday, the 6th day of October next, at Four o'Clock in the Afternoon, at Mr. William Dixon's, the Hare and Hounds Inn, in KESWICK, in the County of Cumberland, unless previously Disposed of by Private Contract, (of which due Notice will be given), all that valuable Freehold ESTATE, called SEATHWAITE, situate in BORROWDALE, in the Parish of Crosthwaite, in the said County; consisting of Three good Dwelling Houses, with convenient Out-Buildings, and containing by Estimation 1200 Acres (more or less) of Arable, Meadow, Pasture, and Wood Land, the whole of the Estate lying very compact, and most of the Fell Fence being nearly new.— Also a very extensive and most exclusive Right of Common on the Mountains immediately adjoining; together with about 1000 excellent Sheep depasturing thereon.

Fig 27: Carlisle Journal 24th September 1836

In 1836, Joseph bought Seathwaite Farm (Fig 27). The farm had been owned by Joseph Birkett (1755-1836) and his wife, Dinah, née Stockdale (1769-1849). They had twelve children, at least seven of whom were living in 1836. Joseph died in August and the farm was advertised for sale in September. Perhaps Joseph wished to provide for all his children and the executors[68] needed to realise the capital. But the change of owner bought no change of tenant – Joseph's son, John (1794-1872) and Thomas

52

(1806-1887) became the tenants of the Fishers. It was a substantial farm with thirty-seven plots in Seathwaite valley, comprising some twelve hundred acres, and including three houses in Seathwaite.

In 1841, Abraham owned other houses in Seathwaite, about seven acres, one house was occupied in 1841 by Charles Stewart (1796-1880), from Walney Island but who spent his working life as a miner at the wad mine. In 1817, Charles had married Sarah (1792-1870), the daughter of Joseph Birkett. They would live in Seathwaite until their deaths.

James Bennett (1779-1854) lived in another Fisher house in Seathwaite – originally from Castleton in Derbyshire, he had married the daughter of William Dixon (1757-1837), the manager of the wad mine. Bennett had lost his sight in an accident at Greenside mine on Helvellyn before 1811 but Dixon had continued to employ him.[69] Bennett's son, Thomas, was also a miner but in 1841 was renting Thorneythwaite farmhouse from Abraham Fisher. Bennett's brother, Matthew, ran the Miner's Arms in Rosthwaite around 1810.

The Fisher family owned or jointly owned three thousand acres of pasture Langstrath Fell, a further seven hundred acres on Coomb Fell, eleven hundred acres on Seathwaite Fell, and a thousand acres on Seatoller Fell. One interesting possibility is that the family now owned some of the fells around the Honister mine as in 1839, a new quarry, Fisher Quarry, was opened up on Yew Cragg.

Despite the ten-year difference in age, Joseph appears to have been quite close to his young brother, Abraham. They both (along with Robert Southey) subscribe to a society for the propagation of the bible.[70] Joseph with his brother donated or left money to build the vicarage adjoining the chapel.[71] It was built in 1842 at a cost of £900, £800 of which had been bequeathed by Joseph and £200 was received from Queen Anne's Bounty. This was a scheme established in 1704 to augment the incomes of the poorer clergy.[72] The first family to benefit was George Newby (1801-1872) who had been appointed to the perpetual curacy of Borrowdale,[73] following the death of William Parsable (1760-1838) who had been the curate for 32 years (as well as the head of Crosthwaite school, known for his quick temper and firm discipline).[74] Newby would also serve for over thirty years.

However, within months, Newby's second wife, Margaret James (née Irving) (1799-1843) died the week before Christmas at the vicarage. Newby sought consolation in poetry, publishing *The Pleasures of Melancholy* in 1843,[75]

> *The sweeping mountains, in their southward range,*
> *Impending o'er the low, romantic Grange,*
> *Their wild confusion curving into line,*
> *As, with terrific mien, they circling join,*
> *Where, clad in matchless beauty, Nature reigns,*
> *Supremely grand, o'er Borrowdale's domains;*
> *Their litt'ring summits, rearward, waving high,*
> *Far as the two-topp'd Scawfell meets the sky—*
> *The dale below, by lake and mountain 'closed,*
> *Small in extent, but with nice art compos'd—*
> *Of rip'ning corn, and meadows strew'd with hay—*
> *Of scatter'd cots along the winding way—*

Although the Cumberland Pacquet felt he was '*possessed of poetic genius*', perhaps Newby was disappointed by the reception of his work. He took to drink, and disciplinary action was taken against him by the church in 1854. But his parishioners loved him: when he retired in 1871, he was given a *'handsomely chased tea and coffee service, an elegant time piece on a stand of black and grey marble and a purse of sovereigns.'*[76]

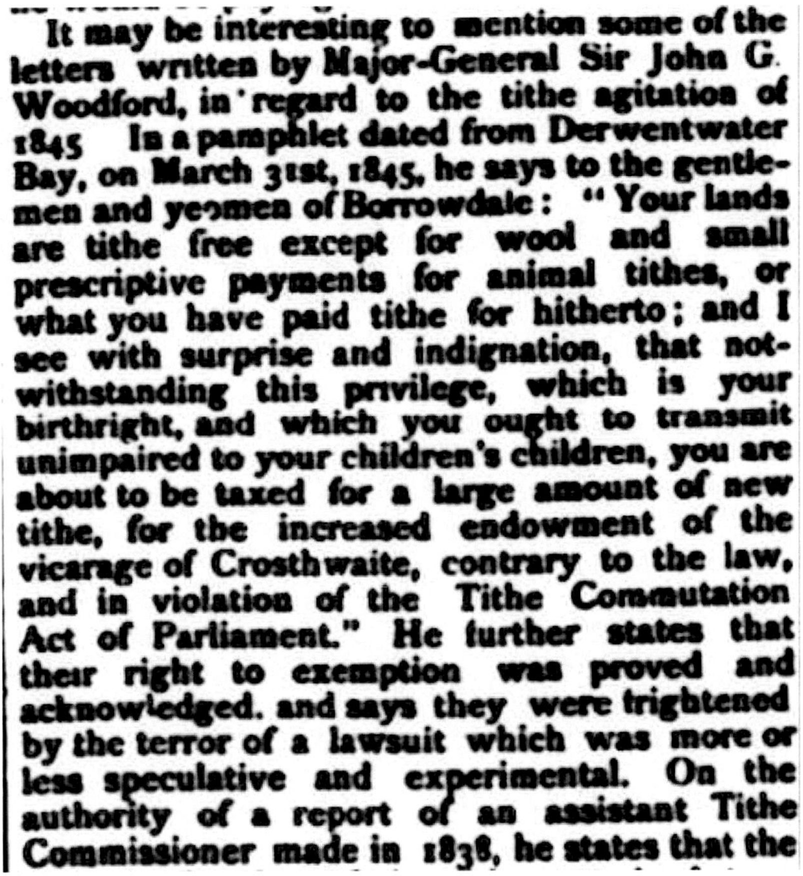

> It may be interesting to mention some of the letters written by Major-General Sir John G. Woodford, in regard to the tithe agitation of 1845 In a pamphlet dated from Derwentwater Bay, on March 31st, 1845, he says to the gentlemen and yeomen of Borrowdale: "Your lands are tithe free except for wool and small prescriptive payments for animal tithes, or what you have paid tithe for hitherto; and I see with surprise and indignation, that notwithstanding this privilege, which is your birthright, and which you ought to transmit unimpaired to your children's children, you are about to be taxed for a large amount of new tithe, for the increased endowment of the vicarage of Crosthwaite, contrary to the law, and in violation of the Tithe Commutation Act of Parliament." He further states that their right to exemption was proved and acknowledged, and says they were frightened by the terror of a lawsuit which was more or less speculative and experimental. On the authority of a report of an assistant Tithe Commissioner made in 1838, he states that the

Fig 27: West Cumberland Times 29th January 1887

Joseph's generosity had ramifications that echoed for forty-five years. The vicarage made Borrowdale even less dependent on the mother church at Crosthwaite which provided fewer and fewer services for the valley. This led to resentment at the imposition of tithes – this was led in the 1840s by Sir John Woodford (1785-1879), who, on his death, was the last British

55

officer alive to have fought at Waterloo where he was an aide-de-camp to Wellington. After retirement, he inherited an estate on the western side of Derwentwater from where he launched attacks, including a failed lawsuit, on the Tithe Commissioners. Forty years later, Borrowdale farmers went on 'tithe strike' (Fig 27) and the church sent in the bailiffs!

Joseph died on 8th August 1839,[77] buried at St Andrew's at a service conducted by George Newby. The press notice reflected that of his father four years earlier, *'a most amiable and unassuming man, truly pious and benevolent; and in him the poor of his neighbourhood, as well as many charitable institutions, have lost a worthy and valuable friend'*.[78]

Notes

[1] *Carlisle Journal 2nd February 1864*

[2] *Grant S., (2006)* The Story of the Newlands Valley *30*

[3] *Crosthwaite F J, (1876)* The Crosthwaite Registers *CW2 225-241*

[4] *Winchester A. J. L., (2001)* Personal Names and Local Identities in Early Modern Cumbria *CW 3 29-49*

[5] *I am in debt to the music scholar and social historian Sue Allan for the information here – her PhD was* Folk Song in Cumbria: a distinctive regional repertoire *(2017); https://www.village-music-project.org.uk/*

[6] *Lucas J.,* History of Warton Parish *(see https://andydenwood.com/music-work-18th-century-style/)*

[7] *Gilchrist A. G., (1939)* Some Old Lake Country Fiddlers *1* The Journal of the Lakeland Dialect Society *16;* see Greg Stephens' CD liner notes on Irwin at https://www.mustrad.org.uk/articles/irwin.htm

[8] *Chappell W., (1855)* Popular Music of the Olden Time *Vol 2 503*

[9] *Brunskill R. W., (1974)* Vernacular Architecture of the Lake Counties *103*

[10] *A lean-to shed where peat was stored*

[11] *Bailey J. and Culley., (1794) G.,* General View of the Agriculture of the County of Cumberland *12*

[12] *The house has had different names (Honister Cottage, the White Cottage etc) but will be referred to as Yew Tree Cottage for consistency – see ch.7*
[13] *Scott J. (1998)* The Kendal Tenant Right Dispute *CW2 169; Harrison P., (2021)* Mountain Republic *134-136*
[14] *Bouch C. M. L. and Jones G. P., (1961)* The Lake Counties 1500-1830 *76*
[15] *Tyson B, (1995)* Rebuilding the Medieval Court House at Keswick *CW2 119 at 126*
[16] *National Trust (2007)* Borrowdale: Historic Landscape Survey *Vol 2 180 – Monument ID 117450*
[17] *Brunskill R. W., (1974) 104*
[18] *Brunskill R. W., (1974) 112*
[19] *Gray E., (2007)* 100 Hunts: A Chronicle of the Trevelyan Manhunt 1898-2007 *101 suggests that the transition from thatch to slate would have been in the late 18th century*
[20] *Brunskill R. W., (1974) 114*
[21] *The evidence for this is genealogical – the 1840 tithe map details ownership and this can be traced back through the generations to Robert Jopson.*
[22] *Gray, E. (2007) 100*
[23] *Gray, E. (2007) 101*
[24] *Written by Hugh Taylor, it is available at https://k-fellfarers.co.uk/ - this section draws on his work*
[25] *Drawn for the High House history – available at https://k-fellfarers.co.uk/*
[26] *Brunskill R. W., (1974) 50 ff*
[27] *National Trust (2007) Vol 1 53*
[28] *Hutchinson W., (1794)* History of Cumberland
[29] *Tyson B, (1995) 126*
[30] *Churches C., (1998)* Women and Property in Early Modern England *23 Social History 165 – this examines the position of women in Whitehaven at that time.*
[31] *CRO Carlisle Q/11/1/81/2*
[32] *Prior to 1752, England followed the Julian calendar by which the new*

year started on March 25th. In accordance with a 1750 act of Parliament, England changed to the Gregorian calendar in use in Europe. December 31st, 1751 was followed by January 1st 1752.

[33] *CRO Whitehaven DLEC/6/4/31/2; CRO Carlisle PROB/1722/AINVX23*

[34] *Churches C, (1998) 165 and 173*

[35] *Mary Fisher, wife of John Fisher of Seatoller, was executrix*

[36] *CRO Carlisle PROB/1738/WINV444*

[37] *A messuage is a plot of land with a dwelling house*

[38] *CRO Carlisle PROB/1744/WINV222*

[39] *CRO Carlisle PROB/1738/WINV444*

[40] *CRO Carlisle - ref DCC 1/56; this would be Johnny Wood. In 1840, the Tithe Map shows a Robert Wren of Longthwaite Farm as owning and occupying this.*

[41] *Tyler I., (1995)* Seathwaite Wad *(workforce appendix)*

[42] *Thomas Gray (1769)* 'Journal of his Tour in the Lake District'

[43] *There is an alternative marriage with a Mary Barnes, on 2nd December 1758 but when Mary died in 1823, the date of birth excludes this as a possibility.*

[44] *Tyler I., (1995) ch 4*

[45] *Tyler I., (1994)* Honister Slate *25*

[46] *Tyler I., (1995) 117*

[47] *CRO Carlisle PROB/1774/W343*

[48] *The couple travelled to New York where their eldest son, John, was born. Thomas was drowned when he fell off the bridge leading to his house in an attempt to retrieve his hat - Carlisle Patriot 9th February 1872*

[49] *London Gazette 3rd November 1829; Braithwaite and Jones continued to trade until 1852.*

[50] *Letter from Southey to Walter Savage Landor 3rd January 1819*

[51] *Sydney M., (2009)* Bleeding, Blisters and Opium: Joshua Dixon and the Whitehaven Dispensary

[52] *Cumberland Pacquet 23rd July 1861*

[53] *Baines, E., (1834)* A Companion to the Lakes of Cumberland, Westmoreland, and Lancashire, In a Descriptive Account of a Family Tour,

and Excursions on Horseback and on Foot *298 ff*
[54] *Baines, E., (1834)* 305
[55] *Tyler I., (1995) 117*
[56] *Green W., (1819)* The Tourist's New Guide to the Lake District
[57] *English Lakes Visitor 21st March 1885*
[58] *West Cumberland Times 20th July 1895 for advert for auction; Maryport Advertiser 7th September 1895*
[59] *CRO Carlisle PROB/1814/W371(B)*
[60] *CRO Carlisle PROB/1826/W27(B)*
[61] *Hall I. (2017)* Thorneythwaite *140 and 214 suggests that Abraham Fisher bought the farm as an investment in 1833. This is unlikely, given the dates as Abraham did not get control of the family money for another six years*
[62] *Carlisle Journal 1/12/1838*
[63] *Westmorland Gazette 7th October 1820*
[64] *Carlisle Patriot 8th August 1829*
[65] *Cumberland Pacquet 7th September 1830*
[66] *Cumberland Pacquet 2nd June 1835*
[67] *CRO (W) DMG/80/1; Carlisle Journal 10th September 1836*
[68] *They were John Birkett, Joseph's son, John Birkett of Rosthwaite and Abraham Fisher*
[69] *Tyler, I. Seathwaite Wad (1995) 132*
[70] *Carlisle Journal 13th December 1834*
[71] *Crosthwaite J. Fisher, (1875-76)* Old Borrowdale *Transactions of the Cumberland Association for the Advancement of Literature and Science 69*
[72] *This was a scheme established in 1704 to augment the incomes of the poorer clergy.*
[73] *Cumberland Pacquet 27th May 1838*
[74] *Parsable was in charge of Borrowdale, Newlands and Gilcrux, living mainly in the last, although he owned a house in Borrowdale.*
[75] *Cumberland Pacquet 9th May 1843; se also Henllywarc or The Druid's Temple (1853)*
[76] *Ulverston Mirror 8th July 1871*

[77] *CRO Carlisle PROB/1839/W704*
[78] *Cumberland Pacquet 13th August 1839*

9: Abraham Fisher (1807-1864)

John Fisher and Agnes Dowthwaite had seven children. Abraham (Fig 1) was the youngest – Abraham was a Dowthwaite family name and Agnes was probably from Smaithwaite in St John's in the Vale. Abraham was christened in St Andrew's on Wednesday 2nd December 1807 It was a calm day but there would be severe gales at the weekend, wrecking boats on the coast.

Agnes had already lost three children who had died in infancy. If she felt a closer bond to her youngest, that would only be strengthened when her eldest son, John, died in his teens in 1814 when Abraham was just seven. Another son, Isaac, died in 1824 in his early twenties. When Joseph died in 1739, in his forties and unmarried, Agnes and Abraham were left by themselves in Seatoller House.

Before his uncle Isaac died in 1819, Abraham would have attended Crosthwaite School (Fig 2), perhaps boarding in Keswick during the week. The school was ruled by the Eighteen Men of Keswick and was remarkable. Neither gentry nor vicar were involved. Tuition was free for all the boys and girls, and, despite its poor amenities (three toilets for the whole school), it produced exceptional results. In 1818, when Abraham was just eleven, the school had two hundred and sixty pupils, far exceeding any other Cumbrian endowed school and including a *'swarm of children from the poorhouse'*. The headmaster was paid the princely sum of £80 pa and there was an undermaster at £30 – perhaps older pupils helped out? In 1821, on the death of

Fig 1: Abraham Fisher circa 1850 – the only likeness of any of the Seatoller Fishers. Perhaps the artist was the sculptor, Joseph Flintoft, who lived for a time in Lyzzick Hall, owned by Abraham

Fig 2: Crosthwaite School: the only known sketch a decade before its rebuild in 1829 (Harrison)

the headmaster, pupils erected a headstone *'thanks to the high principles and indomitable energy of the master, no ill effects came of the dissimilar circumstances of the scholars'.* [1]

After Isaac's death, the Fishers were wealthy enough to send the teenager, Abraham, to a private school – or was the good reputation of the Keswick grammar school sufficient to keep him at home? Perhaps rubbing shoulders and sharing lessons with the children from the poorhouse had its effect on an older and richer Abraham. He would later become one of the Eighteen Men, who were the trustees for the school.[2] Although his education ended when he left school, he would have shared that school experience with many of the Keswickians that he would meet on committees or on the bench, such as the older Tom Spedding. But, unlike Spedding, he did not go to university.

As a young man, he was drawn into country sports. In 1825,

Fig 3: Blencathra fox hounds in Victorian England
(http://blencathrafoxhounds.co.uk/)

at eighteen years old, he held a game certificate,[3] which entitled him to kill game on his own land or on others' property with consent. From 1831, the Game Act constrained hunting certain species as game birds, with open seasons (when they may be shot): grouse could only be shot from August to December, pheasants from October to February and partridge from September to February. Foxes were also hunted by hounds – the traditional, lightly built fell hound was distinctive in having 'hare feet' and long toenails, a genetic adaptation that enabled them to hunt the steep scree and crags of the Lakes and cover up to 40 miles in a day. Packs such as the Blencathra (Fig 3) would visit the different valleys. The Blencathra country covered Borrowdale where they might stay several nights, starting the hunt in the different villages.

...*over such ground it requires a stout heart and a good pluck, in hounds, terriers, and followers of the chase or few foxes would be accounted for. It must be remembered, too, that the hunting is done entirely on foot, in hard frost, or when rain, snow, or bitterly cold winds seep over these wild fells, and I have been out when, owing to the intense cold, the dogs were practically unable to work as they could not take up the drag owing, as the men said, to their noses being frozen.*[4]

John Crozier (1822-1903) took up the mastership of the Blencathra in 1840 and took the hounds to Borrowdale where he would have known Abraham – rather like the old huntsman, Simon Lee, in Wordsworth's poem.

*No man like him the horn could sound,
And hill and valley rang with glee
When Echo bandied, round and round
The halloo of Simon Lee.
In those proud days, he little cared
For husbandry or tillage;
To blither tasks did Simon rouse
The sleepers of the village.*[5]

But the landowners and the valley farmers would have welcomed (and accompanied) the hunt as the best method of controlling what they saw as a pest. And the disruption and damage done by huntsmen on foot was very different to those on horseback, Wilde's '*unspeakable in pursuit of the uneatable*'.

Whether on foot or on horseback, Abraham's involvement in country sports was probably curtailed when, in April 1843, he was seriously injured when his mount, '*young and spirited*', stumbled and threw him.[6] At thirty-six, the poor roads and stony fellsides called out for greater prudence.

Away from the sport, Abraham was soon involved in county affairs. In 1832, he was sitting on a grand jury at Cockermouth

Quarter Sessions.[7] Through his life, he was regularly summoned for both grand jury and special jury duty. The function of the grand jury was to assess the evidence against an accused and to decide whether to send them to trial. Special juries might be summoned to decide a specific question of fact in civil cases. In *Bowman v Bowman*,[8] Abraham (still suffering from injuries after he was thrown from a horse a few months earlier) and his fellow jurors discussed whether old Bowman had the mental capacity to make a will – on his deathbed, he had bequeathed his estate to female first cousins and away from the person who would have inherited, had he died intestate. In another case, *Graham v Ewart* at Carlisle Assizes in 1854, the argument was about shooting rights.[9]

Abraham was qualified to act as a juror being a man and over twenty-one, but he must also have had his own money, at least *'Ten Pounds by the Year above Reprizes in Lands or Tenements, whether of Freehold, Copyhold, or Customary Tenure, or of Ancient Demesne, or in Rents issuing out of any such Lands or Tenements'* (Jury Act 1825). After his uncle Isaac died in 1819, the twelve-year-old Abraham received a legacy of £1000 – presumably this had been wisely invested in land, necessary in order to qualify for jury service. These early courtroom experiences did not deter Abraham and he became a diligent justice of the peace in 1848.

Abraham was well-off but he became rich when his older brother, Joseph, died on 8th August 1839. He inherited the house and the farms and, for twenty-five years, managed considerable landholdings from Bassenthwaite to Patterdale, as well as in Borrowdale. Abraham Fisher was far from the yeoman farmers of his ancestors and more a benevolent squire.

Managing the valley itself provided few problems as there were long-term tenants on each of his farms. Seatoller Farm had been acquired in the 1820s by Abraham's father, John. Soon after, Thomas Wren took over the tenancy, perhaps after his marriage to Sarah Birkett (1794 -1872) in 1824. He was the tenant of most of Abraham Fisher's lands – the fields of High Broad Dale, Low Broad Dale, Plumbtree Howe, Rash, Milbeck Garth, Staley Green, Brackeny Howe and Sandbeds and two thousand acres of grazing on Seatoller Fell. Only the fields immediately adjacent to the house (Little Close and Moss) stayed in Abraham's hands.

At Seathwaite, the Birkett family had sold out to the Fishers in 1836 but then rented the farm and the three sons and daughter Sarah continued to live in the village.

At Thorneythwaite, the 1842 Tithe Commissioners recorded that Abraham Fisher was both the owner and occupier. 'Occupier' did not mean 'resident'. At the 1841 census Abraham was at Seatoller House and employing Henry Dawson as a farm worker at Thorneythwaite while renting much of the rest to Seathwaite miners. By 1851, the miners had been evicted. Henry Dawson had changed jobs, moving to a Threlkeld farm. The farm was now run by a young couple, Thomas Walker (1816-1881) from Newlands and Catherine née Wilson (1817-1865) who had married in 1843 and had moved into Thorneythwaite by the birth of daughter, Hannah, in 1849. Walker would farm Thorneythwaite for twenty-five years. His wife, Catherine, died in April 1865. More grief was to come when his nine-year-old son, Thomas, died in September. Two years later, the eldest child, Robert, would die aged just twenty-two. One bright note came on 11th November 1865 when Thomas married for a second time. The bride was forty-six-year-old Elizabeth Harrison, the long-time housekeeper for Abraham Fisher at Seatoller House. Fisher had died the year before. It was the first ever marriage at St Andrew's and the Rev Newby, well aware of Borrowdale weather, presented the couple with a pair of blankets.[10]

The Fisher empire stretched well beyond Borrowdale. Abraham's father's acquisitions ranged beyond the valley, at one point including the Gate How estate in Hartsop, Patterdale and Lyzzick Hall on the shores of Bassenthwaite. Inevitably there was much to do on the routine day-to-day maintenance and management – Abraham oversaw a complete overall of its machinery of his corn mill at Bishop's Mills attached to Lyzzick Hall before seeking a new tenant.[11]

Abraham also expanded the Fisher empire – in 1843, he bought Bunbury House in Keswick with '*its pleasure grounds and four cottages*'.[12] Bunbury House was associated with Southey's circle as it was owned by Henry Bunbury (1778-1860), uncle of Southey's Cambridge friend, Charles. It had been Miss Jackson's '*Ladies Seminary*' but in 1843, Southey's daughter was living there. Abraham's intention was to turn this into a hotel.[13] If so, he was a businessman before his time as the tourist trade was still sparse - although aristocratic visitors had begun to visit the area.

Perhaps he had advice from Tom Mossop at Lodore. The hotel would have been a watering hole for Abraham on his journeys to and from Keswick.

The worthy host and hostess of the comfortable inn at Lowdore...This well conducted establishment is much frequented during the summer months... but the visits of customers in winter are few and far between.[14]

The only other stop would have been the Miners' Arms in Rosthwaite, nearer home but with a rather rougher clientèle. The Lodore's '*worthy host*', Mossop, might well have had advice for Abraham. He had had aristocracy as guests when the Queen Dowager had visited Lodore in 1840.[15] He had been an energetic innkeeper, fully embedded in community life, proactive in

PURSUANT to a Decree of the High Court of Chancery, made in a Cause Gibson v. Fisher, with the approbation of the Master of the Rolls, at the *Keswick Hotel*, KESWICK, in the County of Cumberland, on THURSDAY, the 6th day of SEPTEMBER, 1866, at One o'clock in the Afternoon precisely, by Mr. C. P. HARDY, the person appointed by the said Judge to SELL the same, in several lots, certain Valuable and Extensive FREEHOLD and CUSTOMARY ESTATES, comprising MANSIONS, MESSUAGES, FARMS, detached CLOSES of LAND, and 2,303 ACRES of Arable, Meadow, Pasture, and Wood Land, called respectively, SEATOLLER, SEATHWAITE, & THORNEYTHWAITE, in Borrowdale, in the Parish of Crosthwaite; High Side, in the Parish of Bassenthwaite; Dancing Gate, in the Township of Under-Skiddaw, and Parish of Crosthwaite; Great and Little Uzzicar, in the Township of Above-Derwent, and Parish of Crosthwaite; Yew Tree, and Brighouse, and Row End, and Wantuwaite, in the Township of St. John's, in the Parish of Crosthwaite; Threlkeld, in the Parish of Greystoke; Two Closes called Castles and Corn Close, in St. John's aforesaid; Four Closes of Wood and Pasture Land, on Whinlatter, near Braithwaite, in the Parish of Crosthwaite; and a lot of Wood Land, called High Ladstock Wood, near Braithwaite aforesaid. A Dwelling house adjoining to High Side Farm. Two Cottages at Stonethwaite, in Borrowdale aforesaid; and a Moiety of Tithe Rent Charge in Under-Skiddaw, and Above-Derwent, in the Parish of Crosthwaite, to the annual value of £51 7s. 6d. The MANSIONS are LYZZICK HALL, in the Township of Under-Skiddaw; and SEATOLLER, in Borrowdale, all in the County of Cumberland.

Fig 4: Cumberland Pacquet 28th August 1866 described the extent of Abraham Fisher's landholdings

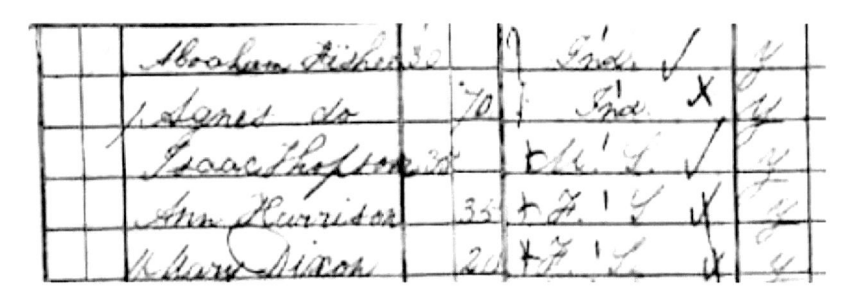

Fig 5: 1841 census return for Seatoller House: the "F S" by Ann and Mary usually indicated 'female servant' and the "M S" by Isaac 'male servant'

organising dances, parties, and sponsoring boats for races on the lake.[16] An entrepreneur, he saw the possibilities in tourism.

But Abraham remained a simple landowner. By the time of his death, he owned farms, houses and land across the district. In 1866, there was a dispute over his will and the Court of Chancery ruled that the estate should be sold. The newspaper prospectus (Fig 4) detailed the lots – it amounted to 2363 acres of freehold and customary land in eighteen lots. There were coloured lithographs of all the lots and a statement of twenty-six conditions, spelling out the details of title and other covenants.

Abraham managed this estate with little administrative or other help. In 1841, he lived (Fig 5) at the house with his mother, Agnes, and three servants to cook, clean and look after the garden – but not to deal with the correspondence or manage the diary.

Abraham and his mother inspired loyalty. Every six months there were hiring fairs in Keswick and yet Isaac Thompson and Ann Harrison worked for the Fishers for at least a decade. And when Mary Dixon got married in 1846, her sister Jane from Seathwaite replaced her. The Fishers were good employers.

Isaac Thompson (1799-1875) was born in Grasmere. His father, also an Isaac (1753-1841), worked across the road at the

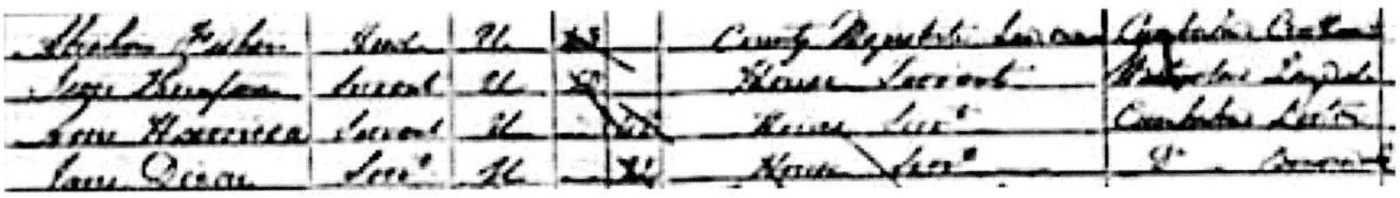

Fig 6: 1851 census return for Seatoller House

farm for Thomas Wren. In the 1850s, Isaac would leave Seatoller after many years. It was at that time that Abraham employed John Mossop from the Lodore as a groom. Was there a falling-out? Or was Isaac, in his fifties, getting a little old? In 1861, he was an husbandman, lodging with Joseph Braithwaite at Sty Beck farm in St Johns in the Vale. From whom did he get his smallholding? As Fig 4 shows, Abraham owned four farms very close to Sty Beck as well as two fields at Castles and Corn Close. It is probably not a coincidence that Isaac was surrounded by land belonging to Abraham. The inference is that he had received a few acres at a peppercorn rent in return for his years at Seatoller House. There was no ill-feeling as, when Abraham died in 1864, he left Isaac a legacy of £100.

In 1871, Isaac was retired and visiting his ex-neighbour, John Braithwaite Fletcher, who had just sold Yew Tree Cottage and was living in Thornthwaite Hall. When he died, Isaac left about £1000. Fletcher and Thomas Walker from Thorneythwaite were his executors. But they left the estate unadministered and in 1882, Margaret Wilkinson from Ambleside, a niece and residuary legatee, had to re-apply for probate. Even that did not go well, as in 1901, William Wilkinson, a waller, made yet another application – the estate by this time was now valued at £1557.

Jane Dixon(1828-1899) followed her sister Mary and worked for the Fishers until she too got married. Her husband was William Keenliside, a pencil maker. For a time, Keenliside

71

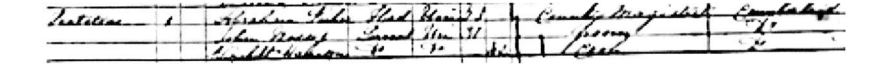

Fig 7: 1861 census return for Seatoller House

was successful and his black pencil works in Keswick employed fourteen men and four boys but in 1884, he went bankrupt[17] and died soon after. Jane, intriguingly, in September 1892 was a passenger on City of Paris from Liverpool to New York and by then was a US citizen.

Another Fisher servant in 1841 and 1851 was Ann Harrison (Fig 6). A local woman, she was born in Lorton around 1803 but there the trail ends. In 1841, there was Sarah Harrison, born 1771, working for John Birkett in Stonethwaite and there was another Ann Harrison, servant to the vicar George Newby and his wife.

In 1861, there were just three living in the house (Fig 7) – Abraham, John Mossop and Elizabeth Harrison. Elizabeth appears to have no connections in the valley or with the other Harrisons. She was born in 1818 at Cardewlees, just south and west of Carlisle. Her father, John, was a stone mason. In 1851, at thirty-three, she was still living with brother, also a mason, and other siblings in Cumdivock, a hamlet close by. How and when did she find her way to Seatoller House?

After the death of his mother in 1847 and Ann Harrison (probably in 1855) Abraham was in need, not just of a servant but a housekeeper. One possibility is Elizabeth was related in some way to Ann. Another might be a word-of-mouth recommendation from one of his fellow magistrates. Abraham frequently visited Carlisle or Cockermouth for Quarter Sessions – he was a justice of the peace and, while minor matters were held at petty sessions in Keswick, he would also attend Quarter Sessions where more serious offences were tried in front of a jury

Fig 8: Allonby and the Ship Hotel in the late 1800s

with a bench of JPs. This was both a legal and social event which many of the county's magistrates would attend.

Abraham travelled around the county – to Carlisle and Cockermouth for Quarter Sessions, to Whitehaven to deal with matters of compensation to be paid by the Whitehaven and Furness Junction Railway,[18] to the coast at Allonby on holiday with his cousin, Grace Gibson (1798-1867), Aunt Dinah's daughter.[19] Allonby (Fig 8) had long been a sea-bathing resort and had added to its repertoire in 1835 by building a suite of hot, cold and vapour baths. It was a popular destination and not just for Cumberland's élite.

Allonby was not to the taste of all visitors. The writers Wilkie Collins and Charles Dickens were on a walking tour in September 1857 when Collins twisted an ankle on the Caldbeck Fells. Seaside air and saltwater was the prescribed treatment and they stayed at the Ship in Allonby, '...*a delightful little Inn, excellently kept by the most comfortable of landladies and the*

73

Fig 9: The Library, Mirehouse (Courtesy of mirehouse.co.uk).

most attentive of landlords.' However, it was dull. A bolting donkey *'was the public excitement of Allonby, and was probably supported at the public expense'.* [20]

Abraham and Grace would have enjoyed the solitude and wildness of the Solway. With them in 1859 was Thomas Story Spedding (1800-1870), his wife Frances (née Headlam) and their four children from Mirehouse (Fig 9).

The Speddings were an old county family. Tom (Fig 10) was baptised at Crosthwaite and may have attended the school (but his father had been at Hawkshead with Wordsworth). Tom went to Trinity, Cambridge where he was awarded a first in civil law in 1821. He had married the daughter of the archdeacon of Richmond in Yorkshire. Like his grandfather, Tom was High Sheriff of Cumberland in 1855. Abraham and he were involved

Fig 10:
Thomas Story Spedding
1800-1870
(Courtesy of mirehouse.co.uk).

as magistrates, on church matters and frequently donated to the same charitable causes. Was Spedding (already chairman of the bench) Abraham's supporter when he was appointed as a justice of the peace in 1848?[21]

A friendship with Spedding meant that Abraham would have shared a range of cultural and social interests. Tom was a Cambridge-educated intellectual, a friend of Thomas Carlyle who visited him in the summer of 1847 at Greta Bank and later at Mirehouse. His letters to Carlyle[22] show how a serious Victorian thought about contemporary affairs and how his religious beliefs played a vital part in that thinking. Fisher did not attend university nor did he write or publish. But through Spedding, in the library at Mirehouse or walking along Allonby beach, he was on the fringe of those great liberal tides of thought in 19th-century art, literature, philosophy, and politics. Through donations Abraham sought to relieve poverty, support education and improve public health, while remaining at heart a conservative landowner. And it was always church affairs that got the most attention.

Abraham's Keswick circle included the Stanger brothers, James (1796-1866)[23] and Joshua (1800-1854). Their grandfather was Joshua Stanger from Cockermouth but their father, James

(1743-1829) was a city merchant in London with Moore, Stanger & Co. He moved back to Keswick in 1813 and built the Dove Cote, neighbour to Southey in Greta Hall.[24] Son James married late, to a widow Sophia Ann Murray née Lynn, the daughter of James Lynn, the vicar of Caldbeck and (from 1820) Crosthwaite.[25] She had married a captain, William Murray,[26] in the 22nd Bengal (Native) infantry, part of the East India Company. Murray died in June 1842 Jubbulpore, perhaps during the Bundela uprising, an early instance of resistance to British colonial rule in India. She returned to Cumberland and married James Stanger on 16th June 1849, presumably with her father officiating. Abraham, a fellow JP, would undoubtedly have been invited.

Twenty-five years previously, in August 1824, in the same church and with the same vicar, Stanger's younger brother Joshua had married the sixteen-year-old Mary Calvert (1807-1890). Her father, William, had been schoolfriends with William Wordsworth, helping him and Dorothy to settle in the Lakes and a friend of Coleridge and Southey – Sara Coleridge and Dora Wordsworth were bridesmaids. The couple moved to London, living in Wandsworth in 1838, although they were back in Keswick regularly – catechising the children from the Sunday School.

The publication of *Lyrical Ballads* in 1798, Coleridge living in Greta Hall, then followed by Robert Southey's appointment as poet laureate in 1813 – all meant that Keswick was a destination for some famous poets and writers. Lamb, Hazlitt, de Quincey, Shelley, Scott, Wordsworth – all stayed at Greta Hall. In 1818, Keats visited Keswick but apparently blanked Southey.[27] You wonder if the schoolboy Abraham hung around the hall gates with his autograph book?

Bott[28] suggests that Greta Hall had only minimal contact

with the ordinary people and that the trail of eminent guests compensated for the lack of Keswick society. That underestimates the depth and vibrancy of the life of Cumbrian gentry.[29] There was a circle of local gentry that not only had had close ties to the Romantics but also wider horizons. As well as the Calverts, down the road towards Bassenthwaite at Mirehouse were the Speddings. Tom Spedding's father, John, had been at Hawkshead school with Wordsworth and Wordsworth's sister Dorothy was a regular visitor to the house. and John Spedding maintained his acquaintance with the poet all his life. John's other son, James, had been at university with Alfred Tennyson and was a life-long friend -Tennyson visited Mirehouse on his honeymoon in 1835, selling a gold medal he won to pay the rail fare.

There were also the practical romantics, doing things with landscapes. Edward Stephenson (1691-1768)[30] had joined the East India Company in 1708 and became successful, dealing in property in Cumberland, London and Essex. He lived in the Governor's House in Keswick. His nephew, Rowland Stephenson (1728-1807) inherited both the Borrowdale land and his uncle's love of the lake and mountains. With Lord William Gordon and Joseph Pocklington, Stephenson bought and developed land around Derwentwater development at the close of the 18th century.[31]

After Southey's death in 1843, a committee was set up to build a memorial. James Lynn, the vicar at Crosthwaite, chaired it. Other committee members included Tom Spedding, the Stanger brothers (Joshua had moved back from Wandsworth), James Henry of Derwent Island and the Hon J H Curzon, son of Lord Teynham. And Abraham Fisher....[32] There were clearly some contentious meetings, not helped by family differences – eighteen months later, they finally decided on the nature of the memorial (a mediaeval shrine made of Caen stone with a recumbent figure of the poet) but were still hunting subscriptions.[33]

Abraham's presence on this committee showed that, at thirty-six, he was firmly established in Keswick society. Perhaps this was not surprising, given his status as wealthy landowner, always willing to make a reasonable subscription or donation to worthy causes. But twenty years previously, the family were limited to a few fields around Seatoller House until the injection of cash from Isaac. Had he overcome the stigma attached to new money?

The impression is that he was a voice to be listened and his views considered. When decisions were to be made, he was in the room but perhaps not the leader. His involvement in church affairs was lifelong – in 1834, Joseph and Abraham were in the congregation at St Kentigern's to hear the Rev Whiteside preach on chapter 2 of Revelations

2. I know your deeds, your hard work and your perseverance. I know that you cannot tolerate wicked people, that you have tested those who claim to be apostles but are not, and have found them false

3. You have persevered and have endured hardships for my name, and have not grown weary.

The church was crowded, and James Stanger and Joseph Pocklington were there. They contributed to the Society for Propagating the Gospel in Foreign Parts with the brothers' names immediately after that of Southey.[34]

This vicarious evangelism was characteristic – James Stanger (who had been baptised in an independent dissenting chapel in London) had been active as superintendent of the Sunday School (sometimes with two hundred children present) and James held an anniversary dinner at his Larthwaite home, especially for the forty teachers but with a few friends well-known to the cause of education, including Stanger's brother Joshua and Abraham Fisher.[35] That evangelical side was also shown in his support, as treasurer, of the Keswick British and Foreign Bible Society.[36] In his will Abraham left substantial legacies of £500 to each of the British and Foreign Bible Society, Church Missionary Society, Religious Tract Society, London Missionary Society, and the Wesleyan Missionary Society.

Crosthwaite was his church of choice, rather than St Andrew's in the valley. Abraham was fully embedded as a congregant. In February 1855, the Crosthwaite incumbent, James Lynn, died and before the funeral there was a small breakfast at the vicarage of family and more immediate friends - along with Abraham and the clergy, there was also Tom Spedding and Arthur Dover from Skiddaw Bank.[37]

Crosthwaite may have been his church but he was supportive (promising £600) of James Stanger's plans to build a new church (St John's) in the east of the town. The project was taken over[38] by John Marshall (1765-1845). The Marshall family, Leeds flax spinners, owned vast areas of land in the Lakes. His son, Henry Cowper Marshall (1808-1884),[39] had been mayor of Leeds in 1843[40] and he bought up Joseph Pocklington's estate but, more relevantly, gathered up most of Seatoller and Abraham's other holdings in 1867.

Henry Marshall's son-in-law, Frederick Myers, was an early incumbent at St John's and used a Marshall legacy to buy land by the church for a public library. In 1855, Henry and Abraham paid £100 for an extension with a lecture theatre on the first floor.[41] Keswick Mechanics Institute had been in existence since 1842, with its own library, reading room and night classes – Abraham helped here too, donating books.[42]

The valley also benefited. In 1845, James Dixon (1824 -),

Fig 11: The desks in the schoolroom at Hawkshead where Wordsworth went to school, similar to Borrowdale School in the 1860s (Courtesy of Hawkshead Grammar School Foundation)

the son of a wad miner in Seathwaite, wrote a volume of poetry with '*displays of fancy and powers of imagery...of no mean order*'[43] and dedicated it to Abraham. He went on to study at Trinity, Dublin and was a curate mainly in Durham and York. Printed by Baileys of Cockermouth, Abraham probably paid for their publication and for James' subsequent education in Ireland.

He was concerned about the valley children generally. At a meeting of Borrowdale ratepayers, George Newby reported that, if an efficient teacher was appointed, Abraham and William Simpson of New York would each give £10 pa towards salary.[44] Within a few years, Abraham was dead but he endowed Borrowdale School (Fig 11) to the sum of £500, which has supported the school into the 21st century.

Abraham's network through the church was extensive and in June 1848, he was appointed to the Commission of the Peace for Cumberland,[45] which entailed sitting as a magistrate at Keswick Petty Sessions. There were about one hundred JPs at that time.[46] A fair proportion would attend Quarter Sessions at Cockermouth or Carlisle (Fig 12) where Abraham and his fellow justices would sit with a jury to hear more serious offences. This was as much a social as a legal event where he would meet with many of the county's gentry and their families.

Prior to 1847, minor criminal matters were dealt with at Cockermouth. There was no county police force - the Cumberland and Westmorland

Fg 12: Carlisle Journal 7th January 1853 – only Tom Spedding and Abraham Fisher were from Keswick

81

Fig 13: Moot Hall, Keswick around 1904 with coaches taking on passengers

Constabulary was only formed in 1856 – and rural Cumberland and Westmorland were notably peaceful.[47] Prior to this there would have been a town constable, presumably appointed and supervised by the Eighteen Men. In 1841, James Adams was a 35 year old police officer, living on Main Street. The constable and the churchwardens referred miscreants to the old manorial court, which may well have exercised jurisdiction over misdemeanours.[48] This court met in the Moot Hall (Fig 13), at the rear of which was a lock up for prisoners:

This lock up house is a detached building in the middle of the town. The site is unobjectionable on the score of health, but it is inconveniently distant from the town hall. There are two cells, each 10 feet long, 6 feet wide, and 8 feet high ... The cell doors open into a small passage which communicates with the street. *The cells appear to be dry at all seasons of the year, but they are quite dark. There are, however, holes for the admission of air. There is no provision for warming. There is no accommodation for a resident keeper, and the place is therefore not secure. Moreover, prisoners in the different cells can talk to each other, and talk to people in the street. In one cell there is a stone bench, with loose straw for bedding; but there is nothing of the kind in the other cell.*[49]

There were just four local justices of the peace: the Stanger brothers, Tom Spedding and John Curzon from Castlette. There was a magistrates' office where the JPs' administrative business would be dealt with but it was not a court. Around 1846, the county commission of the peace created a petty sessional area for Keswick. The new court met regularly on Saturdays. These four would have been instrumental in putting Abraham's name forward to the Lord Chancellor. Almost immediately, the magistrates had to deal with a riot in '*peaceful Keswick*' (Fig 14). There had been some disturbances on hiring day and two local youths were in custody. A crowd attacked the lock up at the Moot Hall and freed the men.

The affair '*has caused the greatest excitement throughout Keswick*' – Abraham might well have wondered what he'd let himself in for. Five years later, there was another 'riot' when there was a strike at Banks pencil factory and returning strikers were assaulted – the 'rioters' were fined.[50] But over the years, a magistrates' lot was routine: offensive language by three pencil makers,[51] furiously riding a pony on Main Street,[52] illegal fishing (the accused had a large salmon under his coat in Main Street)[53] and an odd case concerning the Skiddaw Greys, E Company of the 1st Cumberland Rifles, a volunteer group, who were practising their shooting in the defendant's field where he threw down the target, seen by the officers as an insult to the men. Perhaps Abra-

83

RIOT AT KESWICK.—A most disgraceful riot took place in the generally peaceful town of Keswick on Saturday evening last. As is usually the case on hiring-days, a few squabbles or fights occurred, and between eleven and twelve o'clock the officer, assisted by a person named Bird, from Cockermouth, took two town lads into custody, as the principal promoters of a disturbance then in progress, and conveyed them to the lock-up house. No sooner had this step been taken, than the constable was grossly assaulted; and in an extraordinary short space of time several hundred persons were collected together, and a disposition to rescue the prisoners began to manifest itself. The violence of the mob increased, and the police-officer, after some further rough handling, was glad to make his escape; on which several persons, who were evidently well acquainted with every locality of the town, armed themselves with sledge-hammers and crow-bars, and dragged to the neighbourhood of the prison a tree sixteen feet in length by eight inches square, all of which were brought from different parts, and made available in smashing in the strong door of the building. Whilst this work of destruction was going on below, some of the crowd had mounted the roof and nearly stripped it of its covering, but owing to the strength of the Borrowdale rammels, or flag stones, which formed a kind of inner roof, an insurmountable barrier was presented to any further damage in that respect. The door of the lock-up having been nearly smashed into fragments, the prisoners were released from custody, at which time the building had all the appearance of having stood a siege—the freestone quoins being broken to pieces, with slates and timber scattered in all directions. On Sunday night an attempt was made to fire the prison, for which purpose a quantity of hay and straw was thrown into the premises; but owing to the absence of any great extent of wood among the materials, little damage was done. No doubt proper means will be adopted by the magistrates for the punishment of the ringleaders in these disgraceful proceedings, many of whom, we understand, will be satisfactorily identified. The affair has caused the greatest excitement throughout Keswick and the immediate neighbourhood.

Fig 14: Carlisle Journal 17th November 1848

> SATURDAY, JAN. 30.
> *(Before A. Fisher, S. Z. Langton, and J. J. Spedding, Esqs.)*
> Two men, named *Rigg* and *Holywood*, were charged with being drunk and disorderly.—They were fined 2s. 6d. each and costs.—Holywood deliberately laid the money down, shilling by shilling, and looking at the magistrates, asked :—"Is there any discount?"—Mr. FISHER : We don't allow discount here. (Laughter.)

Fig 15: Carlisle Journal 2nd February 1864

ham should have recused himself as he was a supporter of the Greys shooting competition and annually offered a prize of £5.[54]

Abraham would often sit with the Stangers and Tom Spedding. He enjoyed judicial business, regularly attending Quarter Sessions. Quarter Sessions not only dealt with crime but also (before the creation of county councils) was the local government – rural police, gaols, lunacy committee, bridges, surveyors, setting of county rates.[55] In later years, his name appears first in the press reports, indicating that he was acting as chair of the bench. Normally his words in court are lost but one day, another jokier side of Abraham emerged (Fig 15).

Public health was another issue for Abraham. Soon after his appointment as a JP, he and his brothers-in-arms (the Stangers and Tom Spedding) had a handbill printed, warning Keswickians about the current outbreak of smallpox and the need to get vaccinated (redolent of modern pandemics). There was concern about cholera as well and recommended *'temperance, warmth, cleanliness, proper diet, good ventilation and efficient drainage and sewerage as preventives of the disease.*[56] The newspaper felt that the JPs as members of the Board of Guardians had the power

85

to go further as in a lane off the main street was a '*plot of land embossed with huge middens composed of all imaginable filth, offal and refuse exhaling enough miasmatic gases to poison an army.*' Although a local board of health was set up in 1853, little happened due to the resistance of the ratepayer lobby. Another epidemic in 1861 saw Abraham and his fellow JPs still arguing for proper drainage and sewerage.[57]

There were regular donations for the relief of poverty. In 1862, there was a dramatic downturn in the textile industry in the northwest, the 'Cotton Famine' which led to considerable distress especially in Carlisle. Abraham donated to this,[58] as well as to the Sewing Society for Employing Factory Girls.[59] Closer to home, every Christmas blankets, meals, money were distributed to the poor neighbours in Borrowdale.[60] In his will, Abraham left £255 (£25,000 in 2022 values) for the poor of the different parishes in which he held property

Of course, Abraham was in and out of Keswick frequently and regularly visited Cockermouth, Carlisle and the west coast towns. Did he travel more widely? Tom Spedding and the Stangers visited London regularly as well as travelling abroad. On at least one occasion, Abraham joined them.

On the 14th August 1848, James Stanger wrote to his brother Joshua from Aix La Chapelle, commenting on the channel crossing when he had been accompanied by Abraham and Mrs Murray – this was Sophia Ann Murray née Lynn, the widowed daughter of the vicar of Caldbeck who would marry James Stanger in June the following year. The trio had met on the 9th, Abraham and James at Euston before rendezvousing with Sophia at London Bridge. After the night in Dover, they crossed to Ostend. Sophia's seasickness was soon a thing of the past after breakfast at the Hotel Christophe.

They took the train to Antwerp, which Stanger found quieter

Fig 16: James Stanger to his brother Joshua 14th August 1848 (Wordsworth Trust)

than last year, but was an interesting start for his companions. This is a hint that it was Abraham's first overseas trip. But he was up for the challenge (Fig 16) …

James comments that Abraham *'comes out most wonderfully'* and was seeking information (or endeavouring to) from his neighbours, be they priests in the carriage or whomsoever he was standing next to at the hotel's Table d'hôte. But he was *'hard put to it to comprehend their replies'*. Does this give us a hint of Abraham as curious and outgoing? Or as to his education - and what language was he using? French was Belgium's official language until 1870. But it was German that was dominant in Switzerland and in most of the cities that they visited. French was widely taught in private schools and perhaps at Crosthwaite but German seems to have been taught only in the so-called Dissenting Academies of non-conformist Protestant groups.

By the evening of the 11th, they were in Liege and a visit to Collegiale St Jacques, a late gothic church, with five magnificent 16th century stained-glass windows, which Stanger had '*long wished to see*'. At home in Keswick, he owned pictures of the windows. The next day, they were at the Nuellen Hotel in Aix (Aachen). This was a pious threesome – they visited the cathedral during High Mass (Stanger's letters frequently mention the local churches) and then went to the Lutheran church for an English service. Stanger was not a strong man – he talked of medicine from his Keswick doctor, was overcome by the lack of ventilation at the Lutheran church and later in the trip, made detailed plans as to where to meet his companions if he had to pull out of a projected mountain walk in Lausanne. Abraham and Sophia were hardier souls.

By chance, the group were witnesses to a grand celebration in Cologne. Hotel rooms were scarce, and Stanger had to rush from the station leaving Abraham to deal with the luggage. He was, however, successful in getting a suite of four '*elegant rooms*'.

1848 was the year of revolution across Europe, seeking political and economic reform France had witnessed four hundred food protests in 1846-1847. "*Society was cut in two: those who had nothing united in common envy, and those who had anything united in common terror.*"[61] 1848 saw the end of the monarchy of Louis-Philippe and the establishment of the Second Republic. In Germany, there was, for a time, the prospect of a more unified Germany.

The Cologne celebration of national unity took place from 13th – 15th August.

Following the election of Archduke Johann as imperial regent, the Cathedral Construction Society in Cologne invited him, the King of Prussia and twenty-five deputies of the Frankfurt National Assembly to a new festival.... This festival was probably the single largest and most important celebration of national unity during the Revolution, a complex event rich in political symbolism.[62]

The parade included military bands, choral societies, the civic guard, tradesmen all marching with their tools, masters and foremen separate from the journeymen and apprentices, and five hundred orphans dressed in white. The papal nuncio joined in. Stanger wrote '*Whether we shall be able to gain admittance, I do not know as I have not yet been able to see any programme but we are going to make the attempt*'.

Cologne and Frankfurt were two centres of the spring uprisings. Was this just fortuitous or, in planning the itinerary, were the companions mimicking Wordsworth and Coleridge when they visited Paris in 1797? Was it political voyeurism?

From Cologne, they visited Frankfurt before heading south to Switzerland, visiting the St Gottard pass and then climbing Mount Rigi (Fig 17), just to the east of Lausanne. At 5897 feet, it was much higher than the Cumberland fells and required some 4000 feet of ascent. Stanger admitted to some trepidation in his letters (a railway to the summit was only built in 1880) but he, somewhat heretically, felt that the Lake District hills did not compare to the Swiss mountains.

Stanger and Abraham Fisher returned to Keswick around 16th September, travelling by the mail train and then by '*special conveyance*' from Ambleside. They had been having been away for five weeks. Was this, literally, the trip of a lifetime for Abraham?

There was no great change of direction. He settled back into

Fig 17: Lake Lucerne from Mount Rigi, near Lausanne

his work routine. Press story after press story showed Abraham's concern about public welfare. Anyone so involved in criminal justice, moral education, children's education (and continuing education through night classes) or the relief of poverty, must have thought long and hard about the world and their place in it. The 1848 trip to Belgium, Germany and Swizerland, was evidence of some political involvement. You wonder about Abraham's thoughts when, two weeks after his return, the Carlisle Journal was reporting disturbances at Cologne and troops on the streets and proclamations banning meetings in Frankfurt.[63]

He never sought to become an MP. Parliamentary seats were the monopoly of the upper classes in Cumberland. Abraham left no sign of skill in speaking or writing. Of course, JPs were the *de facto* local government through petty and quarter sessions. He

Fig 18: Illustration from Westall and Martin: Illustrations of the New Testament (1836)

chose to do good in his own world. This man, in the absence of diaries, letters to the editor or lectures, remains tantalisingly out of reach.

However, some of his preoccupations were revealed by his bookshelves. The contents of the house were auctioned in 1867 and the press notice (Fig 19) was usefully detailed, although far from comprehensive. Judging from the dates of publication, Abraham bought books. His religious interests were shown by the four volumes of the bible, incorporating the commentaries of Matthew Henry and Thomas Scott, which was published by the Religious Tract Society – Abraham's involvement in the church was always practical, supporting missionaries and bible societies and he left £500 to that society. Alongside were the more reader-friendly, eight volumes of bible stories, Richard Westall and John Martin's *Illus-*

trations of the Old and New Testaments (1836) (Fig 18).

As part of the Spedding and Stanger circle, Abraham's cultural interests centred around poetry – Byron's *Childe Harold*, Wordsworth, Southey's edition of Cowper's collected works and an 1858 anthology, *The Home Affections, Pourtrayed by the Poets*, collected by Scottish poet Charles Mackay. A recent 1863 volume was *English Sacred Poetry of Olden Time* by Rev L. B. White, also from the Religious Tract Society. Perhaps the *Glossary of Architecture* and *Gems of European Art* were more for the coffee table than a serious interest.

Abraham was aware of the poverty and poor living conditions of the working class. He subscribed to the *Spectator*. In Abraham's day, this was a radical-liberal, anti-Tory, weekly. It was published by Scottish reformer, Robert Rintoul from the first edition in 1828 before its sale in 1858. But Abraham was a landowner, probably hostile to the claims of organised labour and he also read the *Manchester Guardian*. Before C. P. Scott became editor in 1872, it was a different animal. It was founded in 1821 by cotton merchant, John Taylor and decried by more radical papers as '*the foul prostitute and dirty parasite of the worst portion of the mill-owners*'. In 1863, the Guardian's support of free trade led it to support the Confederacy and to denounce Lincoln, somehow convincing itself that, if the South were allowed direct trade with Europe, slavery would cease to exist. Abraham himself may have been equally ambivalent. However, he was strongly anti-slavery and bought Samuel Wilberforce's *Life and Correspondence of William Wilberforce* when it was published in 1840.

Archibald Alison's *History of Europe from the commencement of the French revolution to the restoration of the Bourbons* was published in ten volumes from 1833 to 1843. This interest in modern history was mirrored by travel with books

Broaches, Pins, Buckles, Bracelets, &c. The Oil Paintings and Water Colour Drawings are by Poole, Pether, Ferguson, Newenham, Cocken, H. B. Richardson, T. Knox, Miss Heathcote, W. Davidson, &c., &c. The Library includes Scott's and Henry's 4to Bibles, Wilberforce's Life of Wilberforce and Correspondence, 7 volumes, Emmerson Tennent's Belgium, 2 volumes, Burton's Anatomy of Melancholy, Atkinson's Worthies of Westmorland, Chitty's Burns' Justice, 1845 ; J. Brown's The Forester, the Spectator, Guardian, Tatler, Beattie's Caledonia, illustrated, 2 vols. ; 4to. ; Hall's Ireland, 3 vols. ; Poems by William Wordsworth, illustrations by Birket Foster, elegantly bound in morocco ; Mackay's "The Home Affections of the Poets," illustrated ; Glossary of Architecture, do. ; English Sacred Poetry of the olden time, do. ; Morris's British Birds, coloured illustrations ; Flintoft's Collection of Mosses in the English Lake District ; Wordsworth's Poetical Works, 6 vols., 18mo. ; Cowper's Poems, Gems of European Art, Childe Harold, copiously illustrated ; Alison's History of Europe, 20 vols. ; Southey's Works of Cowper, 15 vols. ; Oke's Magisterial Synopsis, 1858 ; Oke's Synopsis of Summary Convictions, Westall and Martin's Illustrations of the Old and New Testaments, 8vo., &c., &c. The Carriages con-

Fig 19: Abraham Fisher's library – auction advert (Carlisle Patriot 19th April 1867)

including Emmerson Tennent's *Belgium* (1841) and William Beattie's *Illustrated Caledonia* (1838). Samuel Carter Hall and his wife, Anna Maria Fielding collaborated on books on Ireland in the 1840s. Abraham's 1848 trip to Germany showed a curiosity about the world and there may well have been tours around Scotland and Ireland.

The only practical book which related to managing his

estates was James Brown's *The Forester*, a guide to planting and rearing forest trees, published in 1851. There was also a copy of James Flintoft's *Specimens of British Mosses in the Lake District* (1858) – Flintoft was the son of Joseph, the remarkable Keswick cartographer who made a three-dimensional model of twelve hundred square miles of the Lake District.[64] Abraham also subscribed to *A History of British Birds* by the clergyman, Francis Orpen Morris. This was a best-seller, published from June 1850 in monthly parts, each time with four hand-coloured plates, over a period of some seven years.

There was Chitty Burn's Justice and Oke's Summary Conviction. The new taste in crime fiction may have appealed to the magistrate in him. In 1841, Edgar Allen Poe's Chevalier Dupin solved the case in *The Murders in the Rue Morgue* and in 1852, Inspector Bucket was the first English detective to appear in Charles Dickens' *Bleak House*. Sadly, no such frivolous material appeared on Abraham's shelves.

His work as a magistrate meant that Abraham was still travelling around the county. Did he continue to ride his own horse, after his accident in 1843.[65] Perhaps his long-time servant, Isaac Thompson, drove him, although in the stable in the 1860s was a mature, dark brown mare, *'quiet to ride or drive'*. In 1857, he employed John Mossop as a groom. He was the son of Thomas and Margaret who ran the hotel at Lodore. John had worked there with his mother, after the death of Thomas in 1851. But Margaret decided to retire, perhaps with her upcoming marriage in mind. In July 1857, she married William Bowe, a boatman and local guide. Bowe would have been quite an asset to the hotel's business, but Margaret had also got into debt. In March 1857, there was a sale of the hotel furniture for the benefit of creditors. Conveyances were also sold: one carriage, two cars, a gig (Fig 20) ... Did Abraham, now fifty, buy a more

Fig 20: A late Victorian round back gig - a popular mode of transport for gentlemen in during the 1860's. Well sprung with an upholstered seat meant a comfortable ride.

Fig 21: A basket park phaeton – lightweight and compact two seaters, highly fashionable in New York in the 1860s.

Fig 22: Victorian Whatnot

comfortable means of transport for himself to drive, while at the same time employing an experienced driver? At his death,[66] he also owned two phaetons (Fig 21), one with a hood to keep off the rain.

Inside the house, the rooms were comfortable – there was an antique oak cabinet as well as many tables: mahogany telescope, table, fold-down Sutherlands and Pembrokes, round loo tables, card tables (and bagatelle boards). There was much silver plate to go on the dining tables including cutlery, candlesticks, cruet stands, mustard and pepper boxes, cream jugs. There were oak chairs in Morocco covers, sofas, a walnut couch, easy chairs in damask and chintz covers, ottomans and what-nots (an elegant piece of furniture, free-standing, displaying glass, china or perhaps souvenirs from Abraham's European trip).

95

Fig 23: Portrait by Anne Heathcote 1867)

There was a mirror (chimney glass) in a gilt frame above the mantelpieces. On the floor were Brussels and Kidderminster carpets. On the walls were oils and water colours: landscapes by James Poole, moody moonlight scenes by Sebastian Pether, seascapes by Henry Burdon Richardson and portraits by a woman artist, Anne Heathcote (Fig 23).

Upstairs the bedrooms had mahogany wardrobes with marble-topped washing tables with mirrors for dressing. There were feather mattresses with blankets and quilts, as well as a good quantity of linen.

He died on 20th October 1864 after a short illness,

...*one of the oldest families in the county. By far the largest proprietor in Borrowdale and everyone noticed the comfortable looking homestead. AF dwelt among his own people and was looked up to as a pattern in every relation of life. Most liberal to his tenants; constant benefactor to the poor; everywhere his ample means were freely given to alleviation of suffering or for promotion of education or religion. The unostentatious and kindly manner in which he dispensed his charity added to the pleasure of the recipient*[67]

Abraham '*dwelt among his own people*'. Wealthy, living in

a comfortable house, looked after by faithful servants, there was every prospect of a quiet, uneventful life. However, he was on the fringes of those in Keswick who were more educated, more travelled, read more widely and who debated contemporary political and social issues. This rubbed off on Abraham as he was intellectually curious. In religion, he was not satisfied with sedentary Anglicanism, supporting evangelical and non-conformist charities. During the year of revolution in Europe, he embraced the opportunity to visit Germany and Switzerland. And in the dark winter evenings, he would read the *Spectator* or the *Guardian*. But who to debate with? From 1842, there was just his contemporary, Tom Simpson (1808-1872) who had made a fortune in New York, returning to the valley to build Hazel Bank in Rosthwaite. Tom, however, had little education although his son, solicitor John Simpson (1842-1920), was well-read and cultured.

In his 1864 will, away from those who had served him and his family, there were just two people whom he called friends. Edmund Cocken (1806-1873) lived at Hawthorns, Chestnut Hill in Keswick, was a Londoner. As a '*bank proprietor*' he probably did not need the legacy of £250. The other bequest was much more personal. Simpsons had lived at Redmain Hall, near Isel, for generations. Bolton Simpson (1807-1892) as a contemporary of Abraham's and might have attended Crosthwaite School. He graduated from Queens, Cambridge and his first job was as a curate in Buttermere. He was the vicar at St Botolph's in Bossal in North Yorkshire from 1854. Abraham left him his intake, Muddocks, on Buttermere

Abraham had a busy life but perhaps lonely. He had neglected, *'the truth universally acknowledged, that a single man in possession of a good fortune, must be in want of* a *wife.'*

Notes

[1] *Harrison P., (2021)* Mountain Republic *401-403 and 455-458 – the sketch of the school is from Harrison.*
[2] *Cumberland Pacquet 10th June 1851*
[3] *Carlisle Patriot 10th September 1825*
[4] *Gillbanks J., (1906) John Crozier Manchester Quarterly January 1906 - http://blencathrafoxhounds.co.uk/SquireCrozier3.htm*
[5] *Simon Lee: The Old Huntsman (William Wordsworth)*
[6] *Cumberland Pacquet 18th April 1843*
[7] *Carlisle Patriot 20th October 1832*
[8] *Carlisle Journal 12th August 1843; another such was to assess the value of land required for the Lancaster and Carlisle Railway - Carlisle Journal 24th May 1845*
[9] *Carlisle Journal 4th August 1854*
[10] *Westmorland Gazette 11th November 1865*
[11] *Carlisle Journal 11th July 1840 – his friend and tenant, the Rev Monkhouse, showed prospective purchasers the building.*
[12] *In 1851, the tenant was George Minniken, a nurseryman, and the house was on Main Street*
[13] *Carlisle Journal 1st April 1843*
[14] *Kendal Mercury 24 February 1838*
[15] *Carlisle Journal 1 August 1840*
[16] *Uglow S., (2021) Early Tourism in Borrowdale CW3 175*
[17] *Manchester Courier 12th January 1884*
[18] *Cumberland Pacquet 25th March 1856*
[19] *Carlisle Journal 8th July 1859*
[20] *Charles Dickens, The Lazy Tour of Two Idle Apprentices ch 3*
[21] *Kendal Mercury 1st July 1849*
[22] *Fielding K. J., (1986/87)* Carlyle and the Speddings *Carlyle Newsletter No 7 12-20 and No. 8 51-66*
[23] *Westmorland Gazette 3rd March 1866 for an extended obituary*

[24] *Harrison P., (2021) 372 – Harrison mistakes father James Stanger for his son, James*
[25] *Harrison P., (2021) 408 for more on this remarkable family*
[26] *There were two children, William and Charlotte – William returned to India in 1855 and retired and was buried in Corsica: Le Clerc P., (2018)* The Isolated Tomb *West Middlesex FHS Journal 8*
[27] *Bott G. K., (2005 2nd ed)* Keswick *78ff*
[28] *ibid*
[29] *Uglow J., (2012)* The Pinecone *chs 1 and 2 gives a vivid introduction*
[30] *Kaye W., (1966)* Governor's House, Keswick *CW2 340*
[31] *Denman D., (2014)* Lord William Gordon and the picturesque occupation of Derwentwater in the 1780s *CW3 207; D. Denman, Materialising Cultural Value in the English Lakes 1735-1845 (PhD thesis, University of Lancaster) 198ff (at eprints.lancs.ac.uk/61596/1/DenmanThesisEprint.pdf)*
[32] *Cumberland Pacquet 7th November 1843*
[33] *Morning Chronicle 19th May 1845 for list of subscribers*
[34] *Cumberland Pacquet 9th December 1834*
[35] *Cumberland Pacquet 19th January 1847*
[36] *Cumberland Pacquet 22nd May 1855; the branch had been reorganised by James Stanger in 1826 - Cumberland Pacquet 26th May 1857*
[37] *Cumberland Patriot 17th February 1855*
[38] *Harrison P., (2021) 478 for a blow-by-blow account*
[39] *Carlisle Journal 7th September 1865 suggests that the house was originally bought for £1300 by John Simpson of Hazel Bank, Rosthwaite*
[40] *CRO Whitehaven DWM 11/265/3 - records of Marshall family; Leeds Mercury 16th October 1884 for short obituary*
[41] *West Cumberland Times 14th November 1874*
[42] *Carlisle Journal 30th December 1859 5*
[43] *Cumberland Pacquet 10th June 1845*
[44] *Cumberland Pacquet 25th December 1860*
[45] *Kendal Mercury 1st July 1848*
[46] *Marshall J. D. and Walton J. K., (1981)* The Lake Counties *107 and 119*
[47] *Marshall J. D. and Walton J. K., (1981) 99*

[48] *Bouch C. M. L. and Jones G. P., (1961)* The Lake Counties 1500-1830 147; Harrison P., (2021) 486 ff
[49] *Inspectors of Prisons of Great Britain IV. Northern District, Thirteenth Report (Parl. Papers, 1847-8, XXXVI.361), p.116*
[50] *Carlisle Journal 18th March 1853*
[51] *Cumberland Pacquet 28th October 1851*
[52] *Carlisle Journal 27th January 1854*
[53] *Carlisle Journal 29th January 1864*
[54] *Carlisle Journal 29th May 1863*
[55] *Cumberland Pacquet 28th October 1851*
[56] *Cumberland Pacquet 13th February 1849; Bott G. K., (2005 2nd ed) 85-88 for the efforts to counter this*
[57] *Carlisle Journal 13th December 1861*
[58] *Carlisle Patriot 11th October 1862*
[59] *Carlisle Journal 3rd October 1862*
[60] *Cumberland Pacquet 3rd January 1854*
[61] *Tocqueville A, de, (1893)* Recollections
[62] *Sperber J., (1992)* Festivals of National Unity in the German Revolution of 1848-49 *136 Past and Present 114 at 123*
[63] *Carlisle Journal 29th September 1848*
[64] *Harrison P., (2021)* 538
[65] *Cumberland Pacquet 18th April 1843*
[66] *The house and its contents were bought by first cousin, Grace Gibson. She died eighteen months later and the contents were auctioned: Carlisle Patriot 19th April 1867*
[67] *Carlisle Journal 2nd February 1864*

10. Seatoller House: The Guest House Owners after Abraham Fisher

The Fishers lived in Seatoller House for two hundred and forty years but Abraham, like his siblings, died childless. Under the will, he gave,

The residue of my property both real and personal ... to the descendants of the Brothers and Sisters of my late grandfather and grandmother, Joseph Fisher and his wife... and ... to the descendants of the Brothers and Sisters of the whole and half blood of my late Father, John Fisher, of Seatoller aforesaid who may be living at the time of my decease

There was inevitably a dispute over the will.[1] Abraham's grandfather, Joseph, had both a sister, Sarah, who married into the Jopsons at Chapel, and a brother, Caleb, who had taken over the Fisher lands at Grange. Abraham's father, John, had been the eldest with three brothers and a sister. Timothy (1761 – before 1819) had been a Glasgow manufacturer and had left a son, Anthony, and a daughter, Mary. Joseph (1764 – bef 1819) had a son, mentioned but not named in his mother's will. He certainly had a daughter, Mary who had been a beneficiary under brother Isaac's will. Isaac died childless. Sister Dinah (1770-1847) had two surviving children, Daniel and Grace Gibson.

By February 1865, an action had commenced in the Court of Chancery in *Grace Gibson v John Cowley Fisher*. John Cowley Fisher (1807-1887) came from Bridekirk and was, alongside John Fisher Crosthwaite, executor of Abraham's will. Now the lawyers were involved. Press notices were placed by the solicitors advertising for any descendants to come forward.[2] Inevitably and speedily, the court ruled that Abraham's estate would be broken up and the proceeds divided.

The auction of the houses, farms and land and took place at the Drill Hall of the Skiddaw Greys, starting at 1 pm on 6th September 1865 with two hundred people present. Reserve prices had been set by Chancery-appointed valuers. This meant that many lots did not reach this reserve. Uzzicar in Newlands went to Dr Rumney of Keswick[3] but most of the Borrowdale land and properties was sold to Henry Cowper Marshall (1808-1884). Marshall paid £7500 for the Yew Tree, Brig House and Row End and £850 for Howgate Farm, all in St John's in the Vale. He also bought Lyzzick Hall for £6750.

The Marshall family were from Leeds and their wealth came from their flax factories. Henry Cowper had been mayor of Leeds in 1843.[4] He and his siblings owned swathes of Lake District land. But one lot escaped Marshall. Seatoller House was bought for £1300 by Rosthwaite solicitor, John Simpson of Hazel Bank. He was acting on behalf of Abraham's first cousin, Grace Gibson (1798-1867).[5] Grace had been close to Abraham. They had gone on holiday together, to the coast at Allonby.[6] He left her Bunbury House in Keswick with *'its pleasure grounds and four cottages'* and with its tenant, a nurseryman, George Minniken (1807-1871). George would later run the Scafell Hotel in Rosthwaite.

Grace also inherited all Abraham's household furniture, the plate, linen, china, wines and spirits. Buying Seatoller House was not just a gesture for Grace as it was her mother's family home. Grace lived there for eighteen months. Oddly, she never completed the purchase. On 6th March 1867, her solicitor, John Simpson, had drawn the cheque and was on his way to get her signature. She died before he arrived.[7]

At 10 o'clock on Monday 11th March (Fig 1), the funeral

FUNERAL OF THE LATE MISS GRACE GIBSON, OF POWTER HOWE.—On Monday the 11th instant, the remains of this excellent lady were interred at Thornthwaite church with every demonstration of respect and regret. Miss Gibson died at Seatoller, in Borrowdale, for many centuries the seat of her maternal ancestors, and of which she had recently become the owner. The funeral party assembled at 10 o'clock when, according to local custom, the funeral psalm (90th) was sung, and the procession moved slowly through Borrowdale. On reaching Keswick no fewer than 21 carriages and other vehicles formed the procession, and before reaching Thornthwaite several more joined. Here, at one o'clock, representatives from every house in the parish joined, each anxious to show their regard for one who had lived so well amongst them. The Rev. H. S. Short, M. A., the incumbent, read the funeral service with great feeling. Miss Gibson was a representative of the ancient yeomanry of Cumberland of the best type. Her tastes and disposition led her to associate on terms of close intimacy with that class, whilst her society was equally prized by all ranks. Her frank and generous disposition, combined with the most delicate consideration for the failings, sorrows, and wants of others, evinced itself on all occasions. Her hand was ever ready to give to whoever needed, and in dispensing her charity she always counted herself the obliged person. Her piety was unaffected, but, deep, and pervaded her whole life.

Fig 1: Funeral of Grace Gibson - Cumberland Pacquet 19th March 1867

procession assembled at St Andrews – it was a Borrowdale custom to sing the 90th Psalm,

Lord, thou hast been our dwelling place in all generations.
Before the mountains were brought forth, or ever thou hadst formed the earth and the world...
For a thousand years in thy sight are but as yesterday when it is past, and as a watch in the night.

The procession moved slowly through the valley, numbering over twenty carriages by the time it reached Thornthwaite. There representatives from every house in the parish joined in the service.

Grace had not only bought the house but also the contents. Her failure to complete the purchase and her death meant that the trustees of Abraham's estate could proceed with selling both house and contents. There was a four-day auction, culminating at the house itself on Friday 3rd May. By the evening Seatoller House had been emptied of all the books, paintings, furniture and carpets built up by the Fishers over several generations. The carriages were gone from the coach house as had the dark brown mare, the stone roller and other garden equipment had been sold as had a variety of dahlia roots and a few Brahma fowls.[8]

Grace had an aunt, Mary Birkett, the half-sister of Grace's mother, Dinah. Mary had married a Rosthwaite farmer, John Wilson and it was their children who were the main beneficiaries from Grace's will. Unlike Abraham, Grace had a wide social circle and she left small legacies to numerous people. However, there was an odd nod to the past – Abraham's uncle, Timothy, had been a Glasgow manufacturer. His son, Anthony, had become a London doctor and Grace instructed her lawyer to write in a legacy of £1000. However, when she got around to signing the will, she had changed her mind and there was a codicil of the same date as the will revoking this bequest. What had happened?

Another unlucky almost-beneficiary was Caleb Fisher Wilson, a Grange lad, who had become an articled clerk with solicitor Robert Broatch in Keswick, then moving to London and, after qualifying, becoming managing clerk with Helps & Co in Chester. He died very suddenly aged twenty-six, just eight months after Grace.

After Grace's death, there was one person (or maybe two) left in Seatoller House. Abraham Fisher's long-time housekeeper, Elizabeth Harrison, had already left after his death. She received a legacy of £75 from Abraham. She married Thorneythwaite farmer, Thomas Walker, in November 1865, just weeks after Grace Gibson had bought the house. But Abraham's groom, John Mossop, had stayed on. He also received a legacy of £100 and another £50 from Grace. But he was to indirectly benefit from a much larger bequest.

Six days after the 1867 auction, he married Sarah Braithwaite née Stainton (1824-1868). She was the widow of London silversmith, John. There was an odd connection with the Seatoller Fishers, in this case Isaac, Abraham's brother. Isaac had been brought up in Seatoller House but apprenticed to a London goldsmith. Isaac had been in partnership in Cockspur Street with another Cumbrian, Frank Braithwaite. Isaac died, a wealthy man, in London in 1819. Frank, from St John's in the Vale, had carried as a goldsmith. By 1851, he was in his fifties but unmarried. At his Chelsea home, he was surrounded by family. He had taken on his nephew, John Braithwaite (1820-1864), to teach him the trade. John was the son of Frank's brother, Thomas, a captain in the merchant navy.

Also in Chelsea was Frank's widowed brother-in-law, Jackson Stainton. Stainton had worked with him since the 1820s when Frank had been the witness at Jackson's marriage to Frank's sister, Sarah. Their daughter, Sarah, was now behind the

105

shop counter and, in 1852, married John Braithwaite, her first cousin. But in the mid-1860s, Sarah was left alone in London, following the death of her father in 1853, uncle Frank in 1862 and husband John in 1864.

What brought her to Borrowdale is a mystery as she was a London girl, schooled in Lewisham after her mother's death and with only tenuous links to Ennerdale and St John's in the Vale. Another mystery is that her uncle and husband left her poor - John's personal effects in 1864 were under £50. This is surprising since Isaac Fisher, the original partner in the firm, had died a very wealthy man. One clue is in Grace's will when she describes Sarah as '*my relation*'. She set up a trust of £2000, the income to go to Sarah, still a Braithwaite. Grace knew what was in the wind and specified that the income was to be '*free from all marital control*' (a phrase that Abraham had also used in relation to his bequests to women).

Perhaps this enabled John and Sarah Mossop to move to Shorley Croft in Keswick, a large period property on the Penrith Road, nowadays a house with five bedrooms, six bathrooms and front and rear gardens. Was the plan to run their own guest house? That was thwarted when Sarah died seven months after their marriage. The Keswick banker, John Fisher Crosthwaite, was an executor. Thanks to Grace, her effects were valued at under £2000 (£175,000 in 2023 prices). Sarah left £150 to an old servant from Chelsea and other amounts to the family of a friend in London, James Redman Boulton (1823-1885), a civil servant with the Inland Revenue. The income from the residue went to John Mossop and on his death reverted to her Stainton family in Ennerdale.

By September 1867, Seatoller House was auctioned again, with the adverts describing it as a mansion with pleasure grounds and garden. Several surrounding fields were included as the whole comprised twelve acres. Although it failed to reach its reserve at auction (about £1200), it was later bought by Henry Marshall.[9] After Marshall's death in 1884, the farm and Seatoller House (with stables, gardens, paddock and two cottages) were sold again in 1895 to J W Dickinson of Whitehaven for £4500.[10] He was acting as an agent for Henry Wyndham, the 2nd Baron Leconfield (1830-1901).[11] The Leconfield estate owned the mineral rights at Honister.

The ownership passed to the 3rd Baron[12], Charles Henry Wyndham (1872 -1952), inherited the property in 1901. It remained tenanted but when Wyndham died in 1952, the house was transferred to the National Trust in lieu of death duties. The then tenant, John Cockbain (1923-2001), bought the house in 1960[13] with the help of George Macaulay Trevelyan, the initiator of the Trinity Cambridge hunts. In 1977, the freehold was sold to The Lakes Hunts Ltd, a private company set up by the Trevelyan family.

The Tenants
After the death of Grace Gibson in 1867, none of the subsequent owners lived in Seatoller House (until the Cockbains). In 1871, the census enumerated fourteen people in four properties in Seatoller, all owned by Henry Cowper Marshall. There was the farm, run by the widow Ann Jopson (1806-1889) and her sons. There were the two Yew Tree cottages, one with an old couple, John Hird (1794-1872) and his wife, Mary (1790-1873). Sarah Wren (1816-1887), the widow of farmer Isaac, lived in the other half. Richard and Jane Holme and their widowed daughter Sophia (1828-) were living in Seatoller House.

Jane Holme
Jane Holme was the first Seatoller House landlady. As Jane

Briggs (1806-1886), she was born in Bootle in Cumberland, the daughter of a wine and spirit merchant, William Briggs (1776-1844). She was brought up in commerce and was running a grocer's shop in Bootle with her sister, Mary, in 1841. In 1851, after her father's death, she lived in Whitehaven with her mother, Jane (1784-1855) and sisters, making hats.

She was in her 40s when she met and married Richard Holme (1800-1876), a gas engineer, originally from Manchester. He had been married previously and had a married daughter and a son. In 1861, Richard was still working as an engineer in Broughton Mills in south Lakeland and they lived in a cottage in Shuttle Street, close to the Blacksmith's Arms. Jane was clearly accustomed to her independence and was teaching writing and sewing.

Between October 1867 and 1871, the Holmes moved to Seatoller. Jane had visited Seatoller before, perhaps with her father, William, as a young girl. In his will, Abraham left £1000 to be shared between the daughters of his late cousin,[14] William Briggs, who was a Bootle '*mercer and draper*' when he married Jane Hellon in 1802 but by 1841, was a wine and spirits merchant in Furness.

Did Jane come to the funeral? She may well have needed to come to Fisher Crosthwaite's bank to discuss the inheritance on behalf of her sisters, Hannah Jackson and Maria Phoebe Dawson. By then, Grace Gibson may have died and Fisher Crosthwaite (a man with a finger in every Keswick pie) may have discussed the possibility of leasing the house. Who knows?

Relationships with their neighbours did not start well – Richard was brought before petty sessions in Keswick for non-payment of rates (Fig 2^{15}) and objected that he was being asked to pay 10½ d in the pound whereas some farmers were asked for 2½ d. Richard was on good terms with Tom Simpson (1808-1872) of Hazel Bank in Rosthwaite, writing to his daughter in

NON-PAYMENT OF RATES.—*Wm. Holmes*, of Seatoller, appeared in answer to a summons, issued at the instance of the Highway Surveyor of Borrowdale (Thomas Fleming,) to account for the non-payment of highway rates.—Mr. Holmes stated that in the first place the legal formula had not been carried out, no notice having been given of the meeting when the rate in question was levied, and further that some farmers were charged 2½d. in the pound while he was asked for 10½d. in the pound.—The Bench retired for consultation with their clerk, and on resuming their seats informed Mr. Holmes that the matter would be referred to the clerk of the peace for the county, who would state from which side an appeal should be made.—Mr. Holmes, before leaving the court very adroitly quoted a friend's remark, "that it was parish policy to tax our friends, but to evade being taxed ourselves."

Fig 2: Penrith Observer 18th April 1871

New York, who frequently referred to him fondly. Richard tried to persuade Tom to install gas lighting and heating into his home but without success.

By 1871, Richard was seventy-one and Jane sixty-four. Seatoller House was much too large for a retirement home for two elderly people. In an isolated hamlet, far from modern amenities, it seems an odd choice. So odd indeed that one explanation is that Jane always intended to take in paying guests as a means of supplementing their income after Richard's retirement. There are neither visitor books nor newspaper adverts to confirm that this was the plan. Nor does the census of 1871 help as the enumerator visited before the season began. Richard's will described him as a 'gent. Seatoller. But the couple ran a lodging house. Decisively, Tom Simpson in his letters mentioned parties of guests at the Holmes' house. Jane continued to run the business after Richard died in Seatoller on 3rd February 1876.[16]

Jane was probably fit and active for her age. She was also financially astute – her estate consisted of New Zealand government debentures rather than cash and chattels.[17] She would have seen Borrowdale was a good opportunity for a guesthouse. The increase in visitor numbers to the north Lakes had been considerable since the Keswick, Cockermouth and Penrith Railway opened the station at Keswick in January 1865. Coaches now ran excursions past Derwent Water, over Honister, around Buttermere and back to Keswick. New hotels such as the Borrowdale had been built and old ones such as the Lodore enlarged but further down the valley, there was little provision, just the Royal Oak in Rosthwaite. In the 1851 census, no-one in Borrowdale township identified as a 'lodging house keeper'. Travellers could rely on farm hospitality. By 1861, Newton Place, opposite the modern Borrowdale hotel, was a boarding house, in Grange, Ann Wilson, a widow, ran a lodging house and Thomas Fleming had just opened a new lodging house, later the Scafell Hotel in Rosthwaite.[18]

Jane Holme saw the opportunity. Alongside trippers, there were increasing numbers of walkers and climbers. It was the more adventurous tourists who stayed in those remote settings, thought to offer a more authentic Lakeland. Guides to the Lakes had proliferated since Thomas West (*This little delightful Eden.*)[19] They included James Clark (1787 – and very rude about Borrowdale), Wordsworth (1810) Jonathan Otley (1823), William Ford (1839) and Harriet Martineau (1855).

Jane's visitors would also have read the Lake poets, spelling out not just the grandeur of the landscape but hinting at the possibilities of discovery and adventure. A visitor might imagine following in the footsteps of Coleridge,

> *...and on a nice Stone Table am I now at this moment writing to you ... surely the first Letter ever written from the Top of Sca' Fell! But O! what a look down just under my Feet! The frightfullest Cove that might ever be seen, huge perpendicular Precipices, and one Sheep upon it's only Ledge, that surely must be crag! Tyson told me of this place, & called it Hollow Stones. Just by it & joining together, rise two huge Pillars of bare lead-colored stone... I have no shadow of hesitation in saying that the Coves & Precipices of Helvellin are nothing to these! ... I see directly thro' Borrowdale, the Castle Crag, the whole of Derwent Water, & but for the haziness of the Air I could see own House [*Greta Hall, Keswick*]*[20]

There was the indomitable example of Dorothy Wordsworth, aged forty-six, who proudly said that she could '*...walk 16 miles in four hours and three quarters, with short rests between, on a blustering cold day, without having felt any fatigue'*. On October 7th, 1818, she completed a walk with Mary Barker from Rosthwaite to Scafell Pike, a round trip of some fourteen miles and with some three thousand, two hundred feet of ascent.

Visitors would also have been drawn to the wilder and more remote valleys by the greater availability of maps and the prints of sights such as the Bowderstone. There were, of course, the artists. In 1806, John Constable spent two months in the Lakes, half of this in Borrowdale, sketching (Fig 3).

In October 1836, Edward Lear was at the top of Honister Pass, also sketching, in his case the looming and threatening Honister Crag.

As the later Visitors' Books show, Seatoller House has always attracted a *"relatively small, niche market composed of those who wished to contemplate the scenery and savour the*

Fig 3: *Castle Crag (John Constable 1806)*
(Museum of New Zealand – Te Papa Tongarewa)

literary and artistic associations."[21]

Jane's status as a landlady was confirmed in an 1883 directory[22] includes '*Jane Holme, lodgings, Seatoller House*'. When she drew up her will, the witnesses were a local farmer, Daniel Jopson from Chapel, but also a music professor from Leamington Spa, undoubtedly a guest. Jane had built up a reputation – when her successor, Mary Jane Pepper, started advertising Seatoller House as a destination, she carefully included Jane Holme's name in the text.

At the point when Jane Holme was building her guesthouse business, the slate trade was also expanding as a result of a booming construction industry. A group from Ulverston formed the Buttermere Green Slate Company, after negotiations with the

Leconfield estate, signing a lease on 21st October 1879 to exploit Yew Craggs at Honister Pass. By 1881 there were fifty-three men working at the quarry, only seven of whom were valley men. The others came from Cornwall, Wales, Langdale, Coniston and Furness.

Moses Pepper
In 1881, accommodation within walking distance of the mine was in short supply –most of the quarrymen were accommodated in Stonethwaite or Rosthwaite. Just one family were in Seatoller, Moses Pepper (1846-1915), living at Seatoller House. Moses had been a labourer in the Burlington slate quarries at Kirkby Ireleth in 1871 but the next year, he was chairing a meeting of the workforce there, writing to the management to demand that hours be reduced from fifty-eight to fifty-five.[23] He had also been involved in the Kirkby Co-operative Society when it was founded in 1861 as well as in the Quarry Sick Club. He wrote an article on the formation of the Co-op which suggests that he had had a reasonable education.[24]

His abilities must have attracted the attention of the men who set up the company – two were solicitors but John Shepherd Sawrey (1848-1911) was a mining engineer from Ulverston, an inventive man who filed for a patent for pump improvements in 1882 with Alfred Attwood and Henry Woodburne, also of Ulverston. In 1902, there was another patent application in the USA for speak-your-weight scales.

This present invention relates to weighing machines combined with automatic sound-producing mechanism so that the accurate weight of the person or object shall be audibly announced and also, if desired, advertisements or other announcements audibly made or sounds of any other kind produced.[25]

Did Sawrey and his partners headhunt Moses? He had a small family, strong ties to their Kirkby family and was liked and respected at the quarry. There had to be a strong incentive for him to move. This inference is reinforced by the fact that Moses had a management role from the start.[26] This was a responsible position - by the end of 1879, there were already twenty-four men were working at the quarry.[27] And there were the ancillary jobs – Keswick Literary and Scientific Society turned up on 22nd June 1881 where the *'courteous'* manager, *'pointed out the course of the slate veins, their principal features and the mode of quarrying, splitting and dressing the slate'.*[28]

Moses' management role was short-lived. In 1884, Sawrey and his fellow directors brought in Bennett Johns, from Ulverston as manager and secretary with an office in the new Station Buildings at Keswick.[29] He lived with his family in Station Street, and stayed with the company for forty years. Johns produced a critical report on the company's problems in December 1884, highlighting the issues for the men working in the quarry, especially their isolation away from their families. These mirrored the concerns that Moses would have stressed. With Johns often in Keswick, did Moses remain as Johns' right-hand man in the quarries? He referred to himself in later censuses just as a quarryman.

Was Moses lucky in finding somewhere to live so close to his place of work? Or was accommodation part of the deal? Did the company negotiate this with Jane? It is likely that Sawrey and solicitor partner, John Poole, stayed at Seatoller House in their visits to Honister as they sought to close the contract with the Leconfield Estate.

After a full inspection of the quarries, both on the surface and underground, Sawrey and Poole complained that the previous

on "The happiness of married life" in a tone so distinct, so dignified, and so solemn, that, if you had only shut your eyes, you might, without any great stretch of the imagination, have fancied you were listening to an impressive exhortation from some dignitary of the church ; and, on opening them again, you would almost expect to catch a glimpse of the lawn sleeves. Mr. Pepper's reading produced a thrilling sensation. One or two old ladies were observed to wipe a tear furtively away ; and, as to the young ones, I have no doubt that not a few of them then and there resolved to lose no more time but to accept the first eligible offer made them, in

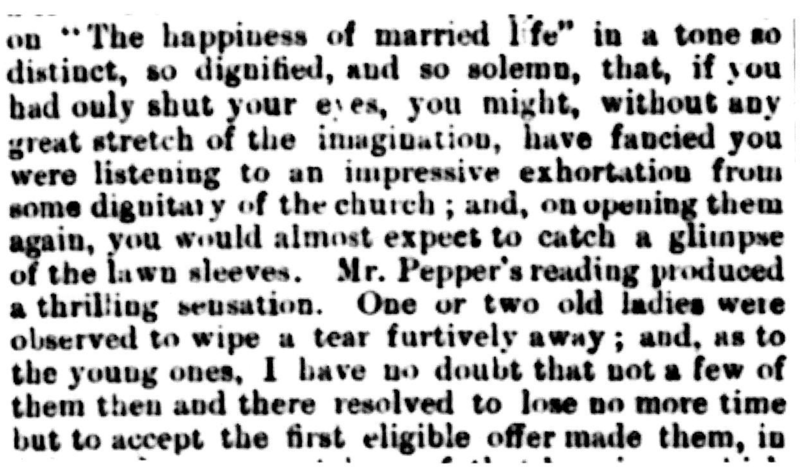

Fig 4: Moses Pepper as a 21-year-old bachelor on the 'happiness of married life' - Ulverston Mirror 23rd February 1867

tenant had robbed the quarries of the best slate... '[30]

Moses' wife was Mary Jane Robinson (1845-1929). They were both from Kirkby Ireleth where they married in 1870. Their daughters, Mary Agnes (1871-1928) and Ada (1875-1944) were both born in Kirkby. Moses and his family were also Rechabites. They were, in origin a strictly teetotal, Israelite sect that also refused to engage in farming. But in 19th century Britain, they were a friendly society, based on their beliefs in temperance. This must have been a plus for Jane Holme as slate miners were a rough lot, not renowned for their abstinence. In the autumn of 1879, the Peppers moved in. For them and for Jane Holme, Seatoller House may have been an ideal solution. For the widowed Jane, not only was it income, another pair of hands to help with the visitors but this young family with their two small girls, only eight and four when they moved to Seatoller, dispelled the prospect of having to live alone in a large house over a gloomy Borrowdale winter.

Back in Kirkby Ireleth, Moses had been a good citizen. In 1867 he had contributed (Fig 4) to the village's '*penny readings*', in the Mission Room in Swan Street, reading an essay on the '*happiness of married life*',

There were concerts to raise money for the reading room at Burlington Slate Works when Moses often performed songs such as '*Forgive and forget*'.[31] He was a brother of the International Order of Good Templars (IOGT), another temperance organisation, named because the original knights templar allegedly drank sour milk, and because the IOGT were fighting 'a great crusade' against 'this terrible vice' of alcohol. In 1874, Moses had hired the reading room and presided over IOGT lectures on the '*curse of drink*'.[32]

The move to Borrowdale meant shouldering very different duties. There were new management responsibilities. His daughters were growing up and in 1884, Mary Jane and Moses had a son, Isaac. And there were the less welcome tasks that every valley (male) resident had to undertake from time to time. In August 1882, Moses found himself on a coroner's jury at Seathwaite. The Rev Pope, a unitarian minister from Spitalfields, in London, died when descending Great Gable in the mist, unwisely trying to jump down a difficult slope.[33] In 1885, it was a local man living at Chapel, road surveyor John Cannon, killed when digging gravel in Salmon Hole, between Seatoller and Honister. Moses was the foreman at the inquest.[34]

He maintained his beliefs and his activism on moving to Borrowdale. Despite working perhaps sixty hours a week, he was involved in many religious and temperance organisations, maintaining that involvement for decades. The Christian Workers Band in Keswick would play and conduct services every Sunday – in 1884 they did this at seven different sites.[35] Moses was their

116

vice president and for ten years organised a Good Friday tea party at Mrs Fleming's in Stonethwaite,[36] which sometimes attracted one hundred.

Moses's religious affiliation was non-conformist and probably Methodist. On Easter Sunday (after the Stonethwaite tea party on Good Friday), he arrived at Applethwaite to preach to their Band of Hope,[37]

> *Nevertheless, God's solid foundation stands firm, sealed with this inscription: "The Lord knows those who are his," and, "Everyone who confesses the name of the Lord must turn away from wickedness."* [38]

For many years around 1890, Moses ran an anniversary service at Grange for the Wesleyan Band of Hope.[39] All this tied into the temperance movement and Moses was a strong campaigner, local speaking at schools and meetings.[40] One success came when, in late 1892, the local valley community, backed by the Buttermere slate company had set up a Mission Room in Rosthwaite. It probably met (despite its advocacy of temperance) at the Mechanics Room at the Royal Oak.[41] Moses appeared indefatigable, but this constant activity took its toll and it was not surprising when he was too ill to address the Temperance Reform Society at Christmas in 1884.[42]

Perhaps temperance was an issue that came close to home for Moses. His uncle, Matthew Pepper (1819-1892) had left Kirkby Ireleth in the south Lakes, as a relatively young man, probably working in the Elterwater slate quarries, also owned by Burlington. Matthew's son, Edward, was summoned to court in 1876 for throwing stones at a constable. Edward did not help matters by being drunk in court and received a prison sentence of two months with hard labour.[43] Perhaps the scandal encouraged the Elterwater family to move to Borrowdale where

117

they found jobs (through Moses?) at Honister. Initially they lived at Thorneythwaite where Matthew had three of his fellow quarrymen as boarders. One of them was John Shaw, one of the "*Langdale Rowdies*" who had caused trouble with Edward. However, Edward settled down, perhaps under the influence of his cousin, and around 1899 was one of the first tenants in New Cottages.

Moses was a political liberal, as might be expected from a spokesman for the workers and a non-conformist. The Representation of the People Act 1884 meant that he was able to vote in a general election for the first time in his life.[44] In the election campaign of 1885, Moses spoke at Borrowdale school in support of the candidate, Henry Howard (1850-1914).[45] John James Spedding (1834-1909), the nephew of Tom Story Spedding and a JP who had sat on the bench with Abraham Fisher took the chair. Howard was a member of the influential family, headed by the Duke of Norfolk – he resigned the liberal whip in July 1886 over disagreements with Gladstone about Irish home rule.

Moses remained involved in liberal politics, sitting on the committee of the Keswick Liberal Association as a Borrowdale representative – with him were George Mounsey, a carpenter from Grange (another temperance campaigner) and William Hudson, a foreman at Honister.

The Liberal governments not only reformed national politics but also local government. Local government, until 1888, was in the hands of magistrates who not only presided over local courts but, meeting at Quarter Sessions, were involved in administrative issues such as the poor laws, weights and measures (trading standards) and the maintenance of roads and bridges. 1888 saw the creation of county councils and in 1893 the government set up elective parish councils (for rural settlements of over one hundred residents).[46]

In December 1894, there was a valley meeting at the school to elect nine members of the first parish council. Borrowdale had a population of 506 but the property qualification meant that only eighty seven were entitled to vote. These split between Grange (thirty five), Rosthwaite (including Stonethwaite) (twenty nine), and Honister (twenty three).[47] At their first meeting, the council co-opted John Simpson from Hazel Bank to be their chair.[48]

Moses chose not to stand, although his friends George Mounsey and William Hudson did. He was already an overseer of the poor – this office was created by the Act for the Relief of the Poor 1597 and the overseer was an elected officials who administered poor relief such as money, food, and clothing or helped youngsters into apprenticeships. In 1893, Moses and Joseph Thomson from Leathes Cottage were confirmed as overseers.[49] The next year, Moses was involved in a committee to improve the Borrowdale Road,[50] along with John Simpson, Hardwicke Drummond Rawnsley, the vicar of Crosthwaite, Roger Bownass, from the Lodore, and Borrowdale's vicar, Rev Heelis. The committee's objectives were to get Big Wood Brow widened and the summit lowered, the road by the lake widened and fenced, Kitty Well (Kettlewell) Brow widened and the summit lowered; Lodore Brow avoided by diverting the road to the right; the steep pull up Eel Brow avoided by diverting the road to the right; the wall at Bowdering End needed strengthening with a hand rail; and at the ugly bend near Rosthwaite, the road should run through the field to the end of the bridge. Who was to pay? The county, the district or the parish? They all had lunch at the Royal Oak but the issue of the road would haunt parish council meetings for another century…

Moses' first attempt to be elected to Borrowdale council was a failure – in March 1896, there was a vote by show of hands and the Seatoller candidates (Moses and Daniel Jopson) came bottom of the poll.[51] However, Daniel objected to the process. In April there was a secret ballot at the school and Daniel and Moses were elected.[52] He served on the council until at least 1907 and often chaired meetings in the absence of Simpson. He was particularly interested in adult education, chairing a technical instruction committee, championing ambulance classes as well as those for nursing, horticulture and poultry farming.[53]

The road remained a constant thorn in the council's side. 1899 had seen a Keswick sensation when the first motor car arrived, driven by the owner of the Queen's Hotel after a 51-hour run from Lancaster. However, it broke down at Bassenthwaite and had to be towed back by horse.[54] By 1903, a rural district councillor complained that the road was *'covered with charabancs, waggonettes and cheap trippers'*[55] The parish council, with Moses in the chair, were debating s.9 of the Motor Car Act 1903, which would enable them either to ban cars or restrict to 10 mph (rather than the statutory 20 mph).[56] The council recommended 10 mph but wanted repairs to the roads so that restrictions could be removed as they harmed the tourist trade. Moses remained a councillor until 1907.

In 1911, Moses and Mary Jane celebrated their fortieth wedding anniversary. He had always left the management of the house to Mary Jane and the census recorded that he was a slate quarryman and slate splitter. There is no sign that he ever considered retirement.

In 1915, the valley lost two of its best beloved residents. On 30th March 1915, John Richardson of Seathwaite Farm was buried. A Cumberland dalesman through and through, at the age of 73, he walked to Caldbeck and the next day, drove his flock of his sheep back to Seathwaite. He was known as the 'king of herdwicks', who had dined with the prince of Wales and hunted with John Peel. St Andrew's was packed with Borrowdale people as well farm families from all the surrounding valleys.[57]

Six months later, Moses was dead. There was no death notice or report of his funeral. Yet St Andrew's would have been crowded for another time that year. He was a tireless organiser, whether it was the Borrowdale school or the Keswick Co-operative, the Band of Hope or the parish council. Whether it be the quarrymen, the schoolchildren, the farmers, or the drinkers, he touched the lives of most of the valley residents. He was a good man.

Mary Jane Pepper
Moses did not come to Seatoller House alone. His wife, Mary Jane Robinson, was the daughter of a Kirkby Ireleth slate river. When she died in 1929, the Yorkshire Post gave her the accolade, "*one of the most noted of Lakeland's hostesses.*"[58] Did Moses and Mary Jane visit Jane Holme in the summer of 1879. Before the move? Jane was then in her seventies and perhaps part of the deal was that some of the cleaning, cooking and looking after visitors to Mary Jane? The Pepper girls would be at school and suspicion is that the guest house was a collaborative effort.

The 1881 census (Fig 5) records the Pepper family as living in the house. In 1881, Jane[59] was in the south Lakes, visiting her sister, Marie Phoebe (1827 - 1898) and her farm labourer

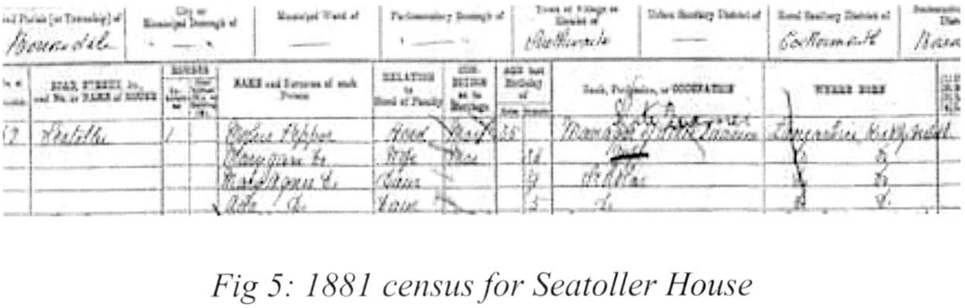

Fig 5: 1881 census for Seatoller House

o'clock, and that Dawson being drunk he went home with him. On arriving at Dawson's deceased was standing in open doorway with a lighted candle in her hand. She went into the house, and Dawson and himself followed. He (Jones) remained in the house about ten minutes. Deceased appeared to be under the influence of drink. At that time she had no cut on her head neither was her face disfigured in any way. Jones says he was sober, and was accompanied by his brother-in-law, who lived at Cleator Moor, and who was on a visit to his house. Mrs. Mary Coward, wife of William Coward, states that when she was called in to see the deceased on the 27th she found her in bed with a large cut at the back of her head. She had a discoloured eye and a bruise on her chin. She saw her many times during the week, and asked her how she got the wounds, but she would not tell her. Dr. Fawcitt having refused to give a certificate as to pro-

Fig 6: Millom Gazette 7th January 1898

husband, James Dawson (1837 -), at Broughton in Furness. Jane had at least six siblings. She stayed in touch – her sister, Hannah, had married John Jackson who ran the King's Arms in West Broughton in Furness and Jane left her niece, Mary Jackson, 19 guineas. Her surviving sister, the youngest, was Maria Phoebe, who had married a farm worker, James Dawson. Jane left her the interest on the New Zealand debentures with the principal going to her nephew, William Dawson, a solicitor's clerk, after Maria's death. Had she had the gift of foresight, Jane may have regretted this (Fig 6) – on Boxing Day 1897, Jackson came home drunk from the Prince of Wales in Foxfield and the evidence suggests he had an altercation with his mother, also drunk and that she fell and hit her head, dying on New Year's Day. No criminal charges were brought – in 1901, Jackson was living and working in Millom.

During Jane's trips away, back at Seatoller, any guests would have been the responsibility of Mary Jane – even at Christmas, there were the braver trekkers, looking for snow and ice on the tops of the mountains. Mary Jane may well have found her niche in running the house and perhaps was urging Moses to look at sites where they might set up for themselves? In September 1882, Field House came on the market and Moses went to the auction at the Borrowdale Hotel.[60]

Jane continued to visit her sister. She was at Bank End, Broughton for the Christmas and New Year 1886 and it was where she died there in January.[61] With her death, the lease of the house expired. It was advertised to let in March[62] and the Peppers became the new tenants around April 1886.

There was another indication that Mary Jane had been straining at the bit to expand and run the guesthouse as a professional business. By July, she had started advertising:

ACCOMMODATION FOR VISITORS – SEATOLLER HOUSE, situated in the midst of the best mountain scenery, at the foot of Honister Pass, on the coach road to Buttermere.... Terms moderate – MRS PEPPER, late Mrs Holme[63]

It was an advert that continues with the nearly same wording

123

SEATOLLER HOUSE to Let, with possession on 25th March next, containing Three Entertaining Rooms, Kitchens, Bedrooms and Out Offices, suitable either for private residence or for a Lodging House, together with Gardens and small Meadow Field, as now occupied by Mr Pepper, who will show the premises.—To treat for the letting apply to Messrs WEBSTER, Son, and BANKS, Land Agents, Kendal.
Kendal, January 25th, 1887.

Fig 7: West Cumberland Times 12th February 1887

for 25 years until December 1910. The reference to the '*late Mrs Holme*' does suggest that Jane had built up a reputation that Mary Jane was not going to jettison. But her speed off the mark in advertising suggests that this was something she had been pressing for. Jane might well have resisted such a commercial approach, perhaps relying on word of mouth, repute and an altogether more genteel approach. Mary Jane was of a different mettle.

However, for a decade there was considerable uncertainty for the Peppers about their landlord and their tenancy. In October 1884, Henry Cowper Marshall had died on his island in Derwentwater.[64] The Peppers may only have secured a short-term lease as in 1887, the house was advertised to let (Fig 7).

Mary Jane carried on business as usual. Eventually on 27th August 1895, the whole of the Marshall estate was put up for auction, including Lyzzick Hall and Dancing Gate Farm (Fig 8). All his Borrowdale estate was included.

down to Mr Collier at £5200. Lot 12 was the freehold messuage called Seatoller House, in Borrowdale, with stabling, coach house, paddock, two cottages and gardens, containing 2a. 2r. 12p., in the occupation of Mr Moses Pepper. Mr Collier was the last bidder at £850. Lot 13 was Seatoller Farm, comprising farm house, out-buildings, and 408 acres of land, with 110 grasses on Seatoller Farm, 10 grasses for 100 sheep on Langstrath Fell, and 1½ grasses for 15 sheep on Comb Fell; and included in the lot was a stock of 413 sheep going on the fells. Mr J. N. Dickinson (Whitehaven) was the last bidder for the lot at £2300.

Fig 8: *Carlisle Patriot* 30th August 1895

Seatoller House (with stables, a coach house, gardens, paddock and the two Yew Tree cottages) were sold to John Norman Dickinson of Whitehaven for £4500.[65] Dickinson was a successful land agent – he lived in Hames Hall in Papcastle - and was acting as an agent for Henry Wyndham, the 2nd Baron Leconfield who owned the mineral rights at Honister and was looking for land to build cottages for the workforce of the Buttermere Green Slate Company.

It would have been a recurring anxiety for Mary Jane, seeing the house advertised for rent and then for sale. No doubt the Leconfield estate acquired their land in Seatoller for sensible commercial reasons. Their slate company shipped most of its slate through the village and a priority would be safeguarding that access. Another motive lay in the need for more accommodation for the workmen. Mountain View had already been built and in 1899, the company would knock down an old barn and erect the New Cottages terrace. But the demand could not have been overwhelming – building controls were virtually

Fig 9: Outside Seatoller House, around 1890

non-existent and the company would have met few obstacles if they demolished Seatoller House and built a small estate on the paddock. Fortunately building controls were in place in 1930 when there was a plan to build twenty-two houses at the farm.

By 1895, Mary Jane's tenure was more secure. She had a burgeoning reputation as a host in a house that was an ideal base for exploring some of the most challenging and beautiful mountains of England. She was well-known locally and there were day excursions for groups such as Keswick Literary and Scientific Society. Through Moses's contacts, fifty-five members of Keswick's Young Men's Bible Class arrived by coach on 22nd June 1899 and had tea in the garden. After an afternoon walk, there was a service in the grounds.[66]

Fig 10: Easter 1895 – Trevelyan logbook cover

An early photograph (Fig 9) may well show the Pepper family. The date is before the building of New Cottages, with the old barn on the right of the picture, with a penny farthing jutting out. The men on the left were probably visitors but teenage Ada Pepper takes centre stage, looking boldly at the camera with her father, Moses in front of her. Mary Jane, in her early forties, stands in the centre of the road with daughter Mary Agnes in the shadows.

With so many visitors, Mary Jane needed the help of her daughters, both of whom would marry quarrymen. Mary Agnes had married John Woodend (1865-1931) in 1895 and Ada had married George Honey (1870-) in 1900. Neither had children so both had the space to help their mother.

That reputation reached nationwide. In the Easter 1895, five young students from Trinity College, Cambridge visited Borrowdale and stayed with the Peppers (Fig 10). They included Geoffrey Trevelyan who would graduate in 1896 and become regius professor of history at Cambridge. He founded the Trinity manhunts in 1898. George Moore, another distinguished academic who became professor of philosophy at Cambridge alongside Russell and Wittgenstein, and Ralph Vaughan Williams, the composer. They kept a logbook of their stay, detailing their walks – Trevelyan was the most adventurous, climbing Great Gable by himself whereas Moore panicked on Castle Crag (...*on a perpendicular precipice called by the natives Castle Crag though indeed it is fit only to be the Devil's Castle*).

When had business taken off? The advertisements may have helped but the house's popularity would have spread by word-of-mouth. Constant links between visitors crop up – it's been possible to identify at least twenty-six as Cambridge graduates. Schools also are part of the network – in June, Merchant Taylor's alumnus Vere Laurence headed up the Trinity Hunt and in September, John Clarke Stobart (1878-1933) brought up a party of boys from the school. A classicist, Stobart went on to become the first director of education at the BBC.

Word might also spread among faith groups: there were a significant number of Quakers staying. In stark contrast, there were also many who were in the territorial army: one group was centred around the 3rd Volunteer Battalion of the Northumberland Fusiliers. Local clubs and associations provided more links: one group included several devotees of the Burnley literary and scientific society. Professional links helped: Meaburn Staniland (1880-1915) was a lawyer in Boston, Lincolnshire who visited in January 1902. Two other young Lincolnshire lawyers, Leonard Porter (1881-1923) and Reynolds Scorer (1876-1958), were staying at the house in May.

And once you had been exposed to the Seatoller experience, you were likely to return. The first surviving Visitors' Book dates from January 1902. In March, for example, a party of young Manchester climbers wrote that this was the best weather for six years. Seymour Gubb (1863-1925) from Southampton recorded that he was on his eighth visit. Twelve years later, on 22nd July 1914, two weeks before Britain declared war, Leo Burley (1873-1921), a British diamond merchant living in Antwerp, stayed at Seatoller House with his wife, Anna. Leo Burley signed the Visitors' Book and made this poignant entry:

Returned after an absence of more than 20 years to find the same unostentatious comfort and the same hospitable care, the same beauty of hill and valley, of rivulet and lake. The European capitals are seething with the violence of men's passions; by the Danube the roar of Austrian artillery has already been heard – and the dark, silent fells around us remain in imperturbable calm.[67]

Those 1902 entries all were remembering the house in 1893-94. The book is some evidence that the visitor footfall had been

Fig 11: Refurbishments at Borrowdale Hotel

substantial from the mid-1890s, and in all likelihood for many years before.

Would any landlord interfere with an obviously successful business? And the Peppers were exemplary tenants – there would not be any headlines such as the *"Langdale Rowdies"*. It was a business plan that relied on "location, location, location" and not necessarily on modern amenities. When the sun failed to shine, it was a Spartan existence for the visitors, especially when compared with the new hotels on Derwentwater.[68]

By August 1897, both the Borrowdale and Lodore had come under a single owner, Edward Francis Felix Cesari (1844-1900). Born in Italy, he had had a distinguished military career.[69] He and his wife had run hotels in Inverness and Dunkald with no connection to the valley or to Cumberland. But in a short period, Cesari modernised both hotels, installed a telephone so that

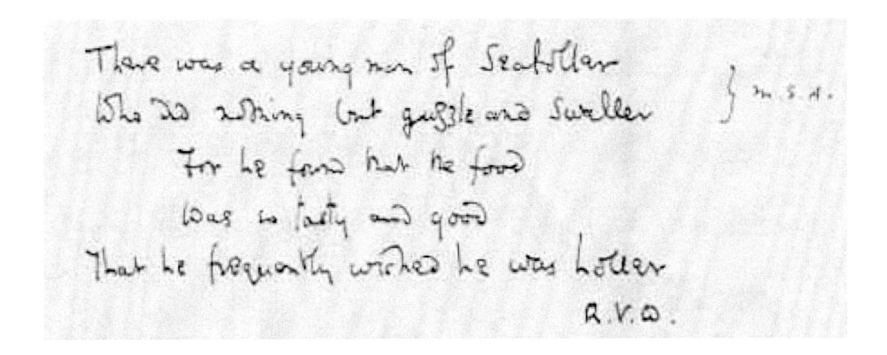

Fig 12: Limerick by Vaughan Williams in 1895 logbook

telegrams could be received and dispatched, made a new path to the Falls and built an excursionists' tearoom at the Borrowdale.[70] The toilet and other kindred arrangements were greatly improved. He was soon advertising that the hotels were, '*remodelled, refurbished, and sanitary arrangements renovated. Fishing, boating, steam yacht. Tariff moderate*' (Fig 11).[71]

The Seatoller House experience was rather different. The only heating was by open fires. Cooking was on a coal-fired range (an Aga only bought in 1949) and this had to do double duty as the only reliable means of drying wet clothes. The water came from a well until a running (but cold) water supply was installed coming from a small stream on the fell. This allowed a toilet to be built. In the bedroom, washing was by cans of hot water. In those bedrooms, there were no cupboards, just hooks on the backs of doors.

Certain aspects of the house, such as the good cooking, compensated. Mary Jane was clearly skilled in the kitchen, as Vaughan William's limerick (Fig. 12) in 1895 makes clear – the glutton, MSA, was Maurice Amos, later a lawyer and judge in Egypt.

The Trinity and Trevelyan Hunts

Maybe this temporary Spartan existence appealed – or maybe it resembled college life - but the house was a favourite lodging place for the young college fellows and students, to read, study, climb and walk. They were mainly Oxbridge but also came from university colleges such as Owen's College in Manchester or Armstrong College in Newcastle. They were often privately educated. In mid-Victorian England, there had been an expansion of boarding schools, such as Cheltenham College (1841), Radley College (1847) or Wellington College (1853). These schools embraced the sort of broader curriculum introduced by Samuel Butler at Shrewsbury (maths, languages, history and not just Greek and Latin) and 'the re-establishment of social purpose, the education of Christian gentlemen' (Thomas Arnold's stated aim at Rugby).

  This ethos of social and moral training was sometimes termed a philosophy of *"muscular christianity"*.[72] A key element was a belief in *"mens sana in corpore sano'*, a healthy mind in a healthy body. Exercise and sport, especially but not exclusively, team sport not only built muscles but also inculcated moral values. Sport required co-operative teamwork, fair play within the rules, respect for the other side while testing your physical prowess to its limits. There was never a "Muscular Christianity Association" nor any organised movement but these tenets both reflected the culture of these schools while also maintaining and reinforcing it. When the schoolboys left the school gates behind them, they took these values with them into universities, colleges and professional life, especially the Army.

  The 1895 group were muscular but showed no great commitment to Christian worship – the logbooks recorded a blank against "Churchgoers" for each of the three Sundays of their stay. Moore sketched out their days in a letter to his father dated 24th March,

We have breakfast at 8 and then work pretty constantly till 1, when we have lunch. Soon after lunch we go out, whatever the weather, till 4 or 5, when we have afternoon tea. Then we work again until till half past seven, when we have dinner. After dinner we have talk, music or reading, then perhaps a little more work, till bed time between 10 & 11

I, Trevy and Wedgwood each have bedrooms to ourselves, the other two sleep in one room. Mrs Pepper is very kind & looks after us very well: one of her daughters generally waits on us. It is an old building of very irregular shape, but comfortably fitted up: we have two sitting rooms, both with low ceilings & the chimneys apt to smoke.

There is a fairly good piano, and fortunately I had brought some music so VW and I both play a bit, we have had some duets & I have sung a little

The logbook is light-hearted but erudite. There was some serious intellectual debate. We get one glimpse of Mary Jane on April 1st when they write a play in which she writes a letter,

Dear Mr Trevelyan

As the girls and I thinks you was quite the handsomest and nicest-mannered of our visitors – which we don't want to say anything against any of the gentlemen, though Mr Amos do frightened us so by his laughing and Mr Moore swears that awful and Mr Wedgwood is so rude and ugly ...so we hopes you will accept of the herewith enclosed stockings for summer wear, which we knitted of ourselves

I am...your most humble servant Emma Pepper

The plot thickens when Mrs Pepper reads the letter and comes to remonstrate with its author Ralph Wedgwood.[73] He jumps into a cupboard to hide. Trevelyan locks him in. April

133

Fig 13: George Macaulay Trevelyan in 1910 with father, George Otto, and son, Theo, who died of appendicitis the following year

Fool! But these young men see Mary Jane (was she known as Emma (MA) to distinguish her from daughter Mary (MB)?) as very kind but someone to be reckoned with.

These groups of students with their tutors, reading, walking and climbing, were common: Exeter College, Oxford came annually to Wasdale. The links between Trinity and Seatoller House have been long-lasting. They evolved into the Cambridge Manhunts, which still take place annually and have shaped the modern history of Seatoller House. One of the originators was George Macaulay Trevelyan (1876-1962) along with the poet, Geoffrey Winthrop Young (1876-1958). During a walking tour of Cornwall in the spring of 1898, Young and Trevelyan, both from Trinity College, Cambridge, apparently discussed Robert Louis Stevenson's *Kidnapped* and subsequently designed a game

Fig 14: Geoffrey Winthrop Young – in 1898 he wrote The Roof-Climber's Guide to Trinity, *in part a parody of early alpine guidebooks, in part a useful reference work for those, like him, who were keen to clamber up Cambridge's highest spires.*

to recreate the excitement of that chase. It was a modification of *Hunt the Hare*, played in English schools since the 16th century, allied to cross-country running, which had developed as a sport in the 1860s.[74] These manhunts began in 1898, often using Seatoller as their headquarters.[75]

The first hunt involved four hares and twelve hounds. The participants were all from Cambridge, mainly from Trinity and included Sidney McDougall (1876-1915), [76] Hilton Young

(Winthrop's brother), bibliographer Walter Gregg, Ernest Barnes, later to be a controversial bishop of Birmingham, lawyer, Sandy Mackay, F W Dobbs, Christopher Wordsworth and Felix Levi.

In June, sixteen Cambridge undergraduates, including Young and Trevelyan, spent four days manhunting across the central mountains of the Lake District. Twelve acted as hounds and four as hares. A touch of the hand was a capture. Trevelyan described one near-capture as 'the most exciting five minutes I have ever had in my life.[77]

Winthrop Young wrote an account of that first hunt, laying out the rules and a detailed narrative of the action.[78] A conscientious objector, he drove ambulances in Italy in the war, losing a leg, but he carried on climbing and was president of the Alpine Club.

In 1901, the Hunt split into two with one organised from Trinity and the other by Charles Philips Trevelyan (1870-1958). Headquarters could be in any one of the central valleys – Buttermere, Borrowdale, Wasdale or Langdale – but after the war, both Hunts were quartered in Seatoller House. Their histories are chronicled elsewhere.[79]

The Visitors of 1902

The first extant Visitors' Book of January 1902 and provides a colourful picture of the comings and goings of that year – which was probably typical of the pre-war period. Outside of the hunts, Seatoller House was normally full - in 1901, the Hunt went to Scotland, to the Rodona Hotel in Roxburghshire because the house was booked up.[80] In 1902 there were at least 180 visitors during the year.

The season ran from Easter until the end of September, with the solitary exception of the New Year, for those who enjoyed climbing in snow and ice. There were just sixteen such guests in January but none in February and for most of March. On the night of the census on 31st March 1901, there were no visitors at Seatoller House. With Moses at the quarry was George Honey, Ada's husband, and John Robinson, Mary Jane's older brother. Son, Isaac, was working at the Keswick Co-op.

Mary Jane and her daughters, Mary Agnes (living in New Cottages) and Ada had two teenagers to help for the season. Mary Nuttall was the daughter of quarryman James Nuttall and Ann née Birkett, living in at No 8 Mountain View. With the family home so close, it was probably that Mary was working at the house in 1902 as well. However, Maggie Sanderson was from further afield – her father, Joseph, was a carter turned horse dealer in Cockermouth – and Seatoller House was seasonal work for six months in the year. In the autumn, she was likely to look for a job nearer home.

In 1902, the Trevelyan Hunt HQ was at the Dun Bull Inn, Haweswater but Trinity's fifth Lake Hunt took place from 18th - 23rd June in Seatoller. The hunt master, Vere Laurence (1876-1934), fellow in history, had been on all five previous hunts as had bibliographer, Walter Greg (1875-1959). A fellow bibliographer, Ronald McKerrow (1872-1940), was on his second. Frederick Sidgwick (1879-1939) was on his third. Sidgwick later founded the publishing firm, Sidgwick and Jackson and McKerrow joined him there. Of the five young men on their first hunt, two would die on the western front, Arthur Turner (1881-1918) and Erasmus Darwin (1881-1915), grandson of Charles. Another, Angus Ferguson (1882-1908), would also die young in 1908, from sunstroke having joined the Indian Civil Service.

Outside of the Hunt members, the clientele was somewhat more diverse, at least sixty per cent came from the northern

137

counties, especially Lancashire. Another ten percent were London-based. There were just a few foreigners – Oscar Watkins (1861-1945) and his wife, a travel agent from Indianapolis, USA, two Italians from Novara and Turin with illegible handwriting; some were colonials visiting home such as Ernest Hill (1872-1917), Professor of Chemistry, Muir College, Allahabad, India; Dietrich Wiencke (1843-1914), working in Newcastle, came with his English wife and daughters.

The visitors were predominantly male (around seventy per cent). There were about fifty women, a third of whom were wives. A Blackburn couple, Charles (1875-1967) and Sophia (1878-1963) Slatter, arrived the day after their wedding. Another couple from Darlington came together, would marry the following year but certainly would have had separate rooms.

There is less educational or occupational data in the censuses or elsewhere on the women. Of those unmarried, half were under twenty-one and with parents or other family. Of the unmarried women, three were (or went on to be) teachers, one was a probationary nurse, two were artists and one was a fellow of St Anne's College, Oxford.

The men were relatively young. A third were between twenty and forty years old. Consequently, around twenty were involved in World War I and, as many were educated in private schools, were commissioned, usually as lieutenants and second lieutenants. Eleven were killed, reflecting the statistic that the life expectancy of a young officer in the trenches was forty-two days.

There were only nine guests aged over fifty. The oldest at seventy-five was Charles Christopherson (1827-1906), a retired ironmonger, born in Keswick. Thomas Dickinson Winder (1831-1905) was also over 70. He had come with his son, John (1881-1956) and they were the only obviously working-class visitors – Thomas was a blacksmith from Kirkby Ireleth and this was a long-term friendship with Moses. Both worked in the Burlington Slate quarries in Kirkby. Thomas Dickinson was the secretary of the Kirkby Co-operative Society when it was founded in 1861. Moses was deeply involved in this and the Sick Club.

Thomas Winder stood out as the visitors were predominantly middle-class professionals, well-educated with at least forty-four attending university, especially Cambridge (twenty-five) or Oxford. There were ten who went to university colleges such as Owen's College in Manchester or Armstrong College in Newcastle. Over twenty would be teachers or academics. Actual or future vicars and lawyers were well represented. There were doctors, civil servants, auctioneer, accountants and merchants, as well as professional artists[81] and designers.

Alongside these white-collar occupations were engineers, colliery owners and manufacturers who ran iron foundries, factories making steam winches and bobbins, cotton mills and chemical plants. The father of Harry Hargreaves Bolton (1886-1915) owned seventeen collieries, employing over one thousand men.[82] These men were predominantly from the north.

The hardy January guests included the town clerk of Boston, Lincolnshire, Robert Staniland (1854-1924). At forty-eight, his best climbing days were probably behind him but he was a keen walker.[83] His son, Meaburn (1880-1915), was with his father. Meaburn was in his early twenties, a sportsman and solicitor. He had fought in the Boer War with the Lincolnshire Regiment. He was killed at Ypres in July 1915, just three months after his brother, Geoffrey.[84]

Also climbing on New Year's Day was a group from the Northumberland Fusiliers. Two were scientists, associated with Durham University. Robert Blyth Greig (1874-1947)[85] became a distinguished agriculturalist, serving on the Scottish Board of Agriculture and Frederick Garrett (1867-1940) taught chemistry at Armstrong College, later Newcastle University. A colleague, John Benson Bainbridge (1872-1942), was a different calibre. From a family that had made money in the drapery business, he was a racing driver who took part in the Monte Carlo Rally – and had his fair share of English motoring convictions.

The private school and Oxbridge connections were never far away. Hilton Young (1879-1960) had just left Cambridge and was reading for the bar.[86] He was the brother of Geoffrey Winthrop Young who, with G M Trevelyan, had developed the Trinity Hunt tradition. Hilton Young was associated with the Bloomsbury Group, friends with Thoby Stephen (1880-1906) and proposed to his sister, Virginia (who later married Leonard Woolf). Hilton had a distinguished war with the Royal Navy. He was later an MP and became Lord Kennett.

In the second week of January, George Chitty (1876-1947), an Eton schoolmaster and George Werner (1877-1915), teaching at Harrow, came to stay. Werner fought in the Rifle Brigade in the war and was killed at Aubers Ridge in 1915. Alongside them was John Clapham (1873-1946), who would become the first professor of economic history at Cambridge.[87]

Perhaps it was a relief for Mary Jane, as January ended, to hear Cumbrian dialect and more down-to-earth talk. Thomas Philipson (1880-1940) was Keswick born into the bobbin-manufacturing firm of Coward and Philipson, centred at Low Briery. He would serve as chairman of Keswick Council and be a force in Keswick and Cumberland Rugby. He was with two Carlisle friends and his cousin, Robert Mandale (1879-1968), whose father was a butcher in St John's St, Keswick. The Mandale family emigrated to Canada before the war.

The house was probably closed to visitors through February

and March but from Easter, there was rarely a week without guests. Over the Easter weekend, a group of climbers from Manchester and its surrounds explored Great Gable – the Kerns Knott Chimney, Arrowhead Ridge, the Great Central Gully and the Doctor's Chimney. It was a mixed group with teachers, cotton manufacturers and a chemist, Norman Sheldon (1876-1946), who became the Chief Inspector of Explosives in India. Manchester Grammar teacher, Henry Joseland (1865-1949), had climbed in Sweden and Charles Hargreaves (1874-1943), son of a cotton manufacturer, was a rock climber for forty years.[88] Both were supporters of the Burnley Literary and Scientific Society as was William Lancaster (1853-1931), a cotton manufacturer and the first Burnley man to climb the Matterhorn.[89] They recorded in the Visitors' Book that they had had their best weather for six years.

A slightly older group of serious climbers comprised four teachers, in their forties. One, Reuben Brierley (1962-1919) from Sunderland, was on his seventh visit – his eighth came in July when he brought his family on holiday. Seymour Gubb (1863-1925), headmaster of Taunton's School in Southampton, was already on his eighth visit. He became a member of the Fell and Rock Climbing Club and when he died in 1925, his ashes were scattered from summit of Great Gable.[90]

In the early spring, these groups of young (and not quite so young) men shared an obsession with climbing, often coming from the same town, with similar occupations, business interests or educational background – in April there was a group of students from Owens College in Manchester and some Darlington curates.

What binds some groups is less easy to decipher – over Easter one visitor was Arthur Simpson (1857-1922), the wood carver and furniture maker, already a master of the Arts and

Crafts movement, who had a workshop in Kendal.[91] He was a devout Quaker who, with his wife, set up settlements for Belgian refugees in the war.[92] What did he have in common with four Chorlton-cum-Hardy businessmen, except that love of the hills? This group were coming to Borrowdale for the first time and deserting their previous haunts in Langdale.

Occasionally there were the solitary walkers. Reginald Hawthorn Hooker (1867-1944) was the son of Reginald Dalton Hooker[93], the close friend of Charles Darwin. Graduating in maths from Trinity, Cambridge, he worked at the Royal Statistical Society and then at the Board of Agriculture. Away from his civil service work, he was a pioneering statistician. In 1902 he spent two weeks at Seatoller in June and then another four weeks in October, at a period when he was working on his most remembered papers on time series analysis.

Another was William Gershom Collingwood (1854-1932), although he stayed just a night. Author, artist, antiquary and, from 1905, professor of fine arts at Reading, he was a friend of John Ruskin and of Arthur Ransome. It was the Collingwood family that provided inspiration for *Swallows and Amazons*. He was President of the Cumberland and Westmorland Antiquarian Society and the Lake Artists' Society

Women had been noticeable by their absence but Madeline Scott (1877-1958), daughter of C P Scott, owner of the Manchester Guardian, came for a week in early April. She wrote *"Delighted with the place and with Mrs Pepper's hospitality"*. Her husband, Charles Edward Montague (1867-1928),[94] was with her. He was *de facto* editor of the paper at this time while Scott was an MP. At the same time, Carl Friedrich Padel (1872-1958), a teacher at Eastbourne College but to become headmaster at Carlisle Grammar and a well-known educationalist, was paying a return visit and this time had brought his sister, Else Clara (1875-1936).

In contrast to the number of all-male pairs and groups, there was just one entry with two women together. Rachel Hill (1853-1930) and Helen Woollacott (1868-1965) were Sunderland schoolteachers, on a two-week summer holiday. However, there were many couples – the Tanners from Bristol (Edgar Tanner (1861-1946) was another lawyer) wrote *'Decidedly one of our most successful holidays. Bicycles and Kodaks*[95] *added much to our enjoyment. Few wet days and those leaving fine cloud effects...'*

The first family group was surprising. Sigismund de Trafford (1853-1936) and his wife Clementina (1856- 1937) owned Croston Hall in Lancashire. He came from an old Catholic family and his grandfather, Thomas,[96] had ordered one hundred and sixteen troopers of the Manchester and Salford Yeomanry to disperse the crowd at St Peter's Field in Manchester on 27th August 1819, the Peterloo Massacre. Sigismund led an altogether quieter life and in April brought his twin sons, Geoffrey (1891-1960) and Reginald (1891-1915)[97] and his daughters Ermyntrude (1883-1964) and Elfrida, (1886-1965) probably with nannies and governesses.

Most families came in the summer holidays. The Quaker connection also re-emerged with the Andrews family (Frederick (1850-1922), Margaret (1879-1935) and Gertrude (1886-1967) from the Friends' school at Ackworth. Reuben Brierley, a teacher-training specialist, returned with his family, wife Sarah (1861-1917), daughters Mabel (1888-) and Gertrude (1889-) and son, Harold. Harold (1891-1916), a draughtsman at Swan Hunter shipyards, was killed on the Somme in July 1916.

Another family to lose a son was that of Thomas (1849-1924) and Augusta (1855-1929) Wilson. He was a schoolmaster at Sherborne in Dorset and they visited with daughters Diana (1887-1969) and Patience (1890 -) and son, Thomas (1883-1916). The weather was not kind:

To Seatoller we came on peak-bagging intent
When we came heaven wept and it wept when we went
Though the fells were in clouds and the dales were in rain
We walked up the mountains again and again

Their son, Thomas Irving, a student at King's Cambridge, wrote this. He later was a schoolmaster at Repton. He joined the Manchester Regiment and was killed on the Somme in November 1916. His sister, Diana Ruth, was a skilled botanical artist.[98]

August must have been a noisy month. Robert Roger (1853-1943), a manufacturer of steam winches from Egglescliffe in Durham, had come to Seatoller in May with his wife. Now he brought a party of ten, including his seven children, ranging in age from 21 to 1. William Hartley (1852-1943), the registrar of Burnley County Court, overlapped with the Roger group, bringing a mixed party of seventeen. Alongside the Hartley children were cousins, Rosamond Tunstill (1885-1970), and Harry Hargreaves Bolton. There were also Dorothy (1887-1970) and Marjorie (1888-1984) from Aspley Guise in Bedfordshire, the daughters of a retired Lieutenant-Colonel of the East Lancashire Regiment, Charles Villiers Somerville Downes (1846-1909). There was some adult company in Herbert Gresley (1876-1941),[99] who would later design the Flying Scotsman and Arthur Ridsdale (1871-1935).

The Visitors' Book has four pages written by Margaret[100] about their activities in cod verse, which was corrected, probably by Arthur Ridsdale. There was some romance in the air as five years later Ridsdale married 19-year-old Margaret Hartley (1888-

1919), seventeen years younger than him. Ridsdale rose to become a Master in the Chancery Division in the High Court. Margaret's brother, Christopher (1886-1917), married Dorothy Downes in 1914. It was a close-knit group and when Susan Hartley (1889-1924) married Perceval Hayman (another lawyer), many of the Seatoller party were guests.[101]

But there are notes in the margins in the Visitors' Book as tragedy would strike the Hartley family. The oldest, Christopher, was in the RFA and killed in 1917 at Ypres and his brother Edmund (1895-1918) served with the Lancashire Fusiliers, was seriously wounded several times and was killed by an exploding shell in 1918. Their cousin, Harry Hargreaves Bolton, died at Gallipoli in May 1915. By 1924, both daughters had also died.

There was an older, loose-knit family group. James Edwin Thorold Rogers (1823-1890) was a high church curate, economist and liberal MP. His four unmarried, adult, children came together in Seatoller in September, including Leonard (1862-1933), professor of maths at Leeds and Clement (1866-1949), a vicar. But it is his daughter, Annie Mary Anne Henley Rogers (1856-1937), who catches the eye. A child model for Lewis Carroll, she sat the Oxford entrance examinations as AMAH Rogers and came top, only for the offer of a scholarship to be withdrawn when it was realised that she was female. She studied and took the undergraduate exams in classics but was only awarded a degree in 1920. A promoter of women's education, she was a tutor and the secretary of the Society of Oxford Home-Students which became St Anne's College.

With the four Oxford Rogers were five Yorkshire Baines cousins, whose family newspaper was the reform/dissent-leaning Leeds Mercury. The connection was on their mothers' side who were both Reynolds from Hampshire, claiming descent from Henry Revell Reynolds (1745-1811), one of the many doctors

145

who attended George III.

Cataloguing these many visitors demonstrates the unique nature of Seatoller House. The house is filled with the energy of precociously talented youth, individuals who would make their mark across most aspects of English society, not merely in politics, the civil service, academia and the church but with industrial manufacturers and designers. Sadly, that mark was too often made on the battlefield.

When Reginald Hooker left on October 25th, this brought an end to Mary Jane's work for the year – except the Cambridge connection lingered for the Trevelyan brothers, Charles and Geoffrey, came for tea on December 8th and Geoffrey stayed for a couple of nights.

***

Moses and Mary Jane Pepper had two daughters, Mary Agnes and Ada and then, after a gap of nearly ten years, a son, Isaac Pepper (1884-1907). Isaac steered clear of both his father's work at the slate mine and his mother's hospitality business, instead working at the Keswick co-operative society. Moses had been involved in the Kirkby Co-operative Society when it was founded in 1861.

The one thing that mattered when I was approaching my seventeenth birthday was whether or not you were going to 'join t' new shop' and the one question discussed by nearly everybody in the neighbourhood was how it could possibly stand when it was 'nobbat two or three Quarry fellows and' a blacksmith' that were starting it.[102]

At Kirkby, there was opposition from the local shopkeepers. The Co-op was run by volunteers such as Moses, sacrificing their leisure hours. They stocked flour, meal, soap, candles, sugar and currants, later expanding and including a 'clogs and shoes'

DEATH OF MR ISAAC PEPPER, SEATOLLER.

Never was so large a gathering of mourners present in Borrowdale Church as on Tuesday, when the remains of Mr Isaac Pepper were laid to rest. Mr Isaac Pepper was assistant grocer to the Keswick Co-operative Society, lodged in Keswick, but returned to his home Seatoller House every Saturday till Monday. On Monday week last, though suffering from cold, he proceeded to work, but rapidly growing worse, retired to his lodgings, and there passed away on Saturday last from pneumonia. His remains were taken to Seatoller, his parents' home. So esteemed was Isaac by young and old, by customers and acquaintances, that the gathering to do respect numbered some hundreds, and many beautiful flowers were forwarded by the bereaved relations, fellow employes, the Co-operative Committee, school children, and friends from Keswick and neighbourhood. "Jesus lover of my soul" was sung and a prayer offered at the door of the house. The cortege was met by the Rev C. A. C. Bowlker, vicar of Borrowdale, at the church, which was unable to contain the whole of the mourners. Two hymns,

Fig 15: West Cumberland Times 11th May 1907

department.

The Keswick co-op had been set up in 1890 when two hundred and fifty people turned up to the January inaugural meeting in Keswick Victoria Hall.[103] The meeting elected Joe Wilkinson as chair. He was the Borrowdale schoolmaster, who lived at Chapel House. Moses shared the lessons learned at Kirkby and was the Keswick delegate to the regional Co-op Wholesale Society meeting in 1903.[104]

Favouritism perhaps? By 1901, Isaac had already started work at the co-op, lodging in Eskin Street and coming home at weekends. In 1907, there was a family tragedy when he died of pneumonia aged just twenty-three. The funeral (Fig 15) was at St Andrew's and so many attended that the church overflowed, reflecting perhaps both Isaac's and his parents' popularity.

Mary Agnes Woodend

Mary Agnes and Ada both married, although neither had children. Mary Agnes (1871-1928) had married John Woodend (1865-1931). He was a slate dresser from Kirkby Ireleth who, by 1893, was working at the Honister mine alongside her father.[105] Mary and John had married in 1895 and by 1901, were living in the new terrace of miners' cottages at Mountain View. A fit woman, she won the Jubilee Sports ladies' race on the football field on 26th June 1897.[106]

Between 1911 and 1921, Mary Agnes and John adopted Mary, from Cockermouth. The 1921 census records her parents as '*both dead*'. In fact, Mary was the daughter of Maggie Cavanagh, born 20th June 1909 in Maryport. She with her mother in Wood Street in Maryport in 1911, along with a dock labourer, Thomas Pattinson. In 1921, Maggie lived a street away, Kirkby Street and worked as a cleaner. Thomas Pattinson also lived a street away in John Street with his mother, still working in the docks.

*Fig 16: Mary Jane Pepper and her daughters,
Mary Agnes and Ada (1898)*

When the decision to adopt was made and through what agency is unknown. Mary was told about her birth and by 1929 she was recorded as '*Cavanagh or Woodend*' when she married Cyril Pepper – he was Moses's second cousin. The couple moved to Essex where Cyril worked as market gardener.

After 1910, Mary Agnes Woodend is said to have taken over the business from her mother and she and John were living at Seatoller House in 1911. Moses filled out the form and listed his wife as "*lodging house keeper*" with no occupation for Mary Agnes. There was plenty to do, however, as the Peppers were now employing both a cook and a housemaid. Mary Jane's young brother, George Robinson was visiting – in 1901, the visitor had been another brother John, a ship's carpenter.

Fig 17: Mary Agnes and John Woodend and adopted daughter, Mary (1922)

There were three Cambridge students. Francis Morland Day (1891-1962) was the son of a Burton on Trent brewer. A schoolteacher and botanist, Day left his herbarium and notes to the Royal Botanical Society at Kew.[107] Philip Spencer Cannon (1889-1955) joined the Lancashire Fusiliers on the outbreak of war and later was in the Indian Army School of Education. In 1923 he wrote *Citizenship in India: Its Privileges and Duties*. He was still in the east in 1939 and was captured and held prisoner by the Japanese. A Canadian, Gordon Stanley Fife (1889-1916) was a history professor in Alberta after Cambridge. He was killed at the battle of Mont Sorrel, a German offensive aimed at disrupting the troop build-up for the Somme.

No 1 company was overrun during the attack, '*almost*

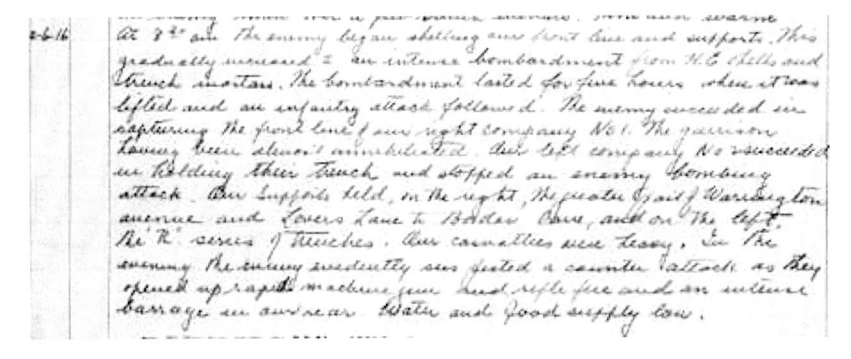

Fig 18: War Diaries: Princess Patricia's Canadian Light Infantry for 2nd June 1916

annihilated', but No 2 company emerged from the bombardment in relatively good order and, for eighteen hours, held out, isolated but with all its officers killed or wounded.[108]

Throughout the First World War, Borrowdale had its share of grief. At the house, the Cambridge Hunts continued into 1916 but then stopped until 1919 [109] but academics and students continued to visit, bringing the bad news about old friends.

After the war, Mary Jane still appeared to have her hands firmly on the family business. On 19th June 1921, there was a national census, at a time when the country was recovering from economic turmoil at the end of the war, exacerbated by a flu pandemic. Although she signed the census form, somewhat laboriously, another person has filled it out on her behalf, recording Mary Jane as *"boarding house keeper"* and her daughter's occupation as *"assisting mother"*. The enumerator almost wrote *'Mary Agnes Pepper'* (*Pep* crossed out and *Woodend* put in).

Three young Threlkeld women were the live-in staff - for two of them, the connection was Cornishman, George Honey (1870-1963) who had married Ada Pepper. His sister, Rose

151

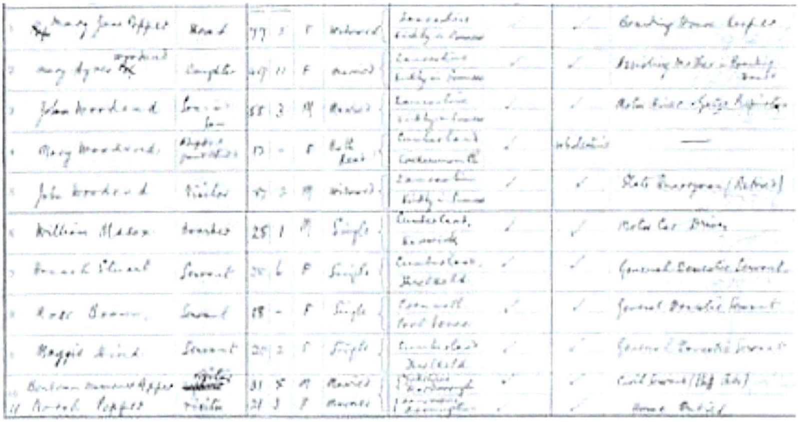

Fig 19: 1921 census Seatoller House

Lavinia, had married in John Brown in Cornwall but on his death in 1900 headed north, with baby Rose Brown, to live near her brother. She then married a Threlkeld lead miner, widowed and with a young daughter, Maggie. Ada Honey would have recruited step-sisters Maggie and young Rose as domestic help. Hannah Stuart (who would be the caretaker of the Borrowdale Institute in 1939) was the daughter of a Threlkeld shepherd.

At Seatoller House, there were no guests but the ties of kinship across the residents are remarkable. Not only did the Threlkeld girls have family links, John Woodend's father, 82 years old and now retired from the slate quarries, was visiting. The only other visitors were Bertram Warrener Pepper and his wife, Norah. Bertram was Mary Jane's nephew by marriage, as he was the son of Moses' brother. Bertram worked at the Inland Revenue in London, although the family would emigrate to South Africa in 1933 to run a hotel.

Like her mother, Mary Agnes may well have been impatient to run the business her own way. Her husband, John Woodend, had already branched out. He had abandoned the slate mine by 1911 and was described as a *"Posting Proprietor"*, referring to the vehicle carrying the letters rather than the mail itself. The local postal service had been run from Rosthwaite post office. In 1901, a young woman, Lizzie Wilson had been the postmistress. By 1911, the Rosthwaite PO had closed down and Woodend must have assumed responsibility for fetching the mail from Keswick, if not delivering it. By 1921, the Rosthwaite PO has re-opened, run by Grace Plaskett and her shoemaker husband, Ernest.

Woodend had an assistant, a local Stonethwaite man, Robert Dover (1881-1936). Robert, one of eleven siblings, married Mary Jane Bragg, the daughter of a Stonethwaite farmer, a few months later. Robert moved jobs, working as a carter for the slate mine, living in Derwent Street in Keswick. By 1921, a young Keswick man, William Mason, had taken over as a driver for Woodend. At Seatoller House, he met Rosie Brown (1903-1964), from Threlkeld, one of the domestic servants. They married at Threlkeld on 24th October 1923. William would carry on driving for a living and in 1939 was a coal delivery driver, living in Eskin Street in Keswick.

Woodend was described as a *'motor hirer and garage proprietor'*(Fig 20). In 1920, there were just 187,000, private, non-commercial, vehicles in the country, although this would double within two years. Buying a vehicle was a considerable investment – the Model T Ford, introduced before the war, still cost about £150 in 1920, equivalent to over £5000 in 2023. Some serious discussion and calculations would have been needed before Mary Agnes and her mother would have agreed to such expenditure. That such an amount was readily available speaks to the success of the business.

Was this mainly a service to pick up guests, arriving at Keswick railway station? The railway had come to Keswick in

153

Fig 20: 'Destination Seatoller' was inevitably for Seatoller House – an identical car appears, parked in the lower photo. The young driver may be William Mason

1864 and the station soon saw touting for business. Early adverts warned likely customers *'Do not be misled by drivers – it is the practice of many hotel keepers to fee the drivers so that families are recommended and driven to the hotel where the driver can get most money'*.[110] Meeting and greeting guests and protecting them from over-charging taxi drivers was all part of the service.

It was a short step from here to hiring out the car and a driver to visitors boarding locally and who wished to explore further afield. There were no press adverts publicising this but Woodend or his driver need only talk to the hotels in Rosthwaite, the boarding houses in Grange or the local farms to ensure a decent take-up.[111]

The 1921 reference to a *'garage'* is puzzling. The house still

Fig 21: A Daimler charabanc with engine trouble on the Kirkstone Pass

owned the stabling and coach house from Abraham Fisher's time so there was plenty of space in the outbuildings to protect any vehicle. Cars were unreliable and breakdowns would have been common whether on the valley roads or on the climb to Honister. If it was a workshop or petrol station, there were no applications to the rural district council for planning permission either at Seatoller or in Woodend's name. However, in 1939, Verdun Jones, a motor mechanic, was living in Top Row.

At his death in 1931, John was a *'charabanc proprietor'*. From the mid-19th century, these trips had become very popular, although in horse-drawn carriages, often arranged by hotel owners. Did he run tours around the district? Were these from Keswick or again based in the valley on a word-of-mouth basis? The classic tour left Keswick and travelled along the shores

155

of Derwentwater, past the Lodore and Borrowdale. Even this road was in poor repair and it remained unclassified until the 1920s.[112] The route led through Borrowdale and over Honister pass where the gradient was such that horse-drawn coaches would get their passengers to dismount and walk up the steepest parts (up to 1 in 4). The return to Buttermere was in even worse state, via a tricky descent, again where the slipper brakes could only just hold the vehicle. Then it was along the valley bottom to Gatesgarth, past Buttermere and back to Keswick via the Newlands pass.

By the 1920s, charabancs were motor-driven but did not travel over the pass. By this point (in 1906-1907), after abortive negotiations with the county council and the rural district council, the mine company built its own road from the pass to Seatoller, avoiding the steep descent down the hause. From 1910, they had invested in a steam traction engine which hauled the slate from the mine to Keswick via Seatoller. In 1926, they were advertising for an experienced driver for their Foden 6-tonner.[113]

This road joined Seatoller, just opposite the bridge to Top Row. There was a gate but access was open to other traffic, on payment of a toll. But, having arrived at Honister, the road surface from there to Buttermere was so bad as to make it impassable to cars. In 1935, the county council eventually built a new road from Seatoller to Honister. They rejected Lord Leconfield's offer to take over and resurface the mine company's road. Instead, the route chosen was the old coach road, alongside the hause itself.[114] Alderman Edmonds of the county council defended the decision on the grounds that it would have cost as much (£2000-5000) to take over the road as to widen and resurface the old carriageway, providing valuable jobs at a time of widespread unemployment.[115] Soon, in 1936, the Cumberland Bus Company, among others, was applying, albeit unsuccessfully, for licences to travel over the pass.[116]

156

Where did John Woodend fit into this in the two decades before his death in 1930? Was he simply a taxi service for his guests – and occasionally renting the car to them? Or was he more entrepreneurial, perhaps running Borrowdale coach trips from Keswick? The local government and newspaper archives provide no clues, with no licence applications or adverts.

Meanwhile, in 1912, Mary Agnes announced the building of two bathrooms with hot running water, heated by a separate stove in the kitchen. It was a radical change as it was a tradition for hunt members and the other visitors to queue for (and share) baths to make the most of the hot water available.

Another tradition was the informality of the dining arrangements, which continue to this day. The dining room had just one or two tables, the evening meal was always at a set time and visitors sat together.

Ada Honey

Towards the end of the Twenties, changes arrived – Mary Agnes died in August 1928. Her sister, Ada Honey, may well have been working with her as the Visitors Book for August 1928 shows no disruption. But when their mother, Mary Jane Pepper, died aged 85 in May 1929, there was a week with no visitors. Then in June 1931, Mary Agnes' husband, John Woodend, also died.

Ada (1875-1944) (Fig 22) ran the house until the Second World War. She had married Cornishman, George Honey (1870-1963), the son of a slate quarryman. George was born in St Teath, Cornwall, close to the Delabole slate quarry. He and his father, John, migrated north to work at Honister.[117] By 1901, he was living in Seatoller House and, astutely, married Moses' daughter, Ada.

Ada and George branched out on their own - Green Bank was a smart Victorian house, up the road towards Keswick, close

*Fig 22: Ada Honey and her cat outside the front door
of Seatoller House (1931)*

Fig 23: The Keswick-Seatoller bus outside the Moot Hall – before 1963

to the Borrowdale Hotel. It was originally built in the 1870s by Watendlath farmer John Green and his wife, Elizabeth on retirement. Elizabeth died in 1903 and by 1911, George and Ada Honey were living there and running a guesthouse. George was still at the mine.

In 1921, the couple were still at Green Bank. George described himself as the boarding housekeeper assisted by Ada and two servants. His widowed father, John, was with them and there were two married couples, the Rigbys and the Woods, on holiday from St Helens, Lancashire. But after the deaths of her sister and mother, Ada and George moved back to Seatoller where she ran the guesthouse until her death in 1944. George, however, was working at Honister again by 1939.

There was still neither gas nor electricity. Gas supplies never came to Seatoller and the 1937 plan for mains electricity fell through. The Mid-Cumberland Electricity Company were to erect overhead power cables to the Honister mine workings.

Seatoller would benefit.[118] But the scheme fell apart amid mutual recriminations between the power company, amenity societies and the slate mine.[119] Seatoller had to wait until the 1960s for an electricity supply.

It was a similar story for a bus route. Although there was a shuttle service between Keswick and Seatoller, the Cumberland Bus Company, among others, were refused licences, which would give them a circular route, through Seatoller, over Honister, around Buttermere and Crummock and returning through Whinlatter.[120]

There was disruption among some of Ada's regulars. In the 1920s, a Lakeland mountain guide, J E B (Jeremiah Ernest Benjamin or Jerry) Wright (1898-1975), based himself at the house, from where he ran rock climbing courses. Alongside him was George Starkey (1900-1974) who assisted with these and also led walking holidays, especially for the Co-operative Holidays Association (CHA).

Wright and Starkey became the moving forces to launch a new mountaineering club and organised a meeting of interested members on 16/17 November 1929. That meeting agreed, subject to the approval of the CHA General Committee, to form the CHA Mountaineering Club, and this was ratified on 10th January 1930.[121]

A few years later, the CHA built Glaramara, just east of Seatoller, opened in 1935,[122] which was intended to be the club's HQ but there was friction over a fatal accident and in 1933 the Club broke away from the CHA, renamed itself the Tricouni Club and reverted to Seatoller House as one of its bases, meeting twice a year. The club was named after the toothed rock-climbing nail invented in 1912 by a Swiss jeweller and watchmaker from Geneva, Félix-Valentin Genecand, alias "Tricouni" (1878-1957). When John Cockbain retired in 1977, he sold Seatoller

House to a consortium of Tricouni Club members and members of the Cambridge Hunts.

September 1939 saw George and Ada by themselves with just Irene Spark as the domestic help. She was the daughter of the landlord at the Lion and Lamb in Crosby Street, Maryport. On the night of September 4th, 1942, there was a fierce storm, floods four feet high rushed down the valley.

That same night at 9pm, a Wellington bomber took off from Finningley airbase near Doncaster on a night-time training mission. Weather conditions were poor and at 10:30 pm, the plane crashed into a crag on High Doat above Johnny's Wood, killing the largely Canadian crew. It was piloted by Flight Sergeant William Sage from Alberta. River levels were high and the RAF rescue team had difficulty reaching the site, although there was little chance that anyone survived the impact. There was Noble Bland at the farm, George Honey at the house, William Jackson at No 4 New Cottages among others – there would have been a search party but there were no press reports of the crash.

There was another rescue party later that weekend on Great Gable involving the professor of medicine at Cambridge, his wife and the headmaster of Eton. The Penrith Observer headlined the accident as *'Professor Falls on Wife'*.[123]

Business was busy during the first years of the war but from September 1943 until April 1946, there were no visitors. Ada died on 2nd January 1944, leaving the not inconsiderable sum of £2346. Despite his sister, Rosie Hind (née Honey) living in Keswick, George returned to Cornwall and to his Cornish roots, living at Delabole where he died in January 1963.

161

Fig 24: Annie Cockbain with Mary Trevelyan (1955)

Post-war

During this period, three Oxford dons became the tenants. What their connection with the valley was remains unknown. Henry Habberley Price[124] (1899-1984) was a Welsh philosopher, based at New College. Christopher William Machell Cox (1899-1982), was a fellow in ancient Greek history at New College until he

TO SAVE DOG.

HOUND TRAPPED IN CREVICE 5 DAYS.

BORROWDALE RESCUE.

To rescue one of the John Peel Hunt hounds which had been imprisoned for five days in a crevice amid the rough crags at Stoneythwaite, in Borrowdale Valley, a young Borrowdale man — William Bell — risked his life on Saturday.

The hound—Ruler—slipped into the crevice during a hunt last Tuesday and, although it could be heard whining, it could not be found.

A search was made each day without success till Saturday, when the hound was sighted on a ledge by two Borrowdale men—Fred Jenkinson and Douglas Cockbain.

They told Bell and the three men climbed to the top of the crag.

From here Bell was lowered on a rope to the rescue.

Later Ruler and the man were hauled to safety.

In spite of being five days without food or water the hound quickly recovered.

Fig 25: Newcastle Daily Chronicle 4th May 1931)

Fig 26: Annie Cockbain with Hunt members 1960. (E Gray, 2002)

became educational advisor to the Colonial Office and then Ministry of Overseas Development. Robert Lowe Hall (1901-1988) was an Australian, a Rhodes scholar who became economics fellow at Trinity, Oxford.

Ada had died during the war, but continuity was assured, however, when the dons sub-let the house to John and Annie Cockbain.

John Cockbain was the son of railway navvy, Mark Cockbain, and Dinah Grigg. He was born near Greystoke with an older brother, Joseph (1881-1917). The brothers were with their parents and grandmother in Mungrisdale in 1891. By 1911, John was working at Honister and lodging with James Nuttall at Mountain View while Joseph was a farm worker. He died on the Somme.[125]

Annie Cockbain (1887-1968) (Fig 24) née Douglas had also

164

Fig 27: John and Betty Cockbain (1977)

migrated into Borrowdale. She was Ada Honey's cousin from the south Lakes and had come to help Ada run the Green Bank guesthouse. In 1912, she married John Cockbain (1883-1972). The couple would have five sons and in 1917, they were living in Stonethwaite with the two eldest, Joseph and Douglas. Apart from time in the army, Joe (1913-2006)[126] would spend his whole career as a rockman at Honister as would brother Douglas (1914-1940). Douglas was more adventurous, narrowly missing serious injury when his motorcycle collided with a car at Red Bank.[127] And he had his moments of fame as a teenager (Fig 25), tracking down and rescuing a lost hound from the John Peel Hunt.

In 1939, John and Annie were in Castle Lodge with the three youngest boys before moving to Seatoller House. The twins, Michael and Norman also took part in rescue operations – upstaging the official mountain rescue team. A twenty-six-year-

Fig 28: 1966 The road by New Cottages

old woman, wife of an Oxford academic, broke her leg on Great Gable. Stan Edmondson from Seathwaite rounded up the twins, borrowed a stretcher and carried the victim back to the farm. It was front page news for the Daily Herald, alongside a US atomic test and the arrest of a Russian spy.[128]

After Seatoller House passed to the National Trust in lieu of death duties, John Cockbain bought it in 1960 with the help of a loan from G M Trevelyan, the initiator of the Trinity Cambridge hunts. Cockbain offered the advertised price and the Treasury accepted this. There was a higher bid and the Treasury planned to put the house on the open market. Intervention by Claud Bicknell, Hunt member, law commissioner and member of the Lake District National Park Planning Board, proved decisive as

Fig 29: 1966 New Cottages gardens

Fig 30: 1966 Seatoller Bridge

Fig 31: Betty Cockbain and her pet fox (Borrowdale Story)

the matter was settled in the Cockbains' favour at a Cabinet committee.[129]

Annie died in 1968. Later that year, her son, John Cockbain (1923-2001) married Elizabeth (Betty) Howard and they took over the business. Betty was the daughter of a soldier, Ernest Alfred Howard (1898-1970) from Sussex. He joined the Royal Sussex regiment in the war but stayed on in the Royal Tank Regiment, eventually leaving the army in 1946. He married Jessie Harrison in 1928 in Richmond, Yorkshire. Betty (1930-) and brother Cyril (1934-) spent much of their early life abroad, including India.

Betty's mother, Jessie, was the daughter of Thomas Morley Harrison and Elizabeth Cowper. By 1921, Harrison was a borer, working for United Steel in the Beckermet iron ore mines but by

Fig 32: Seatoller House garden and pond (2023)

1939 he and Elizabeth were living in Mountain View. Betty and her brother stayed with their grandparents on holiday and for longer stretches – Betty recalled being teased at Borrowdale School for speaking Indian (Hindi?). When the Howard family came back to England permanently, they lived in Yew Tree cottage before moving to Top Row. Her fourteen-year-old brother, Cyril, was one of the Seatoller lads rounded up for the Great Gable rescue in 1948.

By this time, Betty had left school – at fourteen, she was living with her aunt in Ambleside and washing dishes for a living. In 1945 she worked at Yew Crags guesthouse before joining the army for two years. There was a spell at Keswick pencil mill but then she returned to the army for three years until 1954. After that she worked at Seatoller House, before marrying John

Fig 33: Gillian and Geoffrey Trevelyan (1981)

Cockbain in 1968.

John Cockbain had been to Borrowdale School until he was sixteen where he was best friends with William Hind from Stonethwaite and in 1950, he was best man at William's marriage to Dorothy Slee from Grange. He had also been a quarryman, along with his father and his brothers Joseph and Douglas. He was quite deaf. However, at Seatoller House, he drove the local taxi and was the main cook whereas Betty did the sauces and sweets and looked after the house. [130]

In August 1966, there was exceptionally heavy rainfall. Seathwaite Farm took the brunt of the damage but at Seatoller, the first flood saw a wall of water moving down the beck. It moved boulders to block the Top Row bridge. The water came over the road, scouring channels in the road (Fig 28).

Behind New Cottages the backyards and gardens were devastated (Fig 29). The bridge leading to Seathwaite became

Fig 34: Ann Pepper (1995)

impassable (Fig 30). The floodwater poured through the garden and the house, flooding the building to a depth of several inches. Breakfast was served the next morning in wellington boots. Two weeks later there was a second, smaller, flood but with similar results.

***

John and Betty ran the house until 1977 when Betty's back became troublesome and they moved to Rosthwaite. John sold Seatoller House to The Lakes Hunts Ltd, a consortium of Tricouni Club members and members of the Cambridge Hunts. One of these, Richard Ling was a director and later chair of the resultant private company, played a major role in the sympathetic

Fig 35: Jay and Morven Anson

modernisation and management of the House.[131]

The house has subsequently had managers, rather than tenants running their own business. The first of these were Geoffrey and Gillian Trevelyan. From the Trevelyan clan, a nephew of G M Trevelyan, and a Trinity graduate, Geoffrey (1920-2011) worked in publishing as a director at Chatto & Windus, the Hogarth Press and Jonathan Cape. In 1947, he married Gillian Wood (1926-2000). Gillian was the granddaughter of Thomas McKinnon Wood, an under-secretary of state at the Foreign Office and the daughter of Alexander, a Buckinghamshire dairy farmer who died when she was eighteen.

When the Cockbains left, Geoffrey and Gillian uprooted

Fig 36: Trisha and Nigel Dixon from Seatoller House at the wedding of Lucy to Jake

themselves from St Albans in a dramatic change of life. During this period, the garden was re-modelled, especially with the creation of the pond, fed from a stream on the fellside and with an outlet back into the beck. It took on the basic structure of the 21st century garden (Fig 32), which, under the care of Nigel Dixon, received awards in 2022 from Cumbria in Bloom.

Gillian was also renowned for her cooking (as was her successor Ann Pepper), as the house received complimentary reports in the *Good Hotel Guide*.

In 1981, the Trevelyans moved back south and were followed by David and Ann Pepper. In 1998 Ann retired from the management after sixteen years – the last three on her own as she

173

and David had parted.

Her successors, Graham and Christine Welch, lasted just one season. From 1998-2004, Jay and Morven Anson ran the house, '...the cuisine reached new heights and comfort improved'.[132] In 2004, the Ansons retired to run a café and for the next eight years, the managers were Daniel Potts and Lynne Moorhouse.

From 2012, Nigel and Trisha Dixon have run the house (Fig 36). Nigel is a Geordie but Trisha was third generation Borrowdale. Her grandfather, Richard Hutton Thompson (1894-1968) was born in Maryport and by 1911, was an apprentice river at Honister. He married Jane Ann Johnston (1886-1943) in 1917 and by 1931, they had moved to Mountain View. Richard was still commuting to work at the quarry. After Jane's death in 1943, Richard married again in April 1947, to Annie Agnes Benson. Their daughter, Carol, married Michael Hawley. After Trisha's birth, they moved to Stoke but returned to the valley when Trisha was in her teens. The house has gone from strength to strength, winning awards for the gardens, the hospitality and, in 2023, publishing its very own cookbook.

Notes

[1] *CRO Barrow BD TB Wills Box 13/18; CRO Carlisle PROB/1864/W745*
[2] *Cumberland Pacquet 18th July 1865*
[3] *Whitehaven Advertiser 9th April 1867*
[4] *The Marshall family owned vast areas of land in the Lakes; the sale particulars for Seatollercan be seen in the archive of their solicitors, Waugh and Musgrave: CRO Whitehaven DWM 11/265/3; Leeds Mercury 16/10/1884 for short obituary of HC Marshall*
[5] *Carlisle Journal 7th September 1865*
[6] *Carlisle Journal 8th July 1859*
[7] *Carlisle Examiner 14th September 1867*
[8] *Carlisle Patriot 19th April 1867*

[9] *Carlisle Journal* 20th September 1867

[10] *West Cumberland Times* 20th July 1895 for auction; *Maryport Advertiser* 7th September 1895

[11] https://en.wikipedia.org/wiki/Henry_Wyndham,_2nd_Baron_Leconfield

[12] https://en.wikipedia.org/wiki/Charles_Wyndham,_3rd_Baron_Leconfield

[13] Cockbain's offered the advertised price and the Treasury accepted this. It then said that there was a higher bid. The matter was settled at a Cabinet committee (Jones K., (1994) An Economist Among Mandarins: A Biography of Robert Hall *fn* 19 227)

[14] It is unclear what the relationship was. Abraham's mother was Agnes Dowthwaite, probably from Smaithwaite in St John's in the Vale.

[15] William Holmes is clearly an error – there are no Holme(s) in the valley at this time.

[16] CRO Carlisle PROB/1876/W155 Richard's will – gentleman of Seatoller

[17] CRO Barrow BD TB Wills Box 8/77, CRO Carlisle PROB/1886/WCOD44: Jane Holme, widow, probate by Daniel Jopson, Chapel Farm, Borrowdale; CRO Barrow BD TB 31/14/1 solicitor's records - sale book for household furniture, effects, receipts and bill of costs regarding Jane Holme of Seatoller

[18] *Kendal Mercury* 28th January 1860 – there was a tea party for 160 to celebrate opening of the new lodging house

[19] Thomas West, *Guide to the Lakes* (1778)

[20] Letter written to Sara Hutchinson 5th August 1802; a letter the next day recounts his near-death experience descending Broad Stand

[21] Hope D., (2016) The democratisation of tourism in the English Lake District: the role of the Co-operative Holidays Association 8 *Journal of Tourism History* 105

[22] *Bulmer's History and Directory of West Cumberland*

[23] *Ulverston Mirror* 16th March 1872

[24] Geddes R. S., (1975) *Burlington Blue-Grey* 134-135

[25] https://patents.google.com/patent/US803125

[26] *Bulmer's History and Directory of West Cumberland* (1883) refers to him as manager of Buttermere Slate

[27] http://www.dmm.org.uk/company/b034.htm - by 1902, there were over

one hundred employees at Honister and Dubb quarries.

[28] *English Lakes Visitor 25th June 1881*

[29] *Tyler I.,* Honister Slate *(1994) 42*

[30] *Tyler I., (1994) 39*

[31] *Soulsby's Ulverston Advertiser 19th December 1867*

[32] *Ulverston Mirror 17th January 1874*

[33] *English Lakes Visitor 12th August 1882*

[34] *English Lakes Visitor 29th August 1885 and 5th September 1885*

[35] *English Lakes Visitor 20th December 1884*

[36] *Eg English Lakes Visitor 7th April 1888*

[37] *English Lakes Visitor 19th April 1884*

[38] *2 Timothy ch 2 verse 19*

[39] *Eg English Lakes Visitor 7th January 1893*

[40] *West Cumberland Times 21st August 1886 7th January 1893*

[41] *Closely related to freemasonry, Mechanism started in 1757 as a schism of a couple masonic lodges in England. In that year the Independent United Order of Mechanics was founded in Lancaster; Harris H., (2015)* The Order of Mechanics *CW3 183; Harris H., (2019)* A Cumbrian Friendly Society *CW3 195*

[42] *English Lakes Visitor 27th December 1884*

[43] *Lakes Chronicle 2nd August 1876*

[44] *This assumes that he was paying more than £10 pa rent for Seatoller House*

[45] *English Lakes Visitor 14th November 1885*

[46] *Dunbabin J., (1977)* British Local Government Reform *92 English Historical Review 777 at 783*

[47] *West Cumberland Times 8th December 1894*

[48] *West Cumberland Times 22nd December 1894*

[49] *Cumberland & Westmorland Herald 1st April 1893*

[50] *West Cumberland Times 18th April 1894*

[51] *West Cumberland Times 4th March 1896*

[52] *West Cumberland Times 4th April 1896*

[53] *West Cumberland Times 29th August 1901*
[54] *English Lakes Visitor 24th June 1899*
[55] *Cumberland and Westmorland Herald 25th July 1903*
[56] *West Cumberland Times 26th December 1903*
[57] *Cumberland and Westmorland Herald 3rd April 1915*
[58] *Yorkshire Post 29th May 1939*
[59] *She describes herself as c(ivil) engineeer's widow*
[60] *English Lakes Visitor 22nd September 1882*
[61] *Soulby's Ulverston Advertiser 14th January 1886*
[62] *English Lakes Visitor 6th March 1886 – advert inviting offers for lease*
[63] *English Lakes Visitor 17th July 1886*
[64] *Carlisle Journal 17th October 1884*
[65] *West Cumberland Times 20th July 1895 for advert for auction; Maryport Advertiser 7th September 1895*
[66] *English Lakes Visitor 24th June 1899*
[67] *http://www.busheyworldwarone.org.uk/uncategorized/remarkable-coincidence/*
[68] *Uglow S (2021) Early Tourism in Borrowdale CW3 175*
[69] *English Lakes Visitor 7th August 1897*
[70] *Dundee Advertiser 16th July 1898*
[71] *Leeds Times 6 August 1898*
[72] *The phrase was used in 1857 by barrister T C Sandars in a review of Charles Kingsley's novel* Two Years Ago. *Thomas Hughes'* Tom Brown's Schooldays *was published the same year. See Hall D. E.,* Muscular Christianity: Embodying the Victorian Age *(Cambridge 2006)*
[73] *(1874-1956) General manager LNER, knighted in 1924 and baronet in 1942*
[74] *McDonald P.,* The Story of the White Hall Centre
[75] *Gray E., (2007)* 100 Hunts: A Chronicle of the Trevelyan Manhunt 1898-2007; *Dower R., and Trevelyan G., (1998)* The Trevelyan Hunt: The First Hundred Years 1898-1998
[76] *Sidney Macaulay was the son of a manufacturing chemist. After university in Manchester, he went to King's, Cambridge to undertake an MA*

177

in History. He became managing director of McDougall's Flour. He joined the Manchester Regiment in 1915 and was killed at Gallipoli.

[77] McDonald, P. ibid; there is also a vivid description by George Bott in Cumberland Herald 20th June 1998

[78] Gray E., (2007) 4

[79] Gray E., (2007); Dower R., and Trevelyan G., (1998)

[80] Gray, E (2007) 11

[81] Paul Greville Hudson left a pen and ink drawing of a Japanese woman in September

[82] Bolton and two of his brothers, John and Maurice, died in the First World War

[83] Boston Guardian 4th October 1924

[84] http://rosma.co.uk/mw/oba/index.php?title=Meaburn_Staniland

[85] https://en.wikipedia.org/wiki/Robert_Blyth_Greig

[86] https://en.wikipedia.org/wiki/Hilton_Young,_1st_Baron_Kennet

[87] https://en.wikipedia.org/wiki/John_Clapham_(economic_historian)

[88] Burnley Express 13th November 1943

[89] Burnley News 11th March 1931

[90] Penrith Observer 27/10/1925

[91] http://blog.christiandaviesantiques.co.uk/designers/arthur-simpson

[92] Mansergh R., Windermere and Grasmere in the Great War

[93] https://peoplepill.com/people/reginald-hawthorn-hooker/

[94] https://en.wikipedia.org/wiki/Charles_Edward_Montague

[95] Probably the Kodak Brownie or Brownie 2 introduced in 1900

[96] https://en.wikipedia.org/wiki/Thomas_de_Trafford

[97] Third Battalion the Kings Own (Royal Lancaster Regiment) died 9th May 1915 during Battle of Aubers, - Harrow schoolmaster, Charles Werner,who had stayed at Seatoller in January, died at Aubers on the same day.

[98] https://www.dorsetlife.co.uk/2009/01/lady-of-the-palms-and-paddy-fields/

[99] https://en.wikipedia.org/wiki/Nigel_Gresley

[100] There is a very characteristic 'M' in her signature and in the text

[101] *Burnley Express 27ᵗʰ May 1914*
[102] *Geddes R. S., (1975) 134-135 – the quotation is from an article written by Moses on the formation of the Kirkby shop*
[103] *English Lakes Visitor 11ᵗʰ January 1890*
[104] *West Cumberland Times 7ᵗʰ October 1903*
[105] *Tyler I., (1994) Workforce appendix where he is referred to as John Woodend junior*
[106] *West Cumberland Times 30ᵗʰ June 1897*
[107] *Dony J.G., (1963)* Francis Morland Day *Proceedings Botany Society Brit Isles 5(2): 194*
[108] *https://www.canadiansoldiers.com/history/battlehonours/westernfront/mountsorrel.htm*
[109] *Gray E., (2007) 24*
[110] *Bradford Observer 21 June 1870*
[111] *http://thiswascumbria.uk/category/railways/*
[112] *West Cumberland Times 18 April 1894 – hotel owners were still lobbying for improvements*
[113] *Lancashire Evening Post 15ᵗʰ July 1926*
[114] *The Guardian 3ʳᵈ December 1934 – available at https://www.theguardian.com/uk-news/2019/dec/03/honister-pass-road-fears-lake-district-1934*
[115] *Lancashire Evening Post 17ᵗʰ January 1935 – and not giving the Leconfield estate a windfall payout*
[116] *Penrith Observer 18ᵗʰ February 1936*
[117] *Uglow, S. (2015)* Cornish Miners in Borrowdale *(Cornwall FHS Journal)*
[118] *Penrith Observer 14ᵗʰ September 1937 – there was opposition to the plan and it was agreed that part of the cable would be underground: Penrith Observer 9ᵗʰ November 1937*
[119] *Penrith Observer 28ᵗʰ December 1937*
[120] *Penrith Observer 18ᵗʰ February 1936 - the company renewed its application after the war: Penrith Observer 6ᵗʰ December 1949*
[121] *http://www.tricouniclub.org/origins.html*

179

[122] *Hope D, (2016) 105; the building is now privately owned but still run as an outdoor centre and hotel*
[123] *Penrith Observer 8th September 1942*
[124] *https://en.wikipedia.org/wiki/H._H._Price*
[125] *Joseph Cockbain Pte 27348 11th Border Rgt, killed 10 July 1917, buried at Coxyde Military Cemetery; Lancashire Evening Post 21st July 1917 described him as a whipper in to the Blwencathra Foxhounds and to the Cockermouth Beagles*
[126] *Cumberland and Westmorland Herald 27th February 1999 "Joe looks back on 58-year career hewing slate"*
[127] *Lancashire Evening Post 20th July 1935*
[128] *Daily Herald 23rd August 1948*
[129] *(Jones K., (1994); Gray, E. (2007) 55*
[130] *Gray, E. (2007) 43*
[131] *See obituary of Richard Ling in Fell and Rock Journal (2010) 519 at https://www.frcc.co.uk/wp-content/uploads/2016/01/Vol28-2.pdf*
[132] *Gray, E. (2007) 85*

11. New Cottages and Top Row

New Cottages owe their existence to the Honister slate mines. The slate, much valued for its colour and quality, was cut from high on Honister Crag. Originally it was carried on ponies along an old track (Moses Trod, allegedly exploited by Moses Rigg, a whisky smuggler) crossing Dubs Moor, Brandreth and the head of Ennerdale, and from there down into Wasdale.

The earliest formal lease was dated 2nd May 1728 and granted to John Walker *'enabling him extract slate at 'Ewecrag and Fleteworth'*. Prior to 1879, a number of entrepreneurs held leases - Charles Norman around 1750, John Atkinson in 1818, Jopson and Clark in 1840 and Samuel Wright in 1848 – but none of these had much impact on farming life in the valley.

However, by 1870 substantial underground workings were in existence at Dubs, Yew Crag and Honister Crag). It was dangerous work:

Slate from the workings was carried in sleds hauled by the quarrymen along treacherous paths. As these paths crossed steep scree slopes and narrow ledges a stumble could result in a man falling hundreds of feet to his death or being run over and crushed by his own sled. The slate was brought down to the Honister Pass road, the empty sled then being towed back for another load. The extreme physical discomfort of this work is made clear in an account by E. Lynn Linton (1864): 'The noise of the crashing slate comes nearer; now see the man's eager face; and now we hear his panting breath; and now he

Fig 1: New Cottages - at the foot of Honister Pass, it was just over a mile and 800 feet of ascent to get to the mine

draws up by the road side- every muscle strained, every nerve alive, and every pulse throbbing with frightful force. It is a terrible trade - and the men employed in it look wan and worn, as if they were all consumptive or had heart disease'.[1]

Despite the perils, the stress on the body, the slate dust and the extremes of climate, the Borrowdale quarrymen often lived long lives. Looking at a group of approximately one hundred and eighty valley miners in the 19th and 20th centuries, ninety reached seventy and beyond while only twenty-five died before reaching fifty years of age – and five of those were casualties of war. This picture contrasts sharply with other studies - in North Wales the average age of death in 1893 at Blaenau Ffestiniog for those employed at the dressing sheds, where the slate dust was most heavy, was 47.9 years whereas the average age of death for engine drivers and platelayers in the quarry who were least exposed to dust was 60.3 years. Labourers could expect to live until they were 45.3 years of age, while slate miners could only look forward to 48.1 years.[2]

There is no obvious explanation for the contrast. The Buttermere Green Slate Company was a much smaller operation. The rivers and dressers often worked at the entrance of the adits where there was less danger of any concentration of slate dust. The quarrymen were embedded in the community, often marrying local women, the daughters of farmers. Perhaps they benefited from a good diet and healthy lifestyle?

By the early 1870s, the Honister quarries were well developed and working, thanks to the efforts of Samuel Wright. Samuel (1798-1871) had been born in Borrowdale. His father, Anthony (1771-1839) had been a miner and was nearly killed at Quayfoot, near the Bowderstone in 1822 in an accident that killed his fellow worker, Gawain Wren.[3] Anthony then became a slate merchant and Samuel followed in his footsteps. Samuel leased Honister in 1840[4] but he died, unmarried, in 1871 and after his death the mine was dormant for several years.

In the late 1870s, the slate business was expanding as a result of a booming construction industry. The future prosperity of the Honister workings was established when a group from Ulverston (James Barratt, John Poole, Alan Salmon (1859-1946) and John Shepherd Sawrey (1848-1911)[5]) took out a lease, first on Yew Crag where they built a 230-yard-long self-acting tramway and erected barracks for workmen. Then in 1881, as the Buttermere Green Slate Company, they acquired the lease to the Honister Crag and Dubs quarries. Within a few years the company was employing one hundred men and producing three thousand tons of slate per year. There was further expansion in

183

1895, acquiring new quarries in Langdale and the company became the Buttermere and Westmorland Green Slate Company.

A perennial problem for the Honister mine was labour – the remote location and savage weather had meant that recruitment was difficult. There were not enough local men willing to take on the work, although many valley men mixed farm work with quarrying. This shortage of labour meant that wages were somewhat higher and that the employers looked to recruit from other mining centres. Experienced workers were brought in from the quarries of North Wales and Cornwall. The Borrowdale township censuses between 1881-1911 reveal a colony of about twenty Cornishmen, all slate quarrymen, many of them brought up in Medrose, a village close by the Delabole slate quarries.

The new owners at Honister had a network of mining connections in the south Lakes and many quarrymen came north from Coniston and Furness with them. An example was Moses Pepper (1846-1915) and his wife, Mary Jane Robinson (1845-1929), who were from Kirkby Ireleth. The family settled into Seatoller House, probably initially as boarders in 1878. But when the landlady, Jane Holme, died, Mary Jane turned the house into one of the best-known boarding houses in the whole of Cumberland while Moses continued to work as a manager at Honister.

Soon accommodation for these migrants became an issue. The valley farms and cottages had a finite capacity. There were barracks at the mine. There is no evidence on the conditions in these although in other slate mining areas, conditions could be appalling. In North Wales,

[beds] would be separated from each other by a slab of slate, whilst a piece of sacking served as a rug. Furniture in the living room was sparse and crude and usually roughly

> BORROWDALE NOTES.—Work in Borrowdale has been brisk during the last twelve months. The greatest concerns are begun this week. The Honister Quarry Co., are the movers. They have begun ten new cottages at Seatoller, the builder being Mr T. Hodgson, of Keswick. These should add greatly to the dale's population. Being at the foot of Honister, the buildings will be convenient for the men. A greater work is the laying of a tramway to bring slate from Honister to Folley Bridge. The metals have appeared on the place. A find of a valuable metal (ore) vein is rumoured.

Fig 2: West Cumberland Times 17*th* June 1899

constructed by the men themselves. The only light would be from a candle or paraffin lamp. Even when electricity reached the quarry it was never installed in any of the barracks. Newspapers were used as tablecloths, and thick brown paper as curtains, which also kept out draughts at wintertime. Recreation consisted of card games, draughts, dominoes, snakes and ladders, ludo or reading magazines and local newspapers.[6]

The miners must have longed for a normal family life, walking to work, home for dinner, time with the family. In 1893 the Leconfield Estate agreed to spend £1500 on the construction of eight houses at Seatoller to augment the barracks and scattered huts on the quarry site. The building control plans for labourers' cottages at Seatoller were lodged with Cockermouth RDC in 1893.[7] But the land had to be acquired from the Marshall estate

- Henry Cowper Marshall (1808-1884) had bought Yew Tree with the land in 1870. Negotiations dragged on as there was a problem over the right of way to the cottages through the Marshall land.

The work did not start until the summer of 1899. The builders were T & I Hodgson of Keswick (Fig 2) who had built the Grange Wesleyan chapel a few years previously.[8] By now, another terrace, Mountain View, had been completed in spring 1895. New Cottages, which were intended to be the first, followed in 1899[9] and Top Row in 1923.[10] In 1930, there were plans for a further twenty-two house on the farm itself that fortunately never came to fruition.[11]

The New Cottages houses were small for families, who often had four or more children. Downstairs there was a back kitchen with a small utility room/larder outside the back door. The living room had a decent-sized cupboard. Upstairs there were two bedrooms, a box room and a small attic for storage. Outside was a small yard with a narrow garden running down to the stream.

There was running water. This came from a reservoir upstream from the cottages. The reservoir and pipes were on land owned by the farm but New Cottages, Top Row, Yew Tree cottages and Seatoller House[12] all had the right to use the water. This system was probably built or improved when New Cottages were built. Everyone was responsible for repair and maintenance of the system – - each of the cottages was liable for one twentieth of the cost. A 1950s map (Fig 3) shows the water supply and drainage network for the terrace.

In the back yard was an outside toilet, perhaps originally an earth closet. But the water supply map (Fig 3) shows drainage not only via an outlet pipe running along the back walls of the cottages but also a further sewage pipe, which followed the back lane and was connected to the toilets. The drainage pipe led to

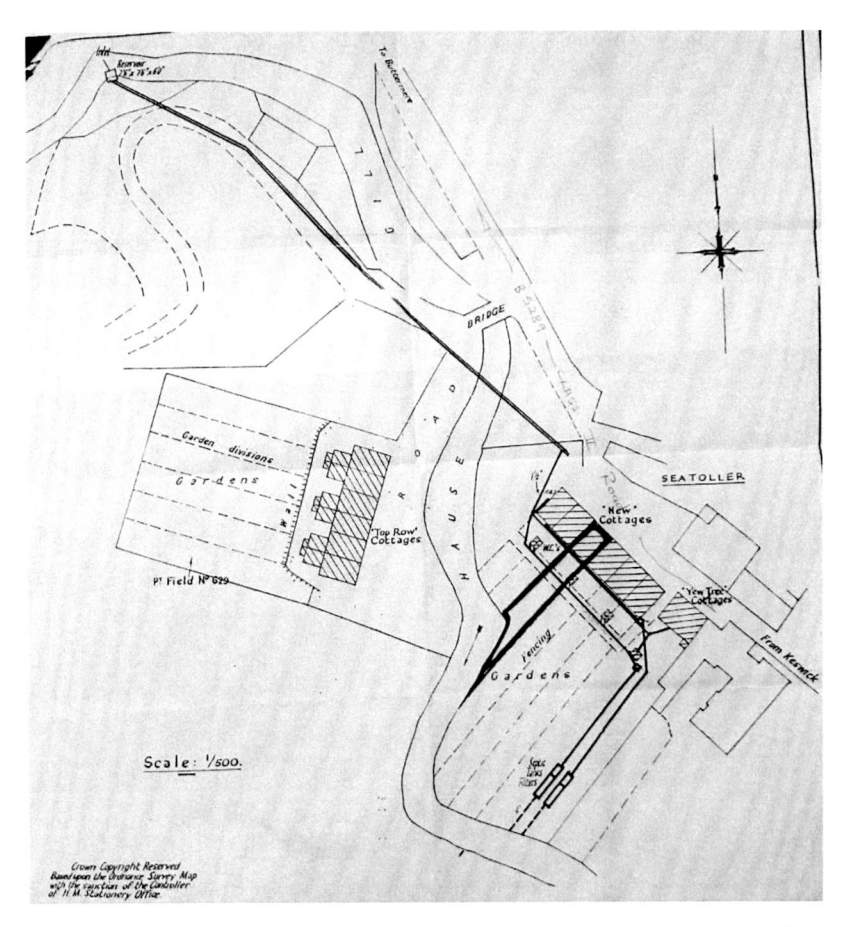

Fig 3: The water supply to New Cottages was from a cistern in the river with drainage into a septic tank in Yew Tree garden

an outfall into the stream via an 'Inspection Chamber Septic Tank and Filter Bed' at the bottom of the Yew Tree cottages garden. Was the sludge used for fertiliser? Although all the residents had rights to use the system, these were linked to obligations to pay for cleaning and repairing. Top Row had its own private system, possibly more advanced as the technology

187

had improved.[13]

The cottages had running water and sewerage from the start – there were fellside cisterns all over the valley so the cistern in the river would not have been an innovation. But when Seatoller House installed some bathrooms and toilets in 1912, they may well have taken advantage of the new water supply? In 1930 the Buttermere Slate Company applied to the RDC for planning permission for sewerage and running water for a further twenty-two houses at Seatoller.[14] The houses were not built but did the company intend a wholly new sewerage system or was it an extension of the one already in existence? It was not until 1968 that a treatment plant was built close to Glaramara, benefiting the whole village (with the exception of Mountain View).

The family washed in a tin bath inside and went outside to the toilet. The installation of bathrooms and indoor toilets only occurred in the 1960s after the 1957 sale of the cottages by the estate.[15]

Heating was always a problem in Borrowdale and was reliant on fossil fuels such as peat, logs and coal. Gas supplies never came to Seatoller and Seatoller had to wait until the 1960s for an electricity supply. A plan for mains electricity had emerged before, in 1937 when the RDC agreed to allow the Mid-Cumberland Electricity Company to erect overhead power cables from Catbells and along the old toll road to bring power to Borrowdale for the first time – more specifically to the Honister mine workings. Eighty-eight houses, including farms and hotels, would benefit.[16] But the scheme fell apart amid mutual recriminations between the power company, amenity societies and the slate mine.[17]

In New Cottages, there was a range in the front room.[18] This was continuously lit, as with the hearths of previous generations. This kept the temperature of the house at a reasonable level.

188

Fig 4: Bath time in a miner's cottage would have been crowded with the children doing their homework and the father washing behind a screen

Water heating was by a brick copper in the scullery. When Top Row was built in the 1920s, there was hot and cold water in the scullery.[19] There was a hot water tank and the water was heated by the range.

After work, the men would wash in tin baths, with a bar of carbolic soap. The baths might well have been stored in the back yard on hooks

Domestic life for the women was manual labour, as it was for the men. Floors covered with oilcloth or linoleum (patented in 1860) would have to be swept and washed and rugs beaten. Coal fires meant that surfaces needed constant dusting, perhaps tables polished with beeswax.

Laundry took time and effort – especially with large families

Fig 5: Laundry drying rack

such as that of Mary Jane Clark, the first tenant in No 1, who had five children. Monday was washing day. Water had to be heated, bedding and clothes scrubbed by hand, using a corrugated metal washboard again using carbolic soap. Whites and coloureds needed to be kept separate, with Reckitts Blue used to keep the sheets whiter. There would be several rinses in cold water and then the washing was put through the mangle. Perhaps the volume of washing was less – while underwear was washed frequently, top clothes might be sponged off. And just one sheet per bed with last week's top sheet becoming this week's bottom sheet.

In the Borrowdale climate, drying the laundry was always tricky, especially in winter. New Cottages had gardens which could be used while there were designated outside drying areas for each cottage at Top Row. Laundry would also be draped on a clothes horse by the fire and in the kitchen, drying racks could be hoisted up on pulleys (Fig 5) – which can still be seen.

Mary Jane would be also juggling a weekly budget. Her husband William Clark's income was wholly from the quarry. Quarries remunerated their workforce by means of a contractual payment known as 'the bargain'. A group of quarrymen, usually four or five would be assigned a particular face of the quarry to be worked over the following month. Many bargains would remain the preserve of a particular family or of close friends and were closely guarded.

At the beginning of each month a negotiation known as 'setting' was undertaken between the workers and the manager with a gang master by which the men were paid a certain amount for finished slates and a lesser amount for dead work. The master would pay the splitters, dressers and rockmen from this. The bargain was an incentive for the workers to produce as much quality material from the face, whilst also being able to earn a wage if the rock was of poor quality. A key component was the quality of the slate – the better quality meant higher earnings but more competition between gangs. A successful month's work may result in a reduced bargain the following month. At the end of the month, there was a settling when the manager would assess slate production and payment was made.[20] The bargain system protected the quarrymen's earnings against the difficulties of working with rock of variable quality; the system allowed the quarrymen to regard themselves as contractors rather than employees.

Discontent over rates could easily escalate. At this time, the quarries of North Wales were responsible for ninety per cent of slate production. On 22 November 1900, 2800 men walked out and began the longest-lasting dispute in the industrial history of Britain – the three-year strike by the men of the Penrhyn Quarry, Bethesda. Chief among concerns was the issue of the 'bargain' and the extent that owners could manipulate the system.[21] Earlier disputes had led to the formation of the North Wales Quarrymen's Union in 1874 but unionism was relatively weak in the industry.

The dispute would have increased demand for Honister slate, benefiting both employers and workers. There is no indication of unrest or solidarity with the Welsh miners. Nor was there any sign of a union (apart from the Mechanics' Friendly Society). The managers at the quarry had limited room for manoeuvre: they were dealing with a small pool of available labour, not easily replaced, and the workforce had strong ties of family, friends and place. The quarrymen might not be union members, but they were united.

After the war, unions gained ground at Honister. In September 1920, quarrymen at Honister and Langdale came out on strike over four Honister men who refused to join the union.[22] It is not recorded which union that might have been. There was the national Society of Masons, Quarrymen and Allied Trades but locally unions were mobilising in West Cumberland as well, such as the Cumberland Iron Ore Miners and Kindred Trades Association.

This was the sole newspaper report of unrest. Tyler suggests that the company let the problem sort itself out as it was not a time when anybody wished to be out of work.[23] Over the previous decade, the Buttermere Green Slate Company's response had been paternalistic, building miners' cottages, employing a 'home missionary' in Rosthwaite, to encourage temperance. All these are indications (no more than that) that the company was relatively enlightened and dealt well with its small and closely knit community of workers – although housing workers in tied

192

accommodation was a useful means of ensuring discipline in the workplace. In 1938, the company took the Honister men and their wives on a trip to see the Blackpool illuminations.[24] Was this an annual 'thank-you'?

The quarry did not employ its quarrymen directly – in the gangs, the gangmaster with his skilled quarries, dressers and rivers were on piece rate, receiving maybe 35s a ton for best slates, 25s a ton for seconds and 25s a ton for best pegs.[25] The rock hands might be paid by the day. The blacksmiths, carpenters, masons etc were company employees.

The lowest day rates at this time were about 4s 6d. In a court case in 1887,[26] Robert and Daniel Dover were prosecuted for failing to support their mother Dinah, who had run a Stonethwaite lodging house but had become a charge on Cockermouth Board of Guardians. Honister wages, it was said, were not less than 4s a day. In 1900, at Ulpha slate quarry, William Woodend was earning 4s 6d for a day's work – a figure that Woodend called a good bargain.[27]

William Clark worked six days a week. As a slate river, a skilled job, William would have earned more than Woodend and might have taken home approximately £6 per month. From this, Mary would have had to find the rent, coal, candles, food (bread, meat, fish, milk, butter, vegetables, sugar, tea), clothing as well as sundries such as subscriptions to the Mechanics friendly society for sick pay.

Rent may well have been kept low, to recruit and retain workers.[28] Were the cottages initially furnished by the company as the cost of tables, chairs, beds would have been considerable? Wood was in abundance and the front page of the English Lakes Visitor[29] showed three coal merchants, all vying for trade and promising prompt attention. Coal itself was cheap.

Candles and oil lamps were a necessity of life. Sourcing

193

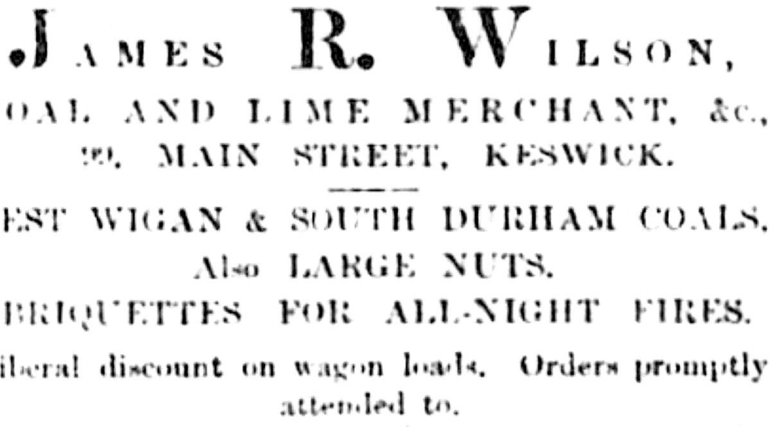

JAMES R. WILSON,
COAL AND LIME MERCHANT, &c.,
99, MAIN STREET, KESWICK.

BEST WIGAN & SOUTH DURHAM COALS.
Also LARGE NUTS.
BRIQUETTES FOR ALL-NIGHT FIRES.
Liberal discount on wagon loads. Orders promptly attended to.

Fig 6: English Lakes Visitor 13th January 1900

these items as well as sugar and tea required some thought. Shops were few and far between, although around 1841, Rosthwaite had two groceries, one run by Mary Coates (1820-1849) and the other by William Park (1809-). There was a surge in village post offices after Rowland Hill's postal reform brought about the uniform penny post from 10th January 1840,[30] but the first indication of a Rosthwaite post office was in 1855 when Harriet Martineau mentioned postmaster, John Jackson (1816-1885).[31] By 1861, Jackson had reverted to his trade as a shoemaker. In 1871, Nathan Coates (Mary Coates' uncle) was the postmaster and his widow, Elizabeth, carried this on in 1881. By 1901, Lizzie Wilson was running the post office. The post office at this time would have carried some limited stock. Down the road towards Seatoller, another grocery had opened at Ivy Cottage by the Stonethwaite crossroads, run by Jane Tamar May (1851-1939) née Jackson, later assisted by her Cornish husband, Edward Jollow May.

JOHN H. WILSON,

GROCER, TEA DEALER,
BAKER AND CONFECTIONER,

Nos. 44 and 46, MAIN STREET, KESWICK

TEA (good value) ... ... 1s. and 1s. 4d. per lb.
 ,, (not to be beaten), ... 1s. 8d. and 1s. 10d. ,,
COFFEE ... ... 1s. and 1s. 4d. ,,
 ,, (pure) ... ... 1s. 6d. and 1s. 8d. ,,
BEST FLOUR ... ... 1s. 7d. per stone
HINDHAUGH'S "H" WHOLE MEAL
 5d. and 10d. per bag
INDIAN MEAL ... ... 9d. ,,
 ,, CORN ... ... 8½d. ,,
CRUSHED OATS ... ... 1s. 2d. ,,
NEW CURRANTS (clean and good) ... 3d. per lb.
 ,, RAISINS ... ... 5d. ,,
TREACLE (1lb. and 2lb. Tins) ... ... 1½d. ,,
SYRUP ,, ,, ... 2½d. ,,
APPLES (Cooking or Dessert) ... 2s. 6d. per stone
ONIONS ... ... 1s. 2d. ,,
WAX CANDLES 3½d. per lb., 9d. per 3-lb. packet
STARCH (Colman's) ... ... 4½d. per lb.

CONFECTIONERY.

Fruit, Seed, Madeira, Bordeaux, and Cokernut Cakes from 6d.

Slab Cakes (own make), Cherry, Sultana, and Eclipse, 6d. and 8d. per lb.; Whole Slabs, 5½d. and 7½d. Eclipse contains Almond Paste in centre.

SOLE AGENT FOR HOVIS BREAD.

Fig 7: English Lakes Visitor 13th January 1900

There was some choice for Mary Jane when she needed to buy things that she could not grow or make at home. There were obviously more shops in Keswick and there were the weekly markets. The valley farmers would take produce to the market and maybe it was possible to hitch a lift?

Otherwise, town trips would never have been casual – there were no bus services until the 1920s. Mary Jane would have to arrange childcare, and she would want to look reasonably smart in public. There would have to be a pressing need for such a trip, perhaps to get dresses for special occasions such as weddings or pots and tools from the ironmongers – although many edge tools might have been acquired through the blacksmiths at the mine. Barbers were for townfolk - cutting hair would have been done at home.

But while Seatoller residents would have visited Keswick irregularly, shopkeepers such as the grocer, John Wilson of Main Street, Keswick, must have seen a market opportunity to take their wares to the customers (Fig 7).

The biggest customers were the modernised and enlarged hotels and boarding houses. All required regular supplies of staples and routine deliveries must have soon become established. By 1897, the Lodore and the Borrowdale hotels were owned by Edward Cesari (1844-1900) who, among other innovations, installed telephones. The Keswick grocers would have not only fulfilled their orders (they had telephones by this point) but also would have visited the farms and hamlets of Borrowdale on a regular basis. For the women at home, the vans would have been a welcome distraction from housework and an opportunity to meet and chat with neighbours.

The family would have been able to grow vegetables and perhaps keep hens in the garden. Other food would have come from the surrounding farms – the explosion of population from

Fig 8: The Co-op mobile shop from inter-war years

1890 to 1910 meant more demand for eggs, milk, dairy products and meat. The farmers were unlikely to ignore this opportunity, which meant that the quality of food for the quarrymen and their families was likely to be good. The visits by the grocers' vans from Keswick provided more variety but also adulteration issues – flour might contain chalk, tea might include other plants, milk might be watered down.

One major advantage of the new buildings was that they had ranges with ovens. The older buildings around the valley would often have had an open fire with all the consequent limitations for the cook. It is unusual to modern eyes but in New Cottages, the range for cooking was in the front room (Fig 9) and there was a brick copper for heating water in the back scullery.[32]

The main skill of the housewife was to make stews and boil potatoes and suet puddings, all to be cooked in the iron pot essential for cooking on an open fire. .... Everything was cooked in the one utensil; the square of bacon, amounting to little more than a taste each; cabbage or other green vegetables in one net, potatoes in another, and the roly-poly swathed in a cloth… by carefully timing the putting in of each item and keeping the simmering of the pot well regulated, each item was kept intact and an appetizing meal was produced. ... Pot pies or pan pies were common because they were easy to cook in an ordinary pan by placing a thick layer of suet pastry over a stew of meat and vegetables, flavoured with onions and herbs. There was little variety of diet. The pudding was sweet or savoury, depending on whether jam, treacle, a few currants, mushrooms, leeks, scraps of bacon, or even hawthorn buds mixed with bacon scraps, were used for a filling. ... If a small joint was bought from a butcher for the Sunday dinner, and there was no oven in the cottage, 'those without oven grates would roast it by suspending it on a string before the fire, with one of the children in attendance as turnspit'.[33.]

One advantage was that bread could easily be baked at home – there were no entries for valley bakers in any of the 19th or 20th century censuses. However, despite the advantages of a modern house and access to the farming community, Mary Jane and the other quarrymen's wives were making do on housekeeping of around £1 per week or less – there could be lengthy periods when stormy or icy conditions prevented the men from working. The border between security and poverty was thin in rural areas as it was in the towns:

The most illuminating study of northern conditions was by J. S. Rowntree, Poverty, a study of town life, reporting on conditions in York in 1901. This contained a detailed analysis of family budgets. The wages of the 24 families investigated varied from the bare subsistence sum of 15 shillings per week to the comparative affluence of 40 shillings. Other factors,

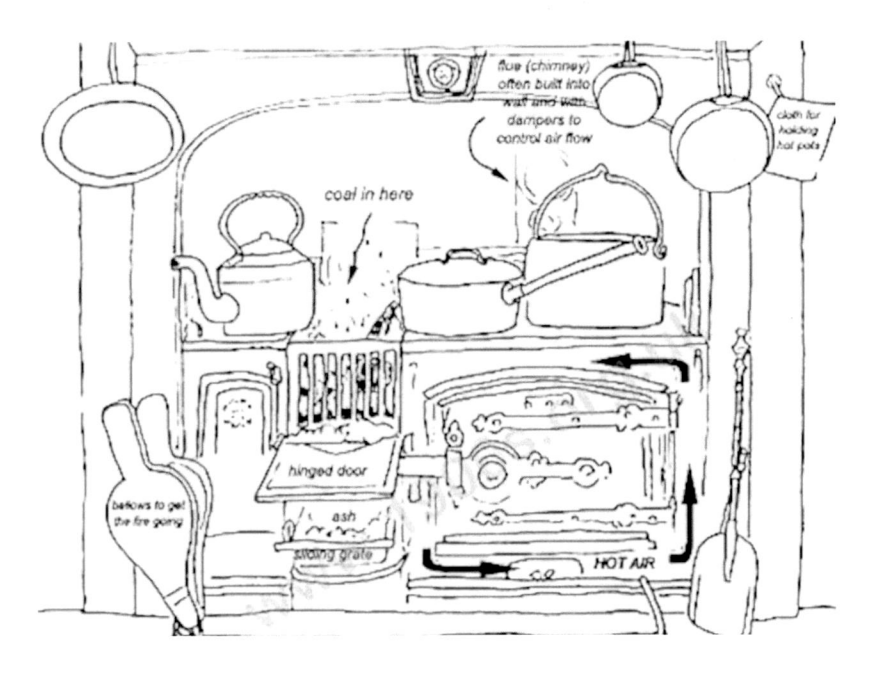

Fig 9: The kitchen range [34]

which determined whether a family was undernourished were the number of children in the family, the skill of the housewife, and whether or not she was a 'working' mother. At the end of his report Rowntree gave a list of the weekly menus of each family. These, from a modern point of view, make very sorry reading. In the poorest, breakfast and tea were identical; bread and margarine or dripping or treacle or jam, and tea. Dinner was rarely a two-course meal. [35]

Away from food, there was also clothing - Mary Jane's children would still have worn clogs to go to school and there were shoemakers in the valley. Edward Coward (1865-1939) from Rosthwaite had made shoes for many years until 1907 when he and wife, Tamar, emigrated to New Zealand to grow fruit.

Mary Jane would have knitted woollens such as socks and sweaters, run up dresses and shirts and mended and darned clothes (as well as for her and William).

The quarrymen's children had one major benefit, a well-endowed school. In earlier times, would the monks of Furness Abbey have run schools for the children of their tenants? Would this have been lost after the Reformation? In 1687, the valley chapel, St Andrew's, was consecrated and through the 18th century, lay readers and curates were appointed – often benefiting from Queen Anne's Bounty, a scheme established in 1704 to augment the incomes of the poorer clergy. In other chapelries, these posts often included the duties of a schoolmaster[35] and this may have been the case with the early Borrowdale vicars, such as John Harrison, who served from 1750-1806. In 1806, there was an advertisement for a curate who could also teach school.[36] This job may have fallen to the incumbents (William Parsable from 1806-1839 and George Newby from 1839-1873) or someone working under their aegis.

The original school was built close to the church under Parsable's guidance in 1826 and its future was secured at the death of Abraham Fisher at Seatoller House. He was involved in education as a trustee for the grammar school,[37] helping extend the Keswick Library,[38] as well as concerning himself with the state of Borrowdale school. He died on 20th October 1864 after a short illness. The press reports all mentioned,

The unostentatious and kindly manner in which he dispensed his charity added to the pleasure of the recipient[39]

The will[40] contained several large charitable bequests, especially to religious and missionary bodies but including a £500 endowment for a teacher's salary at Borrowdale School. By 1894, Kelly's Directory reported that the teachers, Yorkshireman

Joe Wilkinson (1858-) and his wife Susannah (1844-) née Bean, had a roll of fifty children, boys and girls with an average attendance of thirty-nine.[41]

In 1891, there were thirteen children from Seatoller and Mountain View between six and twelve. By 1901, this had doubled to twenty-six and inevitably had led to pressure for the school to be enlarged. A fund was created, [42] and was donated and the new school buildings added. By 1910 the school had a roll of ninety-one children although its average attendance under John Reay was just thirty-eight.

While their fathers and older brothers marched up the hill to the mine, each school day morning, two dozen under-12s, walked in the opposite direction. In 1901, their headmaster was a Devonian, Ralph Pollard (1872-1948), assisted by Gertrude and Florence Spry, daughters of a Cornish quarryman, Charles. Pollard was at the school from 1895 to 1907 and later described the school:

The Cumberland day schools then were very much like workshops or barns. The children were confined in long desks and contributed to the heating of the school. Then the Cumbrian child was vastly different from those children with whom I had been working. Where the Lancashire boy was precocious and far from shy, the Cumberland lad wanted to make sure he was not going to be laughed at and reserved his opinions.[43]

The education would have been confined to the basics but in a 1936 interview, Pollard was clearly progressive and mentioned broader reading including Scott, Dickens and Shakespeare. Fisher's endowment must have given the governors scope to expand the library as well the staff. There was music with regular concerts[44] and an annual prize giving – including

> ROSTHWAITE.
> TECHNICAL EDUCATION.—The classes for instruction in sick nursing, conducted by Miss Catherine Haynes, have been very popular, the average attendance during the course just expired having been 30. Miss K. Armstrong's first lecture on "Poultry keeping and breeding" (illustrated by lantern slides) drew an audience of 33. Mr A. E. Gregory, Mus. Bac., has completed a course of twelve lessons in singing, given by him in Borrowdale School.

Fig 10: English Lakes Visitor 23rd February 1901

prizes for attendance.[45]

There were also popular evening classes at the school (Fig 10) where thirty or more turned up for courses as diverse as nursing or poultry breeding. These adult education classes were backed up by the council's travelling library. In 1950, Cumberland council started a limited service,[46] expanding it to Keswick and Borrowdale two years later. It was still operating in the early 1960s (Fig 11).

Pollard would also have shared his love of football with the pupils. There were sports days at the school as well as some cricket. The annual sports days in the valley were often organised by the Mechanics friendly society: the main sports were fell-racing and Cumbrian wrestling where Stonethwaite's Reuben Dover (1884-1925) had a county-wide reputation.[47] Dover was killed in an accident at Road End, Honister in October 1925.

As soon as he had taken up his post, Pollard was organising a Borrowdale football team, dragooning solicitor John Simpson as president and the Rev Heelis as treasurer. They played their

Fig 11: Betty Howard (centre), later married John Cockbain(right). She worked at Seatoller House from 1954. Mary Mouncey (with the basket) lived at No 3 New Cottages with her husband, Bill. The librarian is on the left with the van driver behind Mary. The little boy was John Jenkinson, born in 1958, the grandson of Seatoller farmer, Noble Bland. (Carlisle Library © cumbriaimagebank)

matches on Dover Jopson's West Garth fields, west of Rosthwaite. Subscriptions were 2s or 1s for the under-14s (which suggests that the game was also played at school). For many years, Keswick Fire Brigade came to the valley for its annual winter outing, playing a match and then to the Royal Oak for tea.[48]

The football ground was used for the Jubilee valley sports on 26th June 1897.[49] Sack races and potato races were mainly for

203

the children but there was 5-a-side for the men and a ladies' race, won by Mary Woodend, from Seatoller House. Elsewhere the children skipped, ran in sacks, ran with eggs and spoons, ran tied to each other, ran over obstacles, ran with potatoes or just ran.

The football team survived the loss of Pollard when he was appointed to a post in Penrith, performing quite creditably in 1908 in the new Keswick and District League and attracting a *'fair gate'*. However, their behaviour on the field left something to be desired – the press opined, after the side's defeat by St John's 'A' XI that it was *'terribly bad form to hold the referee responsible for the reverse'*.[50] In 1935, the schoolmaster, G. Scott, headed an attempt to find land suitable for a valley recreation field, including a bowling green and tennis courts with slate chippings from the mine.[51] Nothing materialised and after the Great War, there were no press reports of any team sports in the valley.

There were few press references to cricket but in 1896, there was an attempt to revive a Borrowdale club. The usual suspects (Pollard, John Simpson and the Rev Heelis) were the prime movers.[52] Little came of this initiative and team sports may have been rare. The Borrowdale Sports took place sporadically alongside the sheep fair. Wrestling was the main attraction, and the press reported the results. In 1860, there were around sixty entrants. In the open competition, John Scott from Little Crosthwaite beat Thomas Tyson from Lorton.[53] John Scott (1838-1903) came from local farming stock and later became a hotelier, owning the King's Arms in Keswick and the Lodore. In 1889, Scott was seized with a 'paralysing stroke' at Gosforth Park coursing meeting.[54] Also taking part, unsuccessfully, was John Mossop, groom to Abraham Fisher at Seatoller House.

In 1902, there was a one-off sports event held at Grange to celebrate the coronation of Edward VII on August 8th. From 1922,

Fig 12: 2022 Fell race at Borrowdale Shepherds' Meet (Steve Uglow)

the meeting became annual with an increasing variety of events for all ages – in 1929 there was a pillow fight. By 1926, the focus was on dogs, both show dogs and trail hounds. There was also a fell race and wrestling with the boys' competition won by John Allison of Mountain View. By 1935, the sports took place on a

Longthwaite field, lent by Benjamin and Elizabeth Pattinson at the farm.

No sports were held during the war but were revived in July 1946. The fell race went up Watendlath Fell – in 1947 it was won by a local, Stanley Edmondson of Seathwaite. In 1955, the meeting was moved to Chapel Farm. In recent years, this has been overshadowed by one of Lakeland's classic fell races, the Borrowdale Fell Race, which covers over seventeen miles and six thousand, five hundred feet of ascent, started in 1974. A less arduous race still takes place as part of the Shepherds' Meet in September (Fig 12).

The Families
No 1 New Cottages
Mary Jane Ramsay (1870-), a miner's daughter and her husband, William Clark (1868-), married in 1889 and were the first tenants in No 1. William was born in Irton, the son of a miner, Thomas (1841-1897) and Mary Ann (1842-1920), née Duke. When William was a child, the family moved around, lodging at Seathwaite in 1881, at Thorneythwaite but then in Keswick where William was a lead miner.

By the time they moved into New Cottages, William was a slate river at the mine and Mary Jane was managing five children. William continued to work for the Buttermere Green Slate Company, even after the family had moved back to Keswick, living in St Herbert Street in 1911. Ten years on, in 1921, William still commuted to the mine.

By 1911 a Cornishman from St Teath, Hanson Tucker (1871-), a slate river and his wife, Annie (1878-1951) née Hetherington from Whitehaven, were living in the cottages. Hanson had been brought up by his grandparents in Cornwall before coming to Borrowdale as a young man. Life must have been lonely, and he was in trouble for drunkenness.[55] Ten years passed before he found Annie Hetherington. Annie and her younger sister, Fanny, worked at Green Bank for a widow, Elizabeth Green, before the marriage at St John's in the Vale. Hanson and Annie's children, Joseph 1910 and Margaret (1911-), were both born in Borrowdale. By 1921, the family had moved to Mountain View, with its bigger houses and gardens and away from the farmyard.

In 1921, William Jenkinson (1887-1980) was living in New Cottages and working at Honister. He had married Elizabeth Dixon (1892-1952) in 1910 and they had two children, William and Beryl. By 1939, the Jenkinsons had moved to Mountain View. Joe and Marjorie Cockbain moved in and would live in the cottage for nearly fifty years.

Joseph Cockbain (1913-2006) worked as a slate miner for 58 years. His parents were John Cockbain and Annie (1887-1968) née Douglas. Annie was Ada Honey's cousin from the south Lakes, who had come to help Ada run the Green Bank guesthouse (near Borrowdale Hotel) and then at Seatoller House. In 1912, she married John Cockbain (1883-1972) who was another Honister quarryman. They ran Seatoller House from 1948-1968, handing over to their son, John (1923-2001) who married Elizabeth (Betty) Howard.

But in 1921, the family were living in Stonethwaite, a short walk to Borrowdale School.[56] Joseph left school when he was 14, immediately starting work at Honister.

I remember I had to walk up to the mine to be there for 7-30am. If you were just a few minutes late you were docked a quarter of the day's wage, so we made sure we were always there on time.

Pay for the teenager was 2s 6d a day. All of the jobs

Fig 13: Joe Cockbain with Mark Weir, owner of Honister mine

(quarryman, splitter and dresser) were manual, working underground with nothing more than candles. Joe was apprenticed for five years and began to work as a river but changed over to dressing slate, cutting and tidying it ready to be sent out. He earned 6s 8d a week and had to provide 22cwt of dressed slate.

Surprisingly there were only three fatalities during Joe's career at the mine, two of whom (William Jackson, and Adam Gregg) were neighbours in Seatoller.

During his youth, Joe's hobby was being a member of the St. John Ambulance Brigade and was also on call to go out to any rescues on the fells and was a keen fell runner. In 1936, he married Marjorie Horsley (1915-1988), the daughter of a

Fig 14: Visit by the Duke of Edinburgh to Honister in June 1966, making no concessions to footwear

Braithwaite lead miner. Through the Second World War, Joseph served with RAMC first with the Abyssinian Company, ending up at Addis Ababa, then in Madagascar, working on a campaign to treat malaria and dysentery and finally in Burma

No 1 was unoccupied in 1939 - Marjorie was living with her widowed mother and siblings in Braithwaite. After Joe returned in 1946, he considered nursing in Newcastle as a career, but it did not pay enough to keep his wife and two young children at the family home in Seatoller. He supplemented his Honister earnings, working as a part-time shepherd for Seathwaite farm with Moss, his own dog, helping to make ends meet. By 1947 he was back at the mine and working underground for £1 a day.

It was hard work but we really enjoyed it. Life was different then. We worked hard and played hard. We had no television, and no radio until after the war...They were happier times although we had to make our own entertainment...Before I was married I would think nothing of dancing until 2-30 in the morning at Rosthwaite dance, walk a girlfriend home to Watendlath, walk back to Seatoller and still get up in time to make it into work for 7-30am on the Saturday...We had a great community spirit at the mine. I always say hard work never killed anybody. Those who work the hardest always come off the best.

Joe and Marjorie applied for planning permission to add a bathroom and improve the kitchen in 1966. They only left Seatoller in 1985 when he, reluctantly, retired.

On 22nd July 1966, the Duke of Edinburgh came on a whirlwind tour of Borrowdale, Ambleside and Windermere. He visited the workings at Honister, passing through Seatoller, no doubt cheered by all the Cockbains, the widows, Betsy Peebles at No 2 and Edith Jackson at No 4 as well as the Blands on the farm.[57] However, the cheering would have been louder eight days later when England won the World Cup!

No 2 New Cottages
Next door to William Clark in 1901 was his sister Nancy (1866-1944), born in Ulpha. Like her brother, she had four daughters. She had married a quarryman, William Thompson (1863-1937), in 1885. William was from a valley family that stretched back generations. His great-grandfather Joseph had been a miner at the Seathwaite wad mine in 1799 and later worked at Honister. His grandfather, John (1802-1854), was a blacksmith, both at the

wad mine and at Honister, before moving into Smithy Cottage at the Longthwaite crossroads. He married Elizabeth Birkett from Seathwaite. Their son, Joseph (1835-1910), carried on as a smith at Grange and living at Leathes Cottage. He in turn married Margaret Dixon, the daughter of Daniel, another black lead miner.

William Thompson was valley through and through, although by 1911, the family were living in St Herbert Street in Keswick – again next door to Nancy's brother. William stayed with the Honister mine, although it was easier work at Keswick railway station as a yardman, organising the shipping of the slate.

In 1911, another rockhand, John Postlethwaite Holmes (1877-1959) was living in the cottage with his wife, Ann née Park (1871-) and four children Violet (1902-) and Annie (1904-) born in Coniston, with Audrey (1907-) and William (1900-) born in Borrowdale. They moved to Egremont where Holmes worked as a gas stoker.

In their place in No. 2 by 1921 was Walter Gaskell (1892-1957) and his family. He was one of eight children of quarryman, William Gaskell (1863-1903) and his wife Martha Allison (1864-1903), who lived in Stonethwaite. In 1903, both Walter's parents and a young sister, Ada, died within a few months of each other. While the two eldest boys, Allison and Walter, were soon working on farms, the family was split up with the other five children living with aunts and uncles in Ireby, Dearham, Carlisle and Gateshead.

Walter had been working on Longthwaite Farm but soon became a quarryman. He met Annie Lancaster (1892-1962) who was in service at Seatoller Farm and they married in 1912. They had four boys, two of whom (Joseph and Walter) were noted fell runners. Forty years later, Walter and Annie were still in Seatoller, in Top Row and sons Cyril and Alfred were also in the village.

211

Annie's niece, Ethel, would follow her aunt and work for Tom Jackson on the farm in the 1930s. And her sister, Emily, and her husband Hilton Middleton would live in Mountain View on their retirement in the 1950s.

In the 1930s, quarryman Robert Hibble (1895-1970) and Hannah Margaret née Smith (1900-1961) were at No 2. Robert was born in Cleator Moor and working as an iron ore miner in 1921. He, Hannah and young son, Robert, were living with his mother-in-law, Jane Smith, at Winder Gate, Frizington. They moved soon after to Seatoller as Robert went to Borrowdale School and won a prize.[58] Four more children, all daughters, were born in Seatoller. In 1925, Robert survived a rockfall, which killed his workmate and famous local wrestler, Reuben Dover (1884-1925). Newly-married Dover was knocked off a ladder when the rock came away.[59]

The Hibble family lived in the cottage until 1946 when they moved to No 6. After them came a Scot, Charles Peebles and his wife, Betsy née Cruickshanks. He was an electrical engineer at the mine, having learnt his trade at Carnoustie where his father was a baker.

The Leconfield Estate sold No 2 in 1957. Betsy Peebles was the tenant, although there was no written agreement. The annual rent was £17 4s and she also had to pay the council rates. Downstairs was a living room with a range and cupboard. There was scullery with a sink and a brick copper and pantry. There were three bedrooms on the first floor. Outside was a toilet with a small garden. The water and drainage were still private.

Nos 2 and 6 were the only ones of the New Cottages terrace advertised for sale in 1957. Arthur Watson Todhunter (1913-1986) bought both. In 1960 he applied for planning permission for a bathroom and toilet for both cottages. Todhunter was the son of a farm manager from Thornthwaite and the brother of John

Todhunter at Stonethwaite Farm. Arthur had been an engineer based in Ulverston in 1939. In 1940 he married Jennie (1912-1972) née Noble. She was also a from a Thornthwaite family – her father William Elwood Noble was motor engineer after the war but killed himself in 1920.[60] In 1939, Jennie was running the Thornthwaite post office with her older sister, Winifred – the PO was just a few steps from Jenkins Hill, the farm managed by Arthur Todhunter's father.

The Peebles remained as Todhunter's tenants. Charles died in 1964 but Betty was on the electoral roll for Seatoller in 1970 and probably remained in the house until her death in 1977.

The house was bought by the Beresford family in the early 1990s and has remained a holiday home for their family.

No 3 New Cottages
In August 1887, Thomas Pepper (1864-1935) married Mary Ann Dover (1869-1927). From her earliest years, Mary Ann's parents left her with her grandmother, Dinah Dover née Tyson (1814-1887). Dinah was the widow of a Crosthwaite farmer but was living as a charwoman in Stonethwaite. Mary Ann and Thomas Pepper knew each other as children. Thomas was one of fifteen children, born in Langdale, the son of Matthew Pepper (1819-1892) and Hannah Miller (1831-1901). Matthew had left Kirkby Ireleth in the south Lakes, to work in the Elterwater slate quarries. In 1850, he married Hannah, the daughter of a Keswick cartman. They lived in Langdale until about 1876 but soon after that, they moved to Borrowdale.

One reason for moving was that Thomas's brother, Edward (see No 4 New Cottages), had served a prison sentence in 1876 when living in Langdale. But the move to Borrowdale was also helped by another event: Matthew was the uncle of Moses Pepper, the son of Matthew's older brother, James (1807-1885).

213

By 1877, Moses was working as the manager of the slate mine at Honister and living in Seatoller House. His influence meant that by 1881, Matthew and three of his sons were working at Honister.

The family lived first at Stonethwaite (1881), Seathwaite (1887) and then at Thorneythwaite (1891) where they rented the cottage across the farmyard from Robert and Jane Jopson. It was crowded at Thorneythwaite. In the farm itself, the Jopsons had six children. In the cottage, there were the Peppers and five children plus one grandson. In addition, Matthew had three of his fellow quarrymen as boarders. Although they may well have stayed at the barracks at the mine during the week, they would be back at the weekend and one of them was John Shaw, one of the *"Langdale Rowdies"* who had caused trouble with Edward. You wonder what his nephew felt as Moses was a Rechabite, a strictly teetotal sect.

Thomas and Mary Ann initially lived in Seathwaite but moved into the new cottage in 1899. The couple carried on the tradition of large families and have eleven children together and by 1911 move back to Derwent St in Keswick where he was later employed by Manchester corporation working on the Thirlmere reservoir.

No 3 was taken by a well-established valley family who had been living at No 5, Thomas Birkett and Annie Jopson (see below). In 1921, Annie and Thomas lived in New Cottages with their daughter, Christina, who was helping Sarah Sands at Seatoller farm. Two other children, Fred and Maggie, were also working for the family at Low Park, Loweswater, where Annie's brother, Dover was farming. On Thomas's retirement, there was a further move within the village and by 1939 he and Annie had moved to Top Row.

In 1939, George McMurdo (1888-1966) and his wife,

Florence née Monkhouse (1889-1953) were living in No 3 with their younger children, John Kennedy (1927-1972) and Florence junior (1928-1999). The son of a Carlisle railway man, George was an electric haulage attendant and petrol locomotive driver at Honister slate quarry. After the war, James and Lily Gardiner lived in the cottage. James Bair Gardiner (1906-1976) was born in Beith, Ayrshire but the family moved to Carlisle. He was one of fifteen children. In 1921, many of the family were employed by fabric manufacturer, Alexander Morton. Several worked as block printers on fabrics but fifteen-year-old James was a 'teaser', combing the raw wool. He married Lily Gregg (1910-1983) in 1931 and they were in Penrith in 1939 when he described himself just as a labourer. After the war, they moved to New Cottages – Lily's parents, Adam and Julia, were from Furness but came to Borrowdale in the 1930s, living in Top Row. Adam was killed at Honister when he was knocked off a ledge by a piece of falling rock and fell 15'.[61]

Cyril Hilton Gaskell (1918-1992) was the son of Walter and Annie Lancaster and was brought up in No 2 New Cottages. He and his wife Sarah, née Foster, applied for planning permission for No 3 in 1956, having bought the cottage from the Leconfield Estate. His parents were in Top Row and his brother Alfred at No 6. After his parents died, he sold to Bill (1910-1989) and Mary Mouncey née Savage (1911-2000). They were both originally from Leeds and lived in No 3 from the 1950s (see Fig 11) until Bill's death in 1989. The house then became the property of the Hunt Trust and is living quarters for the managers of Seatoller House.

No 4 New Cottages
The first tenants of No 4 were Thomas Pepper's brother, Edward (1857-1911) and his wife, Margaret Ann Hall (1858-1929).

215

Edward was the fourth child of Matthew Pepper and Hannah and was born in Keswick, although brought up in Langdale where he worked as a quarryman. He was clearly a difficult young man at first as the Ambleside magistrates fined him £2 for being drunk in April 1876.[62] Four months later he was charged with assault for throwing stones at Constable Gass in Grasmere. Edward did not help matters by being drunk in court and received a prison sentence of two months with hard labour.[63] Clearly this was not a one-off as the press report headed the paragraph "The Langdale Rowdies Again".

After his prison sentence, there are no more press reports of court appearances for Edward. He lived with his parents at Stonethwaite and at Thorneythwaite, having moved with his father to work at Honister. He married his widowed sister-in-law, Margaret Ann Hall (1858-1929), in 1894 in Ulverston RD. She was the daughter of a Coniston copper miner and was the widow of Edward's older brother, James (1855-1888), marrying in 1879. James had died in 1888 and this second marriage was void as it was within a prohibited degree of kinship (and would not be allowed until the Deceased Brother's Widow's Marriage Act 1921). Margaret already had three children with James - John 1881, Hannah 1883 and James 1886 and she would have a further three with Edward - Walter 1895, Albert Edward 1900 and Edward Ralph 1905.

Edward had been living with his parents in Thorneythwaite when his father died at Thorneythwaite in February 1892. His mother, Hannah, died in Little Langdale in 1901. Edward was a quarryman in 1901 and stepson James was an apprentice river. His stepdaughter Hannah was also with them as were the two young boys, Walter and Albert. Walter was at school – and getting a prize for attendance. In 1906, Albert was also at Borrowdale school – and getting a prize for drawing. Another son Edward

Fig 15: Robert Pearson (1883-1968) Margaret Bethwaite (1880-1968)

Ralph was born in Borrowdale in 1905.

In the late 1900s, the family moved again, this time to Vale View, Coniston where Margaret had been born. Edward was a slate dresser. He died in 1911, but his death was registered at Cockermouth – perhaps he had been visiting his brother, Thomas, in Keswick? His son Walter (1895-1917) enlisted in the Border Regiment in 1913 and said that he was born in *'Borrowdale'*. Sadly, Walter only lasted 363 days before discharge as *'unlikely to become an efficient soldier'*. But with the outbreak of war, he was able to re-enlist with the Borders and died of wounds at the Battle of Arras in April 1917.

After the Peppers had left, No 4 was occupied by Robert Pearson (1883-1968) and his family. He was the son of a shepherd, Joseph (1849-1896) and Mary Bennett (1851-1933). As a child in 1891 he was living in Miller's Tenement, Brackenthwaite in the Vale of Lorton.

His wife, Margaret Bethwaite (1880-1968), was the daughter of a Dearham coal miner. In 1901, she was working at

BORROWDALE PATH DISPUTE.

District Council Inquiry.

The Stonethwaite to Borrowdale Church Chapel Field footpath, a gate of which has been locked, has been the subject of a dispute as to whether it is a public footpath or not. The Borrowdale Parish Council reported the matter to the Cockermouth Rural District Council, who held an inquiry in the Borrowdale Institute on Tuesday. Mr. Johnson, Bothel, chairman of the General Purposes Committee, presided, and there were also present Mr. Barraclough, Mr. Tallentire, Mr. A. R. Thomson, Lonning Garth, Portinscale, and Mr. H. T. Pape, Lodore, members of the Cockermouth Rural District Council; Mr. W. Lee, Clerk, and Mr. Simpson, engineer to the Rural District Council. Mr. W. Sumner, Whitehaven and Keswick, represented the owner, Mr. R. Brownrigg, Chapel Field House.

Evidence that they had used the footpath for from forty to fifty years without let or hindrance was given by Mr. John Jopson, Chapel House; Mr. Plaskett, Rosthwaite Post Office; Mr. Jonathan Hind and Mrs. Birkett, Rosthwaite; and Mr. W. F. Askew, Grange-in-Borrowdale, Clerk to the Borrowdale Parish Council

Mr. Sumner did not call any evidence.

The committee of inquiry decided to report back to the Cockermouth Rural District Council that they considered that the footpath was a public one.

Fig 16: Penrith Observer 5th February 1935

the Victoria Hotel in Buttermere. They married in December 1906 and their daughter Mary was born in 1907. In 1911, they were in New Cottages and Robert worked as a labourer at the mine.

They stayed just a few years and, after Seatoller, lived at Croft Home Farm in Buttermere. That was the address when he enlisted with the Royal Artillery in 1916. Robert was called up in 1917 and went to France in the winter of 1917. In April 1918, he was invalided home after being gassed, albeit mildly. By 1939, he was farming at Scales, near Cockermouth. In retirement, they lived at High Lorton, both dying in 1968.

After the Pearsons came the Brownriggs. In 1921, Richard Brownrigg (1888-1975) was a farmhand, working for Sarah Sands at the farm. Living with him were wife Laura née Dover (1889-1978) and son Richard (1913-1996). Laura was the daughter of Reuben Dover at Stonethwaite. Richard was a foxhounds enthusiast and had a puppy, Tempest, which came second at the Blencathra Hunt's puppy show.[64] Richard was a perennial silver medallist, just missing out again in 1922, 1923 and 1924 at the Threlkeld sheepdog trials meet.[65]

Brownrigg moved to Chapel Field House. He was relatively prosperous, although in 1939, he described himself as a labourer. There was an odd incident in 1935, he owned a field by his house and picked a fight with his neighbours when he sought to close off a path across the field. He was rich enough to hire a Keswick solicitor to represent him at the council hearing, although that was money wasted.

After the Brownriggs, the Jackson family stayed in the cottage for over 50 years. William Jackson (1909-1947) and his wife, Edith, lived just across the stream from William's parents who were in Top Row. His father was William James Birkett Jackson (WJB) (1877-1954) and his mother, Olive Ruth Harris

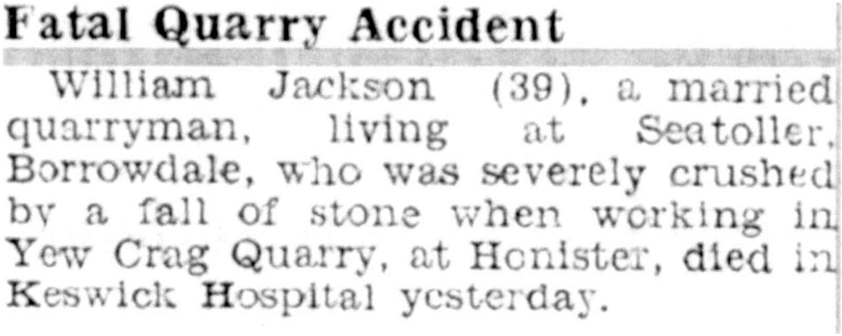

Fatal Quarry Accident

William Jackson (39), a married quarryman, living at Seatoller, Borrowdale, who was severely crushed by a fall of stone when working in Yew Crag Quarry, at Honister, died in Keswick Hospital yesterday.

Fig 17: Yorkshire Post 28th November 1947

(1882-1943). The Jackson family had moved briefly to Idaho around 1907 and that was where William was born in January 1909.

Back in England and short of work in west Cumberland, by 1927 WJB was working as a rock hand at the Honister quarries, and he and Olive were living at Seatoller, probably in the newly completed 6 Top Row. His son, William lived and worked alongside him. In 1929, he married Edith Alice Kelly (1911-1982). Edith was baptised in the Anglican St Oswald's at Warton near Lancaster on 15th October 1911. She was the fourth child of Matthew Kelly (1876-) and Nancy Park Wilson (1878-1922) and her forenames come from two of Nancy's sisters. Nancy was the daughter of Titus and Elizabeth, Warton publicans and hoteliers. Matthew was from Cookley, Worcestershire. Nancy and Matthew had spent a short period in Chester, West Virginia, USA where Mary-Anne, their second child, was born in 1906. But they returned in 1908 and by 1911, Matthew was a navvy on the railways. They were poor, living in three rooms on Main Street, Warton. The family moved to Millom where Matthew worked on the blast furnaces in the steel industry but in 1921, he was out

Fig 18: Edith Jackson outside No 4 with son Bill's car (mid-1950s)

of work.

In 1929, Edith was just 18 at the time of her marriage. It is an intriguing question as to how she met William Jackson but perhaps Edith came to work in a Borrowdale hotel or pub. After the wedding, the couple lived at 4 New Cottages, Seatoller, a stone's throw away from William's parents at 6 Top Row. They had four children but in November 1947, tragedy struck. William was working with his father, WJB, in Cumberland Quarry with WJB on the air winch and William fixing the chain around a clog ready for his father to haul it away. As the chain was being slipped on, the clog moved and crushed William.

Edith was left with four children to bring up on her own (although her parents-in-law were just across the stream). Her life was made much easier by the welfare reforms of the post-war Labour government – there was the NHS for healthcare and the two youngest (Edith and Ralph) had free secondary education. Edith would have benefited from the National Insurance Act 1946, with compensation for the death of William, child benefit and social security. Her eldest son worked at the mine and the family were able to remain in the cottage as tenants.

Her eldest, Nancy (1930-1998) married Stan Edmondson (1926-2003) of Seathwaite Farm in 1948. He was a champion fell runner and sheep farmer. Their children were William Stanley (1950-), born at 4 New Cottages, and Peter (1955-). Peter still farms at Seathwaite.

William (1931-1989) worked at Honister mine as a river. He was part of Keswick Mountain Rescue team in 1948. He married Margaret Mary Ahern in 1961. He and his brother, Ralph, were involved in hound trailing. Bill owned the famous hound, Shannon (Bill's wife was Irish), housed at Victor Brownlee's farm at Stonethwaite.[66]

Edith Ruth (1943-2000) married Robert William Porter (1936-2016) in 1962. He was the whipper in to the Blencathra Hunt. Ralph C (1944-), like his brother, was very involved in hound trailing. Ralph owned the famous hound, Buacail, son of Bill's hound, Shannon and housed at Victor Brownlee's farm at Stonethwaite and trained by Peggy Horsley at Rosthwaite. Ralph married Margaret Saunderson in Millom RD 1966. They farmed at Penny Hill Farm, Boot, Eskdale, Cumbria,

Edith carried on living at 4 New Cottages and in 1953, bought the cottage from Baron Leconfield. Her daughter Nancy had married in 1948 but William, Edith and Ralph were with her until their marriages in the 1960s. It was not until 1967 (and her last child, Ralph, had married and left home) that she had a modern bathroom installed.

Edith died in 1982. After her death, a Leicester manufacturer, Graham Johnson, bought the house, as a holiday home. He sold it in 2014 to Steve and Jenny Uglow, from Canterbury, who now live there.

No 5 New Cottages
The first tenants in No 5 were William Siddle (1866-1932) and his wife, Mary Alice née Benson (1868-1939). William was born in Manchester. His mother, Jane Postlethwaite, was from Newlands but was living in the Cheetham Hill area of Manchester when she met a widowed bricklayer, James Siddall. They married on Christmas Day 1865 in Manchester Cathedral – they were not alone as thirty-six other couples also wed there that day.

Although the couple lived in another Manchester parish, all those who lived within the former parish of the cathedral had the right to be married in the mother church. Christmas Day was always popular and in 1865 was on a Monday. With Sunday off work and Boxing Day as a bank holiday, that allowed three days for the celebrations. At that time, all marriages had to be solemnised between the hours of 8 a.m. and 3 p.m., allowing seven hours, permitting each of the thirty-six couples, if married separately, about 11 minutes for the ceremony. The parish clerk would prepare the register entries in advance so that all that was needed was the signatures of the couple and their witnesses. Other couples were queuing behind them. But there was a practice in Manchester where couples were taken in batches, perhaps six or so, at a time.

James died within a year. Jane was not educated and made her mark on the marriage register. This may explain why her surname changed to 'Siddle' when she returned to the Lakes, after the death of her husband in 1866. With her was little William Henry (1866-1932). In 1871 Jane was a housemaid at

223

Rydal Hall while William was with her mother in Church Coniston. However, he grew up alongside his step-siblings, John and Annie Mary Hunter, after Jane re-married to Joseph Hunter, a quarryman in 1876. They lived in Stonethwaite and by 1881, William was an apprentice at Honister.

Mary Benson was from Troutbeck, the daughter of a road labourer. The couple married in 1890, living for a time with the Bensons. They moved to Seatoller – there were money difficulties and there was an adjudication under the Bankruptcy Acts in 1900.[67] Alongside their own children, John Hunter, William's half-brother, was with them as was baby John Hunter, the illegitimate child of Annie Mary. They would later adopt another child, Ada Sanders. In 1904, there was an accident on Haystacks involving three brothers by the name of Wood, one of whom was killed. William was foremost in the rescue team, recovering the body and taking it to Gatesgarth. He was commended for the '*modest and manly*' way in which he gave evidence.[68]

In 1911, they had all moved to Park Villas in Keswick, and were still there in 1921. Transport had improved as William was still able to work at Honister. Young John Hunter was also back in Keswick with his mother, who was still unmarried and with two more children.

The Siddles were replaced in No 5 by an old valley family: Annie Jopson was the daughter of Dover Jopson, named after his mother, Ann, from Seatoller farm. The picture of the house[69] shows three-year-old Annie with her mother, Margaret née Braithwaite and her grandmother, Ann Jopson with baby brother, Daniel Braithwaite Jopson. Annie (1877-1961) would stay in the village all her life. She married a quarryman, Thomas Birkett, (1870-1952), who was brought up at Castle Lodge, near Longthwaite. He was the oldest child of Joseph, a man who had

224

been a shoemaker for many years, before a stint at the quarries and finally working as the valley postman.

By 1921, Annie and Thomas moved two doors up to No. 3 and John Robinson (1882-) and his wife Florence had taken over the lease. John was born in Borrowdale and brought up in Troutdale. His mother, Jane Robinson née Tweddle was Florence's aunt who was the daughter of Jane's sister, Mary. Florence (1880-1954) was brought up by her grandparents in Greystoke before service at Brockham Park in Surrey. She married John in 1917 and they had a son, John, the following year.

John James Robinson was a quarryman, working at Quey Foot. John and Florence moved back to Troutdale Cottages after his mother's death in spring 1926. Lodging with them in 1921 was Nicholas Bewsher (1888-1944) who was working at Rigg Head quarry.[70] He had been brought up in Grange by his Mounsey grandparents but his wife, Margaret née Bewley (1886-1966) was from Carlisle and by 1939 the family were settled there.

By 1939, No 5 was occupied by Ronald Ovington Wilson (1904-1982) from Auckland in Durham and his wife Martha née Green. He was a general labourer at Honister. They were followed by Joseph and Nora Johnston née Parker. Joseph (1911) could not have had a worse start to life. At the age of one month, he was with his mother, Jane Ann Johnston, in the Union Workhouse at Cockermouth. However, she married Richard Hutton Thompson in 1917 and Joseph was brought up at 4 New Street, Keswick with his step-siblings. In 1931, the family moved to Mountain View – presumably Joseph followed his stepfather to work at Honister. In 1942, he married Nora Parker (1918-) and, after the war, was living just down the road from his mother and stepfather.

225

A WORKINGTON TRAGEDY.

Tearing herself away from her daughter, who had followed her and seized hold of her in an attempt to prevent the tragedy, a Workington widow named Ellen Ray, aged 41, threw herself into the old dock about three o'clock on Saturday morning and was drowned. The woman's husband was swept out of his fishing boat in the Solway during a storm about three years ago, and his death had caused her to be depressed. She went to bed with her four children on Friday night. Early next morning her 16-year-old daughter, Eleanor, who was sleeping in the same room, heard her mother get out of bed, and she asked her where she was going. Her mother said she was going downstairs. The girl got up and followed her mother out of the house. The woman made towards the harbour, and the girl was just in time to catch hold of her. A struggle ensued in the darkness, the girl frantically doing her best to prevent the demented woman from throwing herself into the water. Part of the mother's clothing gave way, and she got free and jumped into the harbour. The girl called for help, and two men named Hadfield and Sharp searched in a boat and found the body still floating, with the head under water. Mr. D. J. Mason, Coroner, held an inquest on Saturday, and recorded a verdict of suicide whilst temporarily insane.

Fig 19: Penrith Observer 20th December 1921

For many years from the 1960s, No 5 was the home of Vincent and Mary Ray. Mary Elizabeth (1928-) was the daughter of John Plaskett and Hannah O'Connor and had been brought up in Mountain View. Vincent Ray (1917-2003) was born in Workington where his father was a dock worker – suing Cammell Laird for unpaid wages in 1905.[71] Later his father was a fisherman and was swept off the boat and drowned during a storm when Vincent was a baby. His father died when he was young. In 1921, his mother, Ellen, was bringing up four children at Sea View, Workington – the two eldest (fifteen and thirteen) were both working for James White, a grocer, in Henry St. The struggle was too great and she drowned herself in December 1921 (Fig. 19).

Did young Ellen and her brother John bring up the two small children, Winnie and Vincent? By 1939, Vincent was working at the Lodore. After the war, in 1947, he married Mary Elizabeth (1928-) née Plaskett. She was the daughter of John Plaskett and Hannah O'Connor and had been brought up in Mountain View.

No 6 New Cottages
In 1901, John Thomas Clark (1876-1943) from Langdale and his Irish wife, Elizabeth née Somerset (1873-1969) lived at No 6 in Seatoller. Elizabeth was the daughter of Cumberland parents, although born in Sligo, Ireland. They were friends of John and Jessie Pepper at Mountain View and in March 1907, the two couples travelled to Harrisburg in Illinois via Liverpool and Boston on the SS Ivernia. The men worked as coalminers - Harrisburg was one of the leading coal-mining centres of the midwest. Three years later, on 15th April 1910, the day of the US federal census, both Johns had been out of work for six weeks. The Clark's lodger, Joseph Birkett, (another valley man) was sharing the same fate.

The Clarks stayed in Harrisburg, becoming US citizens in

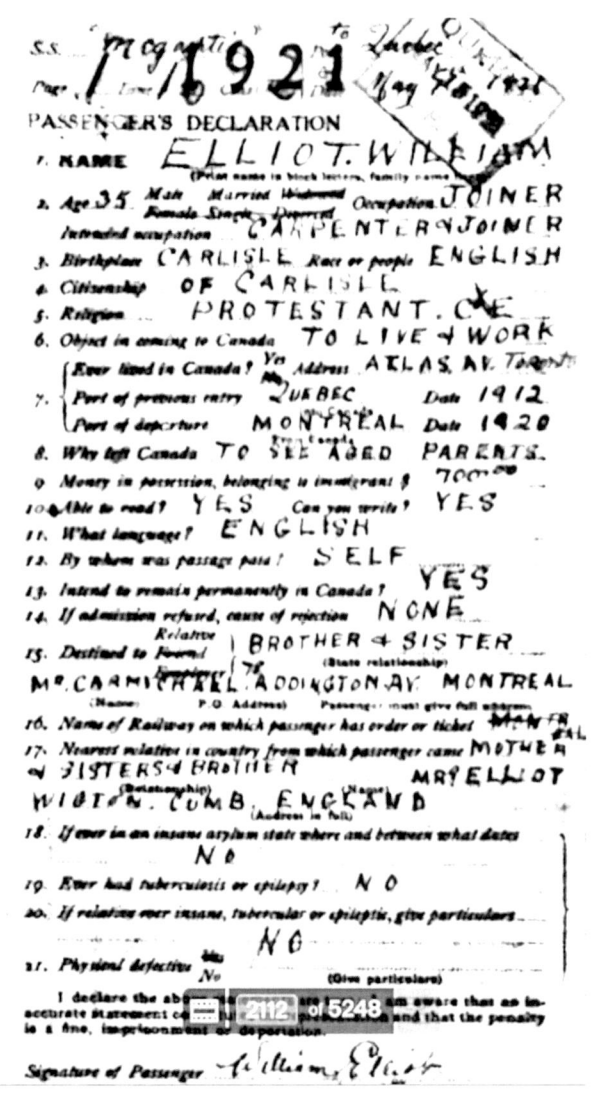

Fig 20: William and Ann Elliot, returning to Canada in 1921, after a trip to Carlisle, apparently an independent republic of which the Elliots were citizens.

Fig 21: Rosthwaite Post Office in Victorian England – in 1891, Martha Thompson née Cannon was the postmistress and deliveries by bicycle may well have been by husband, John

1914 but the Pepper family, travelled back to England on the SS Lusitania in February 1914. The Clarks visited in April, arriving in Liverpool on the SS Mauretania and leaving in August, on the SS Franconia.

By 1911, William Elliot (1886-) and his wife Ann née Hunter (1888-) both born near Wigton were living in the house with their children and Sarah, Ann's sister. He was a joiner and cartwright at Honister. They emigrate to Canada in 1912 where, in 1916, William enlists in the Canadian Expeditionary Force. However, his military career was short as he was discharged the next year. In 1921, now living in Montreal, there was a trip home (Fig 20) for to see their 'aged parents'.

The pull of North America with job opportunities and higher wages is apparent as the Elliots had $700 cash in their possession

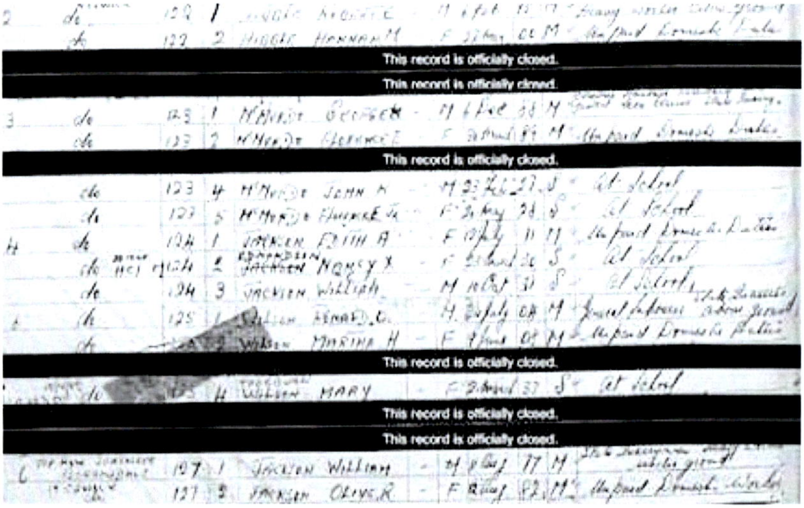

Fig 22: 1939 Register for New Cottages

on their return, equivalent to £7200 in 2023.

By 1921, No 6 had new occupants. Walter Rawes Birkett (1882-) was born a short walk away at Peat Howe and was a quarryman at Honister. His wife, Martha née Porter (1881-) was born at High Row, Threlkeld. Martha's mother, Jane Porter née Birkett (1849-1924), was with them.

Jane and her husband John lived in Threlkeld through their married life where John was a huntsman with the Blencathra pack. Jane was widowed in 1894 and after 1901, she moved to Borrowdale, where her eldest daughter, Eliza, lived with her husband, Jonathan Hind, a coachman. In 1910, Kelly's Directory described Jane as the postmistress in Rosthwaite (Fig.21).

Alongside the PO, Jane also took in visitors with the help of daughters, Alice and Martha – Martha was the cook. In 1912, Martha married Walter – by coincidence, this was the time that William and Ann Elliot leave No 6, heading for Canada. Martha's son, Ralph, was born in Helvellyn St, Keswick in 1913 but her daughter Dorothy arrived in Seatoller in 1915. Martha died in 1933 and five years later, Walter remarried and was the postmaster at Grange.

In 1939, there were two residents in No 6 but both were redacted. After the war, in 1946 Robert and Hannah Hibble (who had been living at No 2) re-located to No 6 but left before 1957 when the cottage was included when much of the Leconfield Estate was sold to pay death duties. In the sale catalogue, the details were the same as for No 2. The exception was that the cottage was sold with vacant possession and yet the catalogue identified Mrs Hughes as the tenant. This was Jessie Hughes and she had been living in No 6 with her husband, George, since moving from one of the Yew Tree Cottages, which was now being converted into a restaurant by the Brookes.

No 2 and No 6 were bought by Arthur Watson Todhunter (1913-1986), son of a farm manager and brother of John at Stonethwaite Farm. He had been an engineer based in Ulverston in 1939. In 1940 he married Jennie (1912-1972) née Noble. In 1939 she was with her sister Winifred, the sub-postmistress at Thornthwaite. Soon, in 1960, he was applying for planning permission for improvements for both cottages.

The Todhunters never lived in their cottages. George and Jessie stayed in the cottage until at least 1978. Jessie (1907-1979) was the daughter of Thomas Morley Harrison and Elizabeth Cowper. Harrison was a quarryman and Jessie had been brought up in Keswick and later Egremont. When she was twenty-one, she married a soldier in the Royal Tank Regiment, Ernest Alfred Howard (1898-1970), the son of a corn miller from Sussex. He had joined the Royal Sussex regiment in the war and stayed on in the Royal Tank Regiment. After the marriage, the family spent the 1930s in India, with trips home when the children (William

231

(1929-), Betty (1930-) Cecil Stanley (1934-) and Ernest (1939-) saw their grandparents in Mountain View. In April 1944, Jessie brought the children home, The SS Franconia was packed with army wives with their children. They left from Port Said and disembarked at Liverpool on 22nd April 1944.

Their destination was Mountain View and were still in the valley in 1948 when Cecil took part in rescuing the wife of an Oxford academic who had broken her leg on Great Gable.[72] And from 1954, after a spell in the army, daughter Elizabeth worked at Seatoller House.

Ernest Howard left the army in 1946 but did not join the family. At some point he and Jessie were divorced. Jessie met George Entwhistle Hughes (1894-1982) in the 1940s. How George Hughes came to the valley is not known. George was born in Wigan. He was a merchant seaman. A tall man at nearly 6', he had a tattoo on his right forearm of clasped hands over a heart. When war broke out, he joined the Royal Engineeers. His military record was chequered as he went absent without leave in July 1918 and was sentenced to eighteen months detention. Later that year, he married Louisa Boyd and they had a daughter, Georgina. George went back to sea but was home and out of work in 1921. Louisa died the following year – Georgina was brought up by her Boyd grandparents and was living with her grandmother, also Louisa, in 1939.

He and Jessie had a son, George Morley Hughes and married in 1956. In the mid-1960s, Jessie and George were living in Seatoller with her parents in Mountain View and her daughter, Betty, working in Seatoller House. Betty and her husband, John Cockbain, ran the guesthouse until 1977.

After Jessie and George left, the cottage was sold to a Liverpool businessman, Norman Cowley. He, his sons, Peter and Tim, and his grandchildren still visit the village regularly.

232

Fig 23: Top Row (Steve Uglow 2023)

Top Row

The 1914-1918 war almost brought the quarries to a standstill and re-starting was difficult. One problem was recruiting new, or regaining past, employees. Many had died in action and the survivors, in general, were not so keen to return to such arduous work. One way to attract workers was the prospect of proper housing and in 1923, six more houses were built at Top Row in Seatoller to attract new recruits,[73] followed in 1927 by a hostel (now the youth hostel) built at the quarry to house some fifty men.

The modern houses have parking spaces but in the 1920s, a 'drying ground' was more important and each cottage was allocated one.

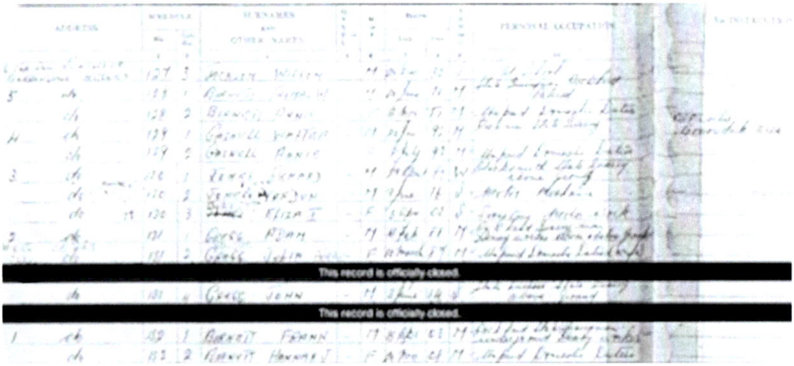
This record is officially closed.
This record is officially closed.

Fig 24: Top Row – 1939 Register

No 1 Top Row

The families in Top Row were often closely linked with those in Mountain View and New Cottages and with the valley farm families. Frank Birkett (living in No 1 in 1939) was the son of Annie Jopson, who grew up on Seatoller farm. Annie's husband was a quarryman, Thomas William Birkett, (1870-1952), who was brought up at Castle Lodge, near Longthwaite. In 1939, Frank's parents were four doors away, living at No 5.

Frank (1903-1977) was brought up in New Cottages but may have tried his hand at farming with William Hodgson at Wigton in the 1920s. He came back to his roots, marrying Hannah Thompson (1908-1953) in 1936. Hannah's father had died when she was just six and she was brought up in Keswick, with her mother taking in lodgers. Frank and Hannah had a son, George (1940-).

Frank was a rockhand at the quarry and like so many quarrymen and farmers, turned out to help when walkers got into trouble. In 1940, two brothers from Hartlepool, slipped and fell to their deaths at Sour Milk Gill above Seathwaite Farm. Frank

Fig 25: Postcard of the workmen's barracks at Honister just after they had been converted into a youth hostel (YHA Archive)

was part of a search team, and it was he who discovered and recovered the bodies at the foot of the waterfall.[74]

After Hannah's death in 1953, Frank moved to Keswick where he lived in Windebrowe Avenue.

The subsequent history of the cottage is unclear but in 1957, M P Newton applied for planning permission to improve the property.

No 2 Top Row
The 1939 Register (Fig 20) showed Adam (1888-1948) and Julia Gregg (1888-1972) née Jewitt living at No 2 with their son John (1914-2000) and Richard (1924-). The family was from the south Lakes in Ulverston - Adam, an iron ore miner from Torver and Julia the daughter of a docker. The family was still in Furness in

235

Fatal quarry accident

Adam Gregg, 60-year-old quarryman, of Seatoller, Borrowdale, died in Keswick Hospital yesterday from head injuries received when he was working at Honister Quarry on Thursday. He was knocked off a ledge by a piece of rock, and fell about 15ft. on to rock below.

Fig 26: Yorkshire Post 12th June 1948

1921, although Adam's brother, William Hornby Gregg, was a quarryman at Honister and living in the barracks (Fig 24). William had been in the Border Regiment for a time and volunteered for the RAMC in October 1914, serving with the BEF in France in 1915-1916.

By 1924, James and Julia had moved north – the birth of their son Richard was registered in Cockermouth. In 1931, daughter Lily married James Blair Gardiner and around 1946, the couple moved into 3 New Cottages, just a stone's throw from Lily's parents. In 1948, there was another tragedy at the mine, just six months after the death of William Jackson, when Adam was killed at Honister (Fig 25). He was knocked off a ledge by a piece of falling rock and fell 15'. He is buried in St Andrew's churchyard. Julia left the valley. She married for a second time in 1956 to John Bowes.

Adolph Beck (1891-1968) was born in North Shields. Did he ever suffer from sharing his name with the victim of one of the most famous miscarriage of justice cases?[75] The Norwegian

Adolf Beck was convicted of fraud, through over-reliance on identification evidence, not just once but twice. A full pardon only came in 1904 and there must have been some Geordie banter as Adolph began work as a draughtsman in marine engineering works. In 1921, he worked at G T Grey & Co in South Shields, which produced engines for many ships built on the Tyne.

He was still working in the same profession in 1939 but by then he was a widower. His wife, Violet née Denny, had died that year and he was living in Tynemouth with his daughter. Ten years later he married again to Marjorie Lockton (1922-1999), a cutter in the Leicester clothing industry. Top Row was a retirement home for Adolph, although Marjorie was considerably younger. He immediately sought planning permission in 1958 to improve the house. After Adolph's death in 1968, Marjorie continued to live in Top Row and was on the electoral roll in 1978.

No 3 Top Row

Perhaps the first tenants of No 3 were Richard Jones (1881-) and his wife Eliza (1884-1928) née Williams. In 1911, the couple were living at Llanymynech with their two daughters, Eliza Irene (1908-) and Hilda (1910-1931). Richard was a blacksmith. By 1916, the family had moved to Cumberland, and in 1921 were living at St Helens Street in Cockermouth with Richard working at the Cumberland Granite Company at Embleton.

The family moved to Borrowdale where Eliza died in 1928. Hilda acted as housekeeper for her father and brother. She was an active member of the Young Helpers Committee and a member of the church choir. She died after a short illness in 1931.[76] By 1939, the older daughter, Eliza, was living at home, a secretary at a motor works. Richard was at the mine and his son Verdun (1916-1988) was a motor mechanic.

The Leconfield Estate sold No 3 in 1957. T Gardner was the

tenant. This may have been Thomas Williamson Gardiner (1908-), the brother of James, living in No 3 New Cottages. In common with the other Top Row cottages (which were sold privately), there was no written agreement between the estate and its tenants The annual rent was more expensive than the New Cottages at £20 8s. The tenant was responsible for the council rates. Downstairs were two living rooms with a scullery with a sink. There was hot and cold water – by the 1920s, hot water tanks heated by a coal-fired range were more common – there was a fuel store outside. There were three bedrooms on the first floor. Outside was a toilet and a small garden. The water and drainage were still private.

D H Tyson applied for planning permission for a bathroom in 1960. By the 1970s there was nobody listed. on the electoral roll.

No 4 Top Row
Walter (1892-1957) and Annie Gaskell (1892-1962) lived in No 2 New Cottages until the 1930s. They moved to No 4 before 1939 and were still there twenty years later but had moved before their son, Alfred Lancaster Gaskell, sold the house in 1955. By the 1970s there was nobody listed. on the electoral roll.

No 5 Top Row
In 1939, Annie Jopson from the farm and quarryman, Thomas Birkett, (1870-1952) were living in No 5. Annie had lived her whole life in the village. They had lived in both No 3 and No 5 New Cottages before moving to Top Row on retirement.

The house was sold to Elizabeth Jane Rosanna Borwick (1885-1979) née Midgley. She was the wife of John Herbert Midgley (1881-1950). Elizabeth's father was from Staveley in Westmorland, a sergeant in the Border Regiment and just before his death in 1896, a drill instructor. Her widowed mother became the manager of Windermere Golf Club. John was a draughtsman and master boat builder on Windermere. Borwicks & Sons was founded by John's father, Isaac, and built many of the famous launches on Cumbrian lakes. There was an engineering department which was associated with early flying boats, constructing floats as well as propellers, together with maintenance and ground support for passenger flights on the lake. John died in 1950, followed two weeks later by the death of her daughter, Kathleen. Elizabeth moved to Borrowdale and Top Row, applying for planning permission in 1956 and was on the electoral roll there until her death.

No 6 Top Row

The first tenants of No 6 were William James Birkett Jackson (WJB) (1877-1954) and his wife Olive Ruth née Harris (1882-1943). They were the parents of William Jackson in No 4 New Cottages. WJB was the son of Hannah Harrington – she was born illegitimate in 1848 but a short time later, her mother had married a Langdale sawyer, James Birkett (1820-1902) and, in a touching tribute, Hannah named WJB after him.[77]

Hannah married William Jackson. William Jackson was an unsettled man and for a short time, the family move to Missouri in the USA. On their return, he worked at the quarries at Elterwater and WJB was born in Grasmere. By 1891, the family were in Herbert St in Keswick and not only William senior but WJB (just fourteen) were working at Honister. By 1911, the family have re-located to the Heights of Lowca in west Cumberland.

WJB left home when he married Olive Harris in Furness in 1903. Olive was born in Peterborough and had come to the northwest with her brother, George, after her mother died in

239

1890. In 1901, just 5' 2" with brown eyes and brown hair, she was working for a Dunnerdale farmer, William Wilson Boow (1862-). How did Olive meet WJB? There is a connection with Borrowdale because William Boow's brother, John (1867-1933), was living in Rosthwaite in 1901 and working in the slate quarries, perhaps alongside WJB.

Perhaps WJB, like his father, was restless and had moved to work in the Furness quarries? In 1904, Olive and WJB's daughter, Hannah, was born in Furness. For a short period, like WJB's father,[78] the family moved to the USA, in this case Idaho. In June 1907, Olive and daughter Hannah travelled to America on the SS Campania. Olive gave her place of birth as 'Keswick'. Their destination was Mullan, Shoshone, Idaho, a town that came into being in the 1880s with discoveries of gold and silver-lead. By 1908, it had a population of 1800 and was still growing. Olive and WJB's son, William, was born there in January 1909.

They failed to find gold. By 1911, they have returned to the bosom of their family and were living next door to WJB's parents in the Heights of Lowca in west Cumberland, albeit everyone in only two rooms. WJB was working as a coal miner. In 1921, the family was at 46 Catherine Street, Whitehaven but WJB, a coal hewer at Lowca, was *'out of regular employment.'* Perhaps that triggered a move back to the quarries as by 1927, WJB was working as a rock hand at the Honister quarries and living at Seatoller, probably in the newly completed 6 Top Row, alongside Olive and son William. Late on in their lives, WJB and Olive have another son, Wilson (1931-1985), the same age as WJB's grandson and Wilson's nephew, William (1931-).

WJB, Olive and Wilson were still living in Top Row. Wilson was just eleven when his mother died in 1943. Four years later, there was a family tragedy when son William was killed in a rockfall in 1947. WJB died in May 1954 – probate was granted to his brother, Richard.

In the 1970s, the cottage was owned by Harold Daynes (1895-1980), a physicist who researched and wrote on the analysis and diffusion of gases. 1970, he applied for planning permission. His son, Roger Daynes (1942-), was a metereologist, working with the British Antarctica Expedition. Mount Daynes in Antarctica is named after him. He has memories of Seatoller,

My parents moved up to Seatoller from North Wales, to where they had retired in 1958. They came to Seatoller sometime in 1971 (I believe the house then cost around £8000) and the planning permission was probably to do with moving a wall to enlarge the front bedroom, taking a foot or two out of the rear bathroom. That is the only major work done on the house while they were there. I seem to remember, at that time, there was only one other house in the row that was permanently occupied...

They moved back to North Wales sometime in about 1977, due to my father's oncoming angina and the fact that the local Keswick bus services were reducing, which made it more difficult for them to shop. They were keen walkers, but the angina stopped this, so they were better off back in North Wales where shops were just around the corner and public transport services were better. They were very friendly with Neil Hunter at the Yew Tree cafe/restaurant, and where I occasionally helped out when I was at home for short periods.

***

Mountain View, New Cottages and Top Row changed Seatoller. From the 1890s until the 1970s, the village was crowded with miners, their wives and plenty of children. It was a noisy, bustling place. In season, there were the walkers and increasingly tourists in their cars. The ageless routines of sheep farming carried on. But the impact of death duties on the Leconfield estate meant

241

that all three terraces were sold, sometimes to the miners themselves or their widows. More often the houses went to outsiders, people moving to the valley on retirement or as holiday homes. In time, more of the houses became holiday rentals although Mountain View and New Cottages kept some permanent residents into the 21st century.

Notes

[1] *(2009)* Buttermere: Historic Landscape Survey Report *Vol 2 172 ff;* Tyler I., *(1994)* Honister Slate *chs 1-5*

[2] *http://www.llechicymru.info/IPSLPay.english.htm*

[3] *Cumberland Pacquet 7th October 1822*

[4] *Tyler, I. (1994) 33ff*

[5] *Sawrey also had an interest in the Seathwaite wad mine. He was convicted of keeping gunpowder in an unauthorised place at the mine: Kendal Mercury 26th November 1880*

[6] *http://www.llechicymru.info/IPSLPay.english.htm*

[7] *CRO Carlisle SRDC/3/2/39*

[8] *English Lakes Visitor 7th April 1894*

[9] *CRO Carlisle SRDC/3/2/264 10*

[10] *CRO Carlisle SRDC/3/2/956*

[11] *CRO Carlisle SRDC/3/2/1227+1273+1274*

[12] *Seatoller House also had water from cisterns on the hillside situated on the farm's land*

[13] *Merdinger C. J., (1953)* The Development of Modern Sewerage. Part II *45 The Military Engineer 123-127*

[14] *CRO Carlisle SRDC/3/2/733*

[15] *CRO Carlisle SRDC/3/2/4445 – a bathroom and toilet at No 2 for A W Todhunter*

[16] *Penrith Observer 14th September 1937 – there was opposition to the plan and it was agreed that part of the cable would be underground: Penrith Observer 9th November 1937*

[17] *Penrith Observer 28th December 1937*
[18] *This information is contained in the 1957 Leconfield sale catalogue*
[19] *ibid*
[20] *This draws on Tonks, A., (2019) 'Wages, welfare and arbitration' - https://oro.open.ac.uk/62655/2/TONKS_A329_RVOR.pdf*
[21] *Tonks, A., (2019) at 11*
[22] *Lancashire Evening Post 3rd September 1920*
[23] *Tyler, I. (1994) 78*
[24] *Penrith Observer 27th September 1938*
[25] *Millom Gazette 19th October 1900 – these rates were given in a court case against the Ulpha Slate.*
[26] *English Lakes Visitor 12th February 1887 – this was a 19th century social security fraud. The outcome was that they were ordered to pay 3s pw each but their mother died a short time after the case.*
[27] *Millom Gazette 19th October 1900 – Woodend was suing Ulpha Slate Company for unpaid wages.*
[28] *The Leconfield Estate sold the cottages in 1957 and the rents mentioned in the sale catalogue were standard market rates for that time*
[29] *English Lakes Visitor 19th May 1900*
[30] *Coase R H, (1939)* Rowland Hill and the Penny Post *6 Economica 423*
[31] *Martineau H.,* Complete Guide to the English Lakes *(in Directory)*
[32] *Property details in Leconfield Estate Sale Catalogue 1957*
[33] *Schofield E., (1971)* Food and Cooking of the Working Class about 1900 *123 Historic Society of Lancashire and Cheshire Journal 151 at 154*
[34] *Join me in the 1900s: a social history of everyday life: https://www.1900s.org.uk/index.htm*
[35] *Bishop of Barrow, (1905)* On the Readers in the Chapelries of the Lake District *CW2 89*
[36] *Cumberland Pacquet 23rd December 1806*
[37] *Cumberland Pacquet 10th June 1851*
[38] *West Cumberland Times 14th November 1874 referring to 1855*
[39] *Carlisle Journal 2nd February 1864*
[40] *CRO Barrow BD TB Wills Box 13/18 – CRO Carlisle PROB/1864/W745*

243

[41] Kelly's Directory *1894*

[42] *West Cumberland Times 22 August 1896; English Lakes Visitor 16th October 1897* for a list of subscribers

[43] *Penrith Observer 5th May 1936*

[44] eg *West Cumberland Times 17 March 1897*

[45] eg *West Cumberland Times 27th September 1902*

[46] *Penrith Observer 23rd February 1960*

[47] *Yorkshire Post 5th October 1925*

[48] *English Lakes Visitor 27th November 1897*

[49] *West Cumberland Times 30th June 1897*

[50] *English Lakes Visitor 21st November 1908*

[51] *Penrith Observer 11th June 1935*

[52] *West Cumberland Times 29th April 1896*

[53] *Carlisle Journal 11th September 1860*

[54] *Carlisle Patriot 8th May 1889*

[55] *English Lakes Visitor 27th May 1893* – John Simpson, solicitor, of Hazel Bank was the likeliest to have such influence

[56] This draws on Joseph's interview published in *Cumberland and Westmorland Herald 27th February 1999*

[57] CRO Carlisle C/C/X/1/81 for itinerary

[58] *Lancashire Evening Post 24th December 1932*

[59] *Penrith Observer 6th October 1925*

[60] *Penrith Observer 6th April 1920*

[61] *Yorkshire Post 12th June 1948*

[62] *Lakes Chronicle 12th April 1876*

[63] *Lakes Chronicle 2nd August 1876*

[64] *Lancashire Evening Post 27th October 1921*

[65] *Penrith Observer 18th September 1923* – oddly always to another R Brownrigg of Bassenthwaite

[66] Clinton S., (2020) All Or Nothing At All *287ff* gives a good account of hound trailing at this time

[67] *Manchester Courier 30th June 1900*

[68] *West Cumberland Times 23rd July 1904*

[69] *See Vol. 1, page 220*

[70] *Opened by William Leyland in the 1830s and run by his grandsons before the war. Later owned by the Buttermere Green Slate Co*

[71] *Maryport Advertiser 12th August 1905*

[72] *Daily Herald 23rd August 1948*

[73] *CRO Carlisle SRDC/3/2/956*

[74] *Penrith Observer 27th August 1940*

[75] *Coates T., (1999). The strange story of Adolph Beck*

[76] *West Cumberland Times 14th November 1931*

[77] *However, Hannah was sent out to work as a kitchen maid in a Grasmere hotel, aged just 13*

[78] *WJB's sister was born in Missouri*

12. Mountain View and Glaramara

Mountain View

In the 1890s, there was industrial unrest in the Welsh quarries.[1] Many of the workers moved north and some worked at Honister where the workforce rose to over a hundred. Pressure on accommodation meant that the slate company applied to turn the old coach house in Seatoller (the building opposite New

Fig 1: Mountain View from Johnny Wood, looking towards Coomb Gill (Steve Uglow)

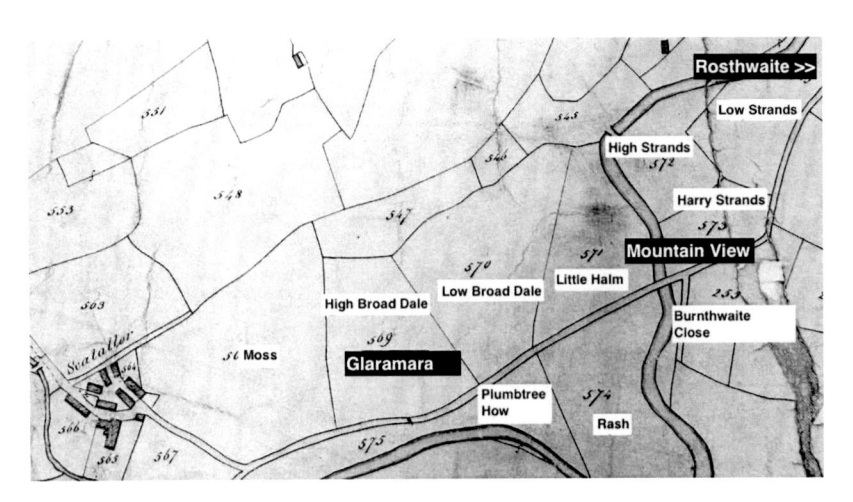

Fig 2: 1842 Tithe Map showing the fields where Mountain View and Glaramara would be built

Cottages) into housing. This did not go ahead. Then, in 1893, the Leconfield Estate bought the land above Yew Tree cottages to build eight houses to augment the barracks on the quarry site. There were applications for planning permission.[2] But the Marshall estate, which owned Yew Tree and Seatoller House raised issues about the rights of way and the plan was put on hold. The company found an alternative, away from the centre of Seatoller, on the Rosthwaite road, where it would build a terrace of eight houses, originally to be known prosaically as Leconfield Terrace but ended up as Mountain View.

In 1842, the field on which Mountain View would be built was known as Harry Strand. It was owned by the Liverpool-based Edward Fletcher, through his marriage to Sarah Braithwaite. In 1870, their son and daughter advertised all their Seatoller and valley lands for sale by auction at the Borrowdale Hotel. Included in this (Fig 3) was 'Harris' Strand. The Fletchers spoke of the land as containing '*many most eligible sites for*

247

```
Lot 4—All those THREE CLOSES:—
   No. on          Names of Closes.          Quantities.
Ordnance Map.                                 A.  R.  P.
   607              High Strand      ...      2   1  38
   608              Harris Strand    ...      1   1  35
   633              Low Strand       ...      3   2  24
```

Fig 3: Mountain View cottages would eventually be built on Harris or Harry's Strand - Carlisle Journal 5th August 1870

building'.

The fields at Strands Bridge were sold in 1871 to Lawrence Harrison, a Penrith solicitor and Lakes enthusiast. Harrison owned other valley land, notably the site in Rosthwaite where Stonethwaite farmer, Thomas Fleming, was expanding his lodging house, which became the Scafell Hotel. On Harrison's death in 1889,[3] his valley properties were inherited by his nephew, Anthony Harrison, who in 1897 donated two fields to the Borrowdale school.[4] Before that, he sold the fields at Strands Bridge to Lord Leconfield in 1890.[5] The land was leased to the Buttermere Green Slate company and would revert back to Leconfield on the termination of the lease.

The company now had an opportunity to house more quarrymen but construction of the terrace of houses, to be known as Mountain View, did not start until March 1894. Land was staked out for twelve houses by William Richardson, a contractor of Millom. The intention even then was only to build eight.[6]

The houses were in two blocks of four with larger, three storey, buildings at each end and two small, two up, two down, houses sandwiched between them. Whether the larger houses were designed for the managers and foremen is not known. The subsequent terraces at New Cottages and Top Row were all the smaller design.

Fig 4: Mountain View from Thorneythwaite Lane, looking north. (Steve Uglow)

Fig 5: the rear of Mountain, looking south (Steve Uglow)

HOUSES OCCUPIED WITHOUT A CERTIFICATE FROM THE COUNCIL.

The Medical Officer reported that the house drains of eight recently built cottages at Mountain View, Borrowdale, for the Buttermere Green Slate Co. were not properly constructed and that the sewage was emptied into an inadequate and imperfectly constructed cesspool, the overflow of which was conveyed into an adjoining beck. Lower down this stream the tenants of three houses at Castle Lodge obtained their domestic supply from this polluted stream, and they demanded that the pollution should be prevented by the Council.—Mr Robinson asked if the cottages had been erected according to the plans passed by the Council.— The Surveyor: No, they have not. I gave notice to Mr Johns that he would have to be summoned. —The Medical Officer: They have neglected nearly all the sanitary requirements necessary. —The Surveyor said he wrote to Mr Johns, and he replied that they were

BETTER THAN ANY OTHER COTTAGES

in the valley. The houses had been occupied for a month.—The Chairman said it was a grave offence. The bye-laws had been infringed in occupying the houses without a certificate.—

Fig 6: West Cumberland Times 6th July 1895 – drainage has been an issue for the cottages into the 21st century

Mountain View was finished within a year and the first tenants moved in – not just humans but also the quarry horses which were brought down daily to the field behind.

However, there were problems, not with the construction but with the council over sewage discharge (Fig 6) into *'an inadequate and imperfectly constructed cesspool'* which overflowed into the nearby stream, polluting the water supply for the houses at Castle Lodge. The response by Bennett Johns, the quarry manager, that the houses were better than any other in the district, cut no ice with the council.

No 1 Mountain View
At No 1 and No 8 (the two end-of-terrace cottages) lived two brothers, William (1857-1925) and James Nuttall (1853-). They were the sons of an iron ore miner from Dalton in Furness, Lancashire. They travelled to Langdale, to work in the slate mines. There the brothers met two sisters, Elizabeth and Ann, daughters of James Birkett, sometime sawyer, sometime labourer, sometime gardener, sometime farmer. In 1880, at St Oswald's in Grasmere, the two brothers married the two sisters - first William and Elizabeth and later that year James and Ann.

The next year William and Elizabeth (1855-1933) moved back to the south Lakes and William worked as an iron miner. They lived at Ireleth in 1881where his father-in-law James Birkett was visiting his granddaughter, Elizabeth, born a few weeks previously. Ten years later, the family were living at Gill Side, below the slopes of Stone Arthur in Grasmere, and by then William was working on James Birkett's farm. It was not until 1897, when their youngest daughter, Ethel, was born that William moved back to mining. Working at Honister, he was rapidly promoted to foreman – a position which explained why the family obtained the desirable end-of-terrace house. Desirable

251

BORROWDALE.

DOUBLE WEDDING.—For the first time within knowledge a double wedding was celebrated at the Parish Church on Wednesday afternoon. The bridegrooms were Messrs Frederick Haigh and Thomas Brown, and the brides, Misses Grace and Mary Nuttall, daughters of Mr Edward Nuttall, Mountain View. At the wedding breakfast the Vicar, during the happily chosen remarks in which he proposed the health of the newly-married couples, referred to the fact that he had been unable to find a record of any similar wedding in the parish. He pleasantly noted the presence on this happy occasion of both the oldest and youngest married couple in Borrowdale. Mr and Mrs Haigh whilst Mr and Mrs Brown journeyed to Sunderland, left afterwards for Blackpool for the honeymoon. The friends, who were a large company, were entertained at a dance in the Schoolroom at night, and the proceedings were kept up till about 3 o'clock on Thursday morning. Music for dancing was played by Messrs J. Tangye and T. Robinson (violin and piano).

Fig 7: The first wedding for 19 years – and a double one (English Lakes Visitor 27th October 1906)

because Elizabeth and William had eight daughters, one of whom died aged seven. Their eldest child, Elizabeth (1881-1904) who had been in service with an Ambleside surgeon, Thomas Mitchell, also died aged just twenty-three. Despite the size of their own family, the Nuttalls also found room for an aunt, Mary Smith, eighty-eight years old and widowed.

In 1906, there came a double celebration (Fig 7) when sisters

Mary and Grace Nuttall were married in a joint ceremony at St Andrews. It was the first wedding at the church for nineteen years and afterwards the party at the school danced until the early hours.

Two other daughters married: in 1912, Florrie (1890-1969) married John Wilson, the manager of a South Shields wallpaper shop. By 1939, she was a widow, living in Portinscale with her stepson Ernest, a bus conductor and her daughter, Grace, a fancy goods saleswoman.

In 1917, Hilda (1895-) married a cousin, Herbert Nuttall (1891-1950). Herbert had been badly gassed during the war and had lost four brothers. He joined the police, working locally. He took a statement from Frank Pepper of Bowderstone (but formerly Yew Tree) when he was accused of stealing a dead pheasant during a shooting party in Braithwaite Wood.[7] As this shows, keeping the peace in Borrowdale was not usually a major task but in 1936, there were disturbances at local dances. On 23rd October, Nuttall was on duty at a dance at the Borrowdale Institute where some Keswick men had become drunk. Committee members tried to throw them out and PC Nuttall had to complete the task. He was a sergeant in Penrith at the time of his death in 1950.[8]

William and Elizabeth were still living in the same house in 1921, William still a foreman at the quarry, working there for thirty-five years. The two unmarried daughters, Rosannah, (1886-1972), and Ethel (1897-1990) were living with their parents. Rosannah was a dressmaker, also employing other women. William stayed in Mountain View until his death in 1925.

After William's death, the house was the home of Richard Hutton Thompson (1894-1968) and his family. Richard was born in Maryport but the family moved to Keswick – in 1901, the family were at King's Head Court and in 1911 in Wordsworth

Street, by which time Richard was an apprentice river at Honister. He married Jane Ann Johnston (1886-1943) in 1917 and they set up home at 4 New Street. By 1921, they had three children (Andrew, George and Mary) as well as Joseph Johnston, Jane's son. Joseph was born in 1911 and at age one month had been with his mother in the Union Workhouse at Cockermouth. Joseph married Nora Parker in 1942 and after the war they lived in New Cottages, just down the road from his stepfather.

Richard and Jane Thompson had moved into Mountain View after the death of William Nuttall. By 1927, there were two more children (Annie and John). The space in the new house would have been welcome and it was more convenient for Richard and his son, George, than commuting to work at the quarry from Keswick. George was a fell runner so may have trained by running to work...

In 1931, Richard was supporting the candidacy of Arthur Carlyne Dixey, the Conservative MP for Penrith and Cockermouth, as were his neighbours, James and Jane Rigg. Dixey had a narrow victory over the Liberals. He stood down at the 1935 election and was replaced by Alan Vincent Gandar Dower who convincingly held the seat over the Labour candidate. The local newspaper printed the names of Jane, Hannah Hibble and six other valley women as supporting Dower. Extraordinarily, the names of the men supporting him were printed in a different section of the paper. Who was separating the sexes? And why?

Jane died in 1943. In 1946, Richard and his daughter Mary were by themselves in Mountain View. In April 1947, Richard married again to Annie Agnes Benson. They had a daughter Carol. The family migrated to the new houses at The Howe in Rosthwaite in the early 1950s when another son, Clifford, was born. (From 2012, Carol's daughter, Trisha, was the acclaimed

Lowther Street, Penrith. Clara Badrock, Rosthwaite, Borrowdale; Elsie Hawkrigg, Rosthwaite, Borrowdale; Laura Brownrigg, Chapel Field, Rosthwaite; Hannah Margaret Hibble, Seatoller, Borrowdale; Jane Ann Thompson, Seatoller, Borrowdale; Jane Rigg, Mountain View, Borrowdale; Jane Porter, Rosthwaite, Borrowdale; Constance Mary Wood, Scawfell Hotel, Rosthwaite.

Fig 8: Borrowdale women nominate the Conservative candidate, Alan Dower, in 1935 election (Penrith Observer 5th November 1935)

cook at Seatoller House, which she ran with her Geordie husband, Nigel Dixon.)

In October 1953, John Taylor (1910-1995) bought the house from the Leconfield estate. He was working as a slate splitter in the Broughton quarries in 1939. He had married a farmer's daughter, Ruth Lavinia Allonby (1915-1986) in 1933. By 1970, they had moved to when they moved to Green Bank guesthouse and their sons, John (1934-2019) and William (1944-) were living in the house. John married Mary Gardiner in 1958 – she was the daughter of Lily and James Gardiner from New Cottages.

In the 1978 electoral roll, Grace Mattinson was the owner. She sold the house in July 1984 to Charles and Gillian Charlesworth. In the 1990s, it was the second home of the Charlesworth family of Hexham.

No 2 Mountain View
The first tenants in No 2 were John (1837-) and Alice Galletly (1834-). John was from Perth and Alice from Crail, Fife. In Scotland, he had worked as a missionary until the 1890s. This

255

KESWICK PRIMITIVE METHODIST SUNDAY SCHOOL

The anniversary services of this school were held on Sunday and New Year's Day. On Sunday Mr Galletly (missioner), Borrowdale, preached two much appreciated discourses to good congregations. A special service, interspersed with solos, duets, recitations, and the dialogue "Gideon," by the scholars was held in the afternoon. The annual festival on New Year's Day was inaugurated by a tea meeting, when the following ladies attended to the wants of the good number who partook of the refreshing cup :— Misses E. Wallace, A. Wilson, D. Bellas, M. and M. E. Littledale, and Martin. A public meeting in the chapel in the evening, presided over by Mr Galletly, was also well attended. Mr Galletly spoke to the children in a very entertaining and instructive manner, and the bairns themselves contributed to the pleasure of the meeting by rendering recitations, special hymns, &c. Mr S. A Birkbeck presided at the organ. The services, the proceeds of which go to the reduction of the Sunday School debt, were in every way satisfactory.

Fig 9: West Cumberland Times 3rd January 1903

One answer may be that the company was indirectly on a moral (or perhaps reputational) mission. In the 1890s, the quarrymen were hard men who played hard as well – their regular pastimes were gambling (pitch and toss, quoits at 5s a throw), wrestling but also blood sports such as rabbit coursing and cockfighting.[9] And they would get drunk[10] – in 1893 PC Scott was outside the vicarage when he encountered a young Cornish miner, Thomas Benoy, from Seatoller, who was drunk and used '*very bad language*'. Benoy was tried at Keswick Petty Sessions but Benoy's companion that night testified that '*they were talking among themselves in an ordinary way*' and there was no drunkenness or language. Case dismissed. But at the same sessions, another young Cornishman, Hanson Tucker, (who would later live with his family in Seatoller) was fined 10s for the same offence.

PC Scott had been sent especially to Borrowdale after serious complaints to the Chief Constable.[11] There was friction between the valley community and the incomers, perhaps particularly the Cornish, who, unlike the Coniston miners, were far from home and lacked the family connections that so often linked the quarrymen from Furness, Langdale and Borrowdale. Life consisted of early rising, a walk to the mine, hard, backbreaking and dangerous work in weather that was often wet and cold, long days, walk back to lodgings, eat, sleep. Repeat. It was not surprising that on his day off, Sunday 7th May 1893, Thomas Benoy was drunk.

A few months before, in late 1892, the local community, backed by the company had set up a Mission Room in Rosthwaite. The meetings were at the Mechanics Room at the Royal Oak.[12] The room was there for unattached young men to visit on Sundays, for prayer, to drink tea, read books and, perhaps, meet young valley women. Indeed, Thomas Benoy told

MISSION ROOM.—At tea party in connection with this institution was held on Friday evening, and, considering the inclemency of the weather, both it and the subsequent meeting were well patronised. The following presided at the tea tables :—Mrs. Turner (a visitor), Mrs. Birkett, Mrs. May, Mrs. Smith, and the Misses Johns, assisted by Mrs. Burns and the Misses Birkett, Jenkinson, and Gillbanks. The room was decorated with evergreens and texts, the gift of the Misses Slack and Kemp, and was comfortably filled with an appreciative audience. Mr. Johns presided, and also accompanied the singing on an American organ kindly lent by Mr. C. Spry. Gospel temperance addresses were delivered by Mr. Turner, the newly-appointed evangelist ; the Rev. W. J. Bain, Keswick ; and the Rev. A. J. Heelis, vicar of Borrowdale. The addresses were interspersed with hymns and songs. Mrs. Turner sang " The skipper and his boy," and Miss G. Johns " The Better Land." Though the mission room has been in existence but a few months, it has a Sunday evening service, a Sunday School, a Sunday morning prayer meeting, a Band of Hope, and latterly, through the kindness of Miss E. Langton, what will probably be the nucleus of a lending library, the lady named having given to the room three dozen books.

Fig 10: English Lakes Visitor 14th January 1893

the court that he had been to the Mission on that Sunday. In the New Year, the press reported on a tea party (Fig 10).

The press report named Mr Turner as the newly appointed

evangelist. The 'mission' is clear – Turner addressed the audience on the gospels and temperance and there had previously been a Band of Hope meeting, a temperance organisation, an innovative feature of which was "Signing the pledge". The Mission Room was evangelical in nature. Were the Sunday services complementing those at St Andrew's? The Anglican vicar at St Andrew's, Arthur Heelis, brother-in-law to Beatrix Potter, delivered a temperance address. The 1910 Kelly's Directory refers to the Mission as non-sectarian in character.

There was an appreciative audience. Was Seatoller's Moses Pepper (1846-1915) in that audience? A quarry foreman, he lived at Seatoller House. The Peppers were Rechabites, a strictly teetotal sect, and Moses was an active campaigner. He addressed local meetings[13] of the Band of Hope. As a person of local influence (a parish councillor, overseer to the poor), Moses may have sought to improve the manners and customs of the miners and been involved in setting up the Mission.

Where does the missionary's salary come from? The company had set up the Buttermere Slate Quarries Church Mission[14] which provided accommodation at Mountain View and presumably also contributed to the salary and running costs of the Mission Room. There was further company involvement. '*Mr Johns presided* 'and has 'volunteered' his daughters (who have been ferried out from Station Road in Keswick) to help with the tea. This was Bennett Johns (1851-1943), one of the senior managers for the Buttermere Green Slate Company. A Yorkshireman from Skipton, he had been a mine agent in Coniston before joining the Honister mine in 1884, retiring in 1926 after forty-two years.[15]

There was a strong Cornish feel – Jane Tamar May (née Jackson) was married to Edward May from St Teath; Charles Spry (1860-1929) had set down strong roots in Borrowdale and married Rebecca Simpson (1859-1928). Spry's Cottage is in Rosthwaite, opposite the Scafell Hotel. The American organ was probably a small pump organ but may have been a present from Rebecca's sister, Margaret (1857-1917), who had married Henry Arthur Dutton (1862-1922) and was living in Rochester, New York.

John Galletly was the successor to Mr Turner. After some years, the Galletys moved to Dorset where two of their children, Alexander and Alice, lived. His place was taken in 1907 by a young man from Millom, Frederick Darvell (1882-1937). Darvell was a cheerful and popular young man who was chairman of the village football team. Darvell was more light-hearted than Gallety. Aged twelve and living in Seascale, the West Cumberland Times gave him the first prize for a child's comic essay: *...after receiving a lesson on gravitation in school one afternoon, I came home and astonished my sisters by explaining to then that if it were not for gratification, we would all be spinning about in the air.*[16]

After three years, in January 1910, he moved on to a '*more populous*' centre. The Rev Bowker praised his work and Borrowdale FC presented him with a travelling clock.[17] But the next year, Darvell has moved into No 2, working as a home missionary. In 1915, he married a Newlands woman, Isabel Thwaites. She was the daughter of a Newlands farmer, and she taught in a council elementary school. Their first child, Elaine, was born in Borrowdale in 1916.

In 1921, Mary Annie Brown née Nuttall (1882-) and her husband Thomas have moved houses from No 4 to No 2. Her sister, Florrie was staying with them. She was normally in South Shields, where she had married John Wilson, but she had brought her stepson, Ernest, and her daughter, Grace, to visit. The Browns were still living in Borrowdale in 1931 when their daughter,

Maud (1907-2002), married Tom Wilson Gibson (1902-1956) from Braithwaite. For a short time, he was a policeman in Surrey, but they ran the Dukes Head in Armathwaite from 1946-1956.

By 1939, Mary Brown (but not Thomas) was living in Grange and Charles and Betsy Peebles had moved into No 2. A Scottish couple, Charles was the son of a baker in Carnoustie, in 1921 working as apprentice electrician; just along the coast, Betsy was the daughter of a Dundee tailor. Charles' work involved dealing with the installation, repairs and maintenance at the slate quarry generating plant. He also volunteered with Cockermouth ARP as a driver. After the war, they moved to 2 New Cottages where they lived until the 1960s.

After the war, William Nuttall junior (1881-) and his wife Edith Mary (1880-1959) née Randle, were living in No 2. He was the son of James and had lived with his parents at No 8 Mountain View and, after his marriage in 1910, he and Edith lived in No 7. There had been a sojourn in Little Langdale where William worked in the quarries, but they were now back on the Borrowdale electoral roll until the 1960s. He was a contributor to Wilfred Pickles' Home Service programme, *Down My Way* in 1947.[18] In retirement, he corresponded with the Lancashire Evening Post, re-telling the stories that his father, James, had told him about the famous whisky distiller, Lanty Slee (1802-1878) (Fig 11).

William died in July 1961 at his daughter's home, Oaks Farm, Loughrigg. Mary Beatrice (1911-1999) had married a farmer, Joseph Park in 1940. She remained the owner of Mountain View and in 1964 applied for planning permission for a bathroom.

By 1970, Eric and Marie Cockbain were living in the cottage. Eric (1940-) was the son of Joe and Marjorie Cockbain and had been brought up with his sister Mary Gwen at No 1 New

261

An elderly correspondent, Mr. W. Nuttall, of Mountain View, Borrowdale, has been writing to me about Lanty Slee, the almost legendary Lake District whisky distiller and smuggler to whom I have referred on more than one occasion. Mr. Nuttall's father knew Lanty, who died at a great age in 1878, and so far as I know Lanty's son, Adam, is still alive and will now be in his ninetieth year.

Mr. Nuttall tells me of a partner Lanty once had in his sideline and although he does not say so, I think this might have been Neddy Mawson, of Langdale. At all events, Lanty said to his partner: " If ivver I'se te'an thou mun folla an' me'ak sew'er thou gits t'worm." One day Lanty had the misfortune to be " taken " and was bundled with his equipment into a farm cart and driven towards Kendal.

Evidence had gone

At Skelwith, Lanty pressed his escort to allow him a drink, but this was refused, as was a second request at Ambleside. When the Lowwood Hotel was reached, however, he managed to persuade his escort to join him in several drinks and they must have been in some time. When they came out Lanty had to support himself on the cart, but he was able to look inside and see that his partner had done his job well, for the " worm " had disappeared.

Fig 11: Getting the better of the excisemen - Lancashire Evening Post 11th September 1953

Cottages. Marie née Doran (1942-) was the daughter of an iron ore miner from Whitehaven. By 1978, nobody in No 2 was registered on the electoral roll.

No 3

The Bainbridges, Miles (1853-1928) and Mary Jane (1854-) were the first family to move into No 3. They were married in Manchester in 1879 – Mary Jane was from Salford but Miles was another Coniston quarryman. By 1892 they were living in Borrowdale where their youngest child, Agnes was born. In 1896, Miles was head of company at Road End, a quarry that was going forward and finding good slate at a rate of 45 tons a month.[19]

Miles was much involved in the community. The Liberal government in 1893 had set up parish councils for rural settlements of more than one hundred residents. Through the 19th century, the male franchise had been extended but the property requirement meant that rural labourers were excluded until the 1880s (Fig 12). Even then women, or men under twenty-one or adult men living with their parents were unable to vote.

In December 1894, Borrowdale township had a population of five hundred and six, of whom eighty-seven could vote. At a meeting at the school, fourteen were nominated for nine seats but five withdrew. Miles and his neighbour, William Hudson, were elected.[20] Miles attended regularly, and the high-profile issues were usually (as in the 21st century) flooding and the state of the roads and bridges. The parish council were against the road across Styhead to Wasdale – *'those who want it should pay for it'*. However, by 1911, he opted for a less demanding job and moved to Keswick as a market gardener.

In 1911, Joseph Birkett (1880-1943) and his wife Sarah Margaret née Nicholson (1880-1966) were living in No 3 with their young son, Walter. His father, also Joseph, was from the

THE GROWTH OF THE FRANCHISE

BOROUGHS	COUNTIES OUTSIDE BOROUGHS	COMMENTS
1832:		
The traditional franchise of each borough continued with the addition of householders (occupiers, whether owners or tenants) of property assessed as worth £10 a year	Freeholders with property worth 40s a year. Copyholders renting property rated at £10 a year. £10 leaseholders with at least 60-year leases. £50 leaseholders with at least 20-year leases. Any tenant paying more than £50 a year	By 1833, about 814,000 had the vote (1 man in 7) – richer industrialists, merchants and substantial farmers.
1867:		
Every adult male householder resident for a year and heads of families lodging in unfurnished rooms paying £10 a year in rent	Any owner or leaseholder of property rated at £5 a year, or tenant of property rated at £12 a year	By 1866, about 1,430,000 had the vote. By 1868, about 2,500,000 had the vote (1 man in 3)
		This now included most men working in towns and cities but excluded rural labourers
1884:		
No change	Same voting qualifications as granted to the boroughs in 1867	By 1883, about 3,200,000 had the vote. By 1885, about 5,900,000 had the vote (2 men in 3)
		Most rural labourers now received the vote but still excluded were women, heads of households who shared houses and adult males living with their parents

Fig 12: Expansion of the right to vote
(Cumbria Record Office, Whitehaven)

Seathwaite farm but had become a shoemaker before turning to more lucrative work at the quarries. Joseph junior married in the spring of 1907 – just a few weeks after the wedding, his workmates and neighbours, John Thomas and Elizabeth Clark from New Cottages and John and Jessie Pepper at Mountain View, travelled to Harrisburg in Illinois where they worked as coalminers. Three years later, on 15th April 1910, the day of the US federal census, Joseph Birkett, had also travelled to Illinois, was living with them and, like them, out of work.

Joseph returned to England by 1911 but, undeterred by his previous experience, set off for the USA again. On 28th March 1913 the family arrived in Boston on SS Ivernia, heading to Harrisburg, Illinois. They were still there in 1920 with Joseph working as a coalminer. Indeed, naturalisation papers were submitted. But there was a major change of heart and on 19th September 1921, Sarah and the children returned on SS Campania and on 10th March 1922, Joseph arrived back in Liverpool on SS Baltic. They settled in Keswick where in 1939, they were in Wordsworth Street with Joseph back in the slate quarries.

In 1921, Annie Clymo née Hasseldine (1873-1964) filled out the census form for No 3, only for her name to be crossed out and replaced by that of a New Zealander, John Roberts, (1876-). Roberts lived in Selkirk in Scotland where he was a woollen manufacturer. His Scots wife, Agnes Amelia (1879-), son and servant were also in No 3 – presumably on holiday.

Annie meanwhile was at the Station Hotel in York, again on holiday? Annie was born in King's Lynn in Norfolk but had been working in London when she met and married a Cornishman, Thomas Clymo (1872-1907). A talented musician, he was organist and choirmaster in Illogan before spending some years in London. After the wedding, they lived in Newton Abbot where he was organist at a Bible Christian chapel while working as a saddler and harness maker. They moved to Chepstow, still associated with non-conformism. His death came about from eating tinned salmon. His funeral was crowded and subsequent press reports long and detailed.[21]

Whether Annie was involved with the Methodists before she met Thomas will not be known. But by 1911, she was a Wesleyan deaconess at the Temple Street in Keighley, a large chapel only completed in 1905. Now she was the replacement for Frederick Darvell, the home missionary, employed by the Honister slate company, who had been living in No 2 until 1916. The company's missionary zeal hadn't abated. Kelly's Directory has Annie Clymo based in the Rosthwaite Mission Room throughout the 1920s. Methodism remained strong in the valley with the

265

Grange chapel (completed in 1893) having two Sunday services in the 1950s. Emmie Mounsey of Grange remembers . . .

Grange Methodist Church has always been an important part of my life since I came to live here in 1956. There was no heating in the church, just an old stove in the back that we used to roast chestnuts on. We had a very good congregation in those days with two services on Sundays. Local preachers came from all over the circuit, and I remember some very lengthy sermons. In recent times, membership of the church has dwindled away, and I am the only Wesleyan left in the village.

Annie Clymo was part of that - although by 1939, she had moved from No 3 and was combining chapel services with running a guest house at Rigg in Grange. In 1939 at Mountain View, a quarryman, William Jenkinson (1887-1980) and his family had moved from New Cottages. He was the fourth generation of Jenkinsons to work in the Borrowdale quarries, his great-grandfather recorded as working at Honister in 1824. William had married Elizabeth née Dixon (1892-1952) in 1910 and they had two children, William and Beryl. Tom, William's older brother, was living at No 5.

By 1944, William Jenkinson had moved to Lake Road in Keswick and James and Mary Noble were the tenants. They stayed until the early 1960s. James Noble (1894-1968) was the son of James (1863-1941). Although born in St Day in Cornwall, James senior was brought up in Barrow, working with ships and their engines – in 1901 he was a stoker. He married a Barrow woman, Harriet Holland. James junior attended Thwaite Street School in Barrow until September 1903 when he '*left the district*'. His father took a job with the steam launches on Windermere, living in Newby Bridge in 1911 and in 1921, at

Blue Hill, Ambleside. Times were hard and Harriet was fined for the theft of a purse from Miss Tyson's tobacconists in Market Place.[22]

By 1911, James junior was independent, first working as a groom at Graythwaite Hall, Ulverston but his employer, Thomas Sandys, died in October 1911. James was twenty when the war broke out but there is no record of army service, nor can he be found on the 1921 census. But in 1927, he married Mary Wilkinson (1902-1954). She was the daughter of a Keswick boatman. By then, James junior was working as a quarryman, living at Braithwaite in 1939 before moving to Mountain View when the Jenkinsons left.

In 1965 Irene Margaret Shepherd applied for planning permission for alterations and additions and she was living in No 3 in 1970, along with George Leonard. Soon after the house was sold to John and Mary Whitehead who again undertook improvements and were on the electoral roll in 1978.

No 4 Mountain View

The first tenants were Annie and George Kirkby. He was a smith, son of a Langdale *'black and white' smith*.[23] However, the family soon moved back to Langdale. By 1911, Thomas Brown and Mary Ann Nuttall had moved in.

Mary (1882-) was the daughter of William and Elizabeth Birkett. She grew up at Gill Side, below the slopes of Stone Arthur in Grasmere, helping out on grandfather James Birkett's farm. When her father moved back to Honister and into No 1 Mountain View, Mary was living and working at the Borrowdale Vicarage for the Rev Edward Penson – probably grateful for the space as there were five sisters back home. In 1906, she married a waller, Thomas Brown (1884-), from Keswick. He worked as a mason and stockkeeper at the mine. It was a double celebration

267

BORROWDALE VISITOR'S ESCAPE.

A NIGHT IN THE SNOW.

Honister Workmen's Timely Rescue.

In the early hours of Saturday morning Messrs. T. Brown, Mountain View, and R. Pearson, Seatoller, were proceeding to their work at Honister, when they had a very unusual experience. Getting nearly opposite the top of High Cow Park intack, which is about half-way from Seatoller to Honister, they heard a distressing cry for help. Answering back to the call, another cry was heard. Hastening towards the direction of the cry, and shouting as they went along, they crossed the ghyll, and on getting over the wall and proceeding up the intack, came across a gentleman in a very exhausted condition. The morning being rather dark, and the severe blizzard just making a good start, the difficulty the two men were placed in can be imagined. Mr. Brown, who has passed three examinations in "first aid," saw that something immediate had to be done to save the gentleman's life. He was unable to stand, but they managed to get him over the wall and ghyll safely and the old road was reached.

Fig 13: Cumberland and Westmorland Herald 18th January 1913

when Mary and her sister Grace were married in a joint ceremony by Edward Penson at St Andrews (Fig 4). It was the first wedding at the church for nineteen years. Mary and Thomas went to Sunderland for their honeymoon.

Thomas had also had first aid training which proved lifesaving (Fig 13) for a man who got lost, walking back to Buttermere from Borrowdale. The man was soaking wet, having fallen into the ghyll and was 6' and fourteen stone. Thomas and Robert Pearson from Seatoller managed to get him to the mine office, sent William Siddle to Hasness for help, found dry clothes and hot coffee and brought him back from hypothermia.

By 1921, Mary Annie and Thomas had moved with daughter, Maud Elizabeth (1908-2002) to No 2 Mountain View. No 4 was now the home of William Allison (1878-) and his family. Another quarryman from Brigham, William married to Edith Broad (1871-1911) and they had four daughters. In 1921 two daughters were working in the valley - Eleanor was at High Lodore farm and Sylvia was at the Vicarage. William had been widowed in 1911 and had been living with his young children in Stonethwaite. Four houses away in Stonethwaite was Thomas Rigg with his wife, Agnes, and their daughter, Agnes Jane (1891-1972). In 1913 William married Agnes Jane, quite a leap for a young woman to take on two stepdaughters of ten and eight. She had help as her mother and father also moved to Mountain View, two doors away at No 6. Agnes Jane also had a son and daughter of her own. And in 1926 at the Borrowdale Sports, the boys' wrestling competition was won by John Allison of Mountain View.[24] There was a big change in 1939 when the family move to Bingley in Yorkshire and William became a poultry farmer but still living with his retired in-laws, Thomas and Agnes Rigg.

The cottage stayed in the family as it was taken over by William's brother-in-law, James Riley Rigg (1894-1963) and his

Fig 14: Luchini's ice cream van (Old Cumbria Gazetteer). Alongside the mountain wear shop, George Fisher, and Booths supermarket, Luchini's icecream vans are the best known of Keswick businesses

wife, Jane Boyd (1896-1957). In 1911, James had been living with his parents, Thomas and Agnes in Stonethwaite. James and his brothers moved with their parents to No 6 in 1916. Thomas and his sons were all slate quarrymen. James's oldest brother, John, was killed on the Somme in 1916 and 1917 had seen the near loss of another brother, Thomas.

James and Jane were still in Borrowdale in 1945 when their son Brian (1933-) won the Sir Hugh Walpole prize at Borrowdale School.[25]

After James's death in 1963, the cottage was taken over by Patrick Joseph Rogers. He may have been from Northern Ireland and a serviceman with the Royal Enniskillen Fusiliers. In 1939, he lived in Rotherham and was the foreman of a gang laying electricity cables. There were links with Cockermouth and the Luchini family. Louis Luchini was from Lucca, came to Glasgow before moving to Workington and starting his Italian ice-cream business (Fig 14). His wife, Sarah, was from Workington.

Their daughter, Mary Evelyn (1909-1979) was a shop-assistant in the family business in 1939 when she met Rogers. They married in 1941. After the war, he went to Zambia (Northern Rhodesia), working as a linesman. He travelled back to England in 1951 (although intending to return to Africa) on the SS City of Paris. His address in England was 60 Main Street, Cockermouth, the home of the Luchini family. By 1967 he had bought No 4 and was applying for planning permission to install a bathroom. Probate showed that he died at the cottage in 1975. Mary Evelyn lived in Main Street, Cockermouth until her death in 1979.

After Joe Rogers, the house has been owned by the Crockford family and, more recently, the Campbell family of Cockermouth.

No 5 Mountain View
The first family to live in No 5 were the Birds. James Bird (1858-1932) was a Cornishman from Medrose, a village close to the Delabole slate quarries where he and his younger brothers were working in 1881. The oldest brother, William, had headed north and, by 1881, had settled into Borrowdale – James followed him. In 1885, he married Elizabeth Lawson (1864-1955) from Thurstonfield near the Solway, the daughter of a tanner. How a Cornish miner met a Solway girl is a mystery, but the ceremony was on 11th March 1885 at Burgh by Sands. They lived initially at Chapel.

In 1890, brother William was killed. James had been working alongside him. James was part of William's gang, working on contract with the Buttermere Green Slate Company. Some stone was preventing them from getting at the slate that they were after. After two days of failed attempts, on Saturday

*Fig 15: Bull Gill winding drum with Nag Back incline behind
(B Moore Collection)*

21st the other gang member, Robert Wilson (1870-), bored a hole into the stone for blasting. William was working underneath it when a piece dislodged, fell and killed him instantly. His brother James heard a shout and found William dead.[26]

James became a contractor with the Buttermere Green Slate Company. This meant that he was his own master, heading up a gang. In 1896, there were at least twelve gangs with James and his men working at Windy Brow in the Nag Back part of the quarry (Fig 15).[27]

James and Elizabeth moved into the newly built terrace and stayed there until the outbreak of war. In 1916, they were at Rose Cottage in Rosthwaite, running the post office. Of their four sons, three joined the army – Thomas was too young. Fortunately, two survived: William Sydney (1893-1968) was with B Company of the 2/4 Borders in Peshawar, then in India in 1919; and Edwin James (1899-1970) was with the 1/4 Cheshires at Bornheim on the Rhine.

The eldest boy was George Lawson Bird (1889-1917). Like his father, George worked at Honister, a skilled river. On 4th December 1915, he signed his attestation papers - like so many Borrowdale young men, he joined the Border Regiment. He was a private, regimental number 23847 and in the 1st Battalion. George was 5' 8" and weighed 10 stone with a *'convergent squint'* in his right eye and upper dentures. Initially he was posted to the Army Reserve but was called up on 10th February 1916.

Some of his training in those early months of 1916 was at Seaford, Sussex – in April 1916 he had a bout of German measles in Seaford Hospital. On 2nd July 1916, George embarked for France. He joined his battalion on 14th July but then was posted to the 177th Tunnelling Company on 5th August. Between November 1915 and August 1917, the unit was stationed in the Railway Wood-Hooge-Armagh Wood area of the Ypres Salient,

273

Fig 16: George Lawson Bird 1889-1917

where it was engaged in mining activities against the Germans on the Bellewaerde Ridge.

This posting lasted until 7th October when he rejoined his battalion, only to be posted to a Pioneers Brigade on 14th October. It's not clear what this posting was but pioneer battalions were raised and numbered within existing infantry regiments, where possible recruits were men who possessed transferable skills from civilian life. As a miner, accustomed to tunnelling, George stayed with them until 10th March 1917 when he rejoined the Borders Battalion.

The 1st Battalion was involved in heavy fighting at Arras and Monchy-le-Preux from 12th April until the third week of May. They spent the remainder of May and most of June at Candas, in the Picardy region of the Somme, making the most of their time away from front line action - *"comfortable, clean little village, beautifully situated."* On 26th June, the Battalion went back to Belgium on the banks of the Yser Canal. They entrained at Doullens for Proven where they were moved by bus and then route march to their new accommodation in the support trenches of the Canal. Without any delay they were involved in active patrolling on the front line, a duty that often amounted to needless casualties. The next three weeks were spent at Proven, the small village they had spent time at more than once before. On 4th July 1917, George was killed in action.[28] A party was ordered to provide cover for a working party digging a trench. With this done, George and his comrade got back into the trench but because it was very muddy, they went along the top – George was hit by a German machine gun bullet that passed through his head. Immediately unconscious, he died thirty minutes later on his way to the first aid post. His comrade described him as *"the most sincere mate I have ever had and was very popular in his company"*.[29] He was buried at Bard Cottage Cemetery, Ypres, Belgium. In October 1917, his mother Elizabeth received his personal possessions – some letters and photos, a wallet, a religious book and his cap badge. On 10th January 1922, she acknowledged the receipt of the British War Medal and the Victory medal awarded to George.

The family were still in Rosthwaite in 1921 – father James and son William were working at the mine, Edwin was a carpenter and Thomas was apprenticed at the Keswick branch of the grocer, J&J Graham, a firm which is still going strong in Penrith.

In the cottage in 1921, there was an odd trio – granny, daughter-in-law and baby granddaughter, all from the Midlands. Ellen Ada née Stanley (1866-1937) married Fred Spencer Yates and they had two boys, Reginald and Herman. But at the time of the 1921 census, their marriage had disintegrated – Fred, a civil engineer, was boarding in Warwickshire and describing himself (falsely) as a widower. Worse was to follow as within a year he was convicted of embezzlement and imprisoned ((Fig 17).

Soon after, he took a ship to South Africa to join his son, Reginald. He died there. Ellen perhaps was avoiding the social stigma with the help of daughter-in-law Valerie née McCain, who

275

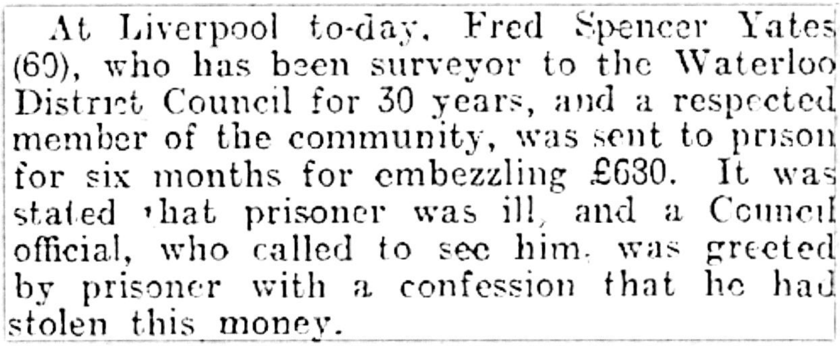

> At Liverpool to-day, Fred Spencer Yates (60), who has been surveyor to the Waterloo District Council for 30 years, and a respected member of the community, was sent to prison for six months for embezzling £630. It was stated that prisoner was ill, and a Council official, who called to see him, was greeted by prisoner with a confession that he had stolen this money.

Fig 17: Edinburgh Evening News 19th May 1922

was married to Herman. The three-month-old baby, Edith Margaret would have distracted them both. But they were tangential to the Borrowdale story.

In 1928, a quarryman Tom Jenkinson (1886-1980) and his brother George (1899-1972), aided by the Seathwaite Edmondsons, helped a walker with a broken ankle down from Styhead.[30] In the press report after the 1928 rescue, Tom was reported to be from Seatoller and so may already have moved into No 5 Mountain View.

Mountain rescue was not co-ordinated at that time, reliant on farmers and quarrymen. There were some professional mountain guides who were often involved such as J E B Wright based at the Seatoller House in the 1920s, from where he ran rock climbing courses. In 1932 the Rucksack Club and the Fell and Rock-Climbing Club combined to produce a suitable mountain stretcher and a list of first aid equipment. The Thomas stretcher was deemed the most suitable as the design allowed the end carriers to see their feet and avoid stumbling, and the wooden runners gave sufficient ground clearance to allow easy movement across rock, scree, grass or snow. Along with a double Thomas

Fig 18: A mountain rescue party at Stockley Bridge – happily the stretcher has not been needed

splint, wooden arm splints, iodine, bandages, kettle, primus stove, an eiderdown, feeding cup and urine bottle, the new stretchers were to be left at designated posts, such as Styhead, for use as required.[31]

After the war, a Borrowdale Mountain Rescue team (now Keswick MRT), run by Colonel Rusty Westmorland, was formed after an accident on Great Gable in April 1946. Two experienced climbers had been tackling a climb called Shark's Fin when a gust of wind blew one of the men from his sloping hold. He fell onto a ledge, his femur broken. Their subsequent rescue was a long and laborious twenty-one hours, much of it endured without food, in foul weather and darkness — exhausting for everyone involved.

The mountain rescue teams were, *mainly local guides and amateur climbers, who know their own zones like the backs of their hands and whose telephone numbers are known to all hostels, hotels and police stations in their area. They are unpaid but are pledged to turn out whenever a human being is in trouble in the mountains. Each team is equipped with rucksacks containing medical stores, an eiderdown bag, a leg splint, a specially designed stretcher, a paraffin stove, a lantern, candles, hot water bottles and a kettle.* [32]

Tom Jenkinson was a fourth-generation quarryman. He had married Hilda née Bragg (1892-1952) in 1913. In 1921, Tom was quarrying slate with his brother, Fred. The family were in Egremont and Tom and Hilda had three surviving daughters, Hilda, Sarah and Annie. Tom Jenkinson and his family were at No 5 in 1939, neighbours to his brother William at No 3. Daughter Sarah was disabled, Hilda was a parlourmaid to a retired iron master at Brockleside and Annie was working for a recently retired East India merchant, Robert Bazley, at Leathes Head.

Tom and Hilda left the valley and from 1946, Richard (1912-1993) and Annie Jackson née Myers lived in the house for over forty years. They had a daughter, Olive, (1937-). Annie Myers (1915-2001) had several links with the valley. Her father, Roland Myers (1884-1958), and his uncle, Ezekiel, came from Torver to work at Honister and in 1906 they were boarding with William Nuttall at No 1 Mountain View.[33] In October 1905, at St Andrews, Ezekiel married Jessie Richardson from Seathwaite and Roland married Annie Plaskett from Stonethwaite. Roland and Annie went south, living at Holme Ground, Coniston but his brother Ezekiel turned to farming at Wall End Farm in Langdale.

Perhaps Annie returned to her valley relatives after the death of her mother in 1934. She married Richard Jackson in 1937 and their daughter, Olive, was born the following year. After Richard's death in 1993, she is listed by the Rev Rooke as still living at Mountain View. By 1998 the house had been sold to Caroline Ingamells, a Keswick dentist, and her husband, Nick.

From 2010, the house has been owned by Peter and Jean Hutchinson. Peter Hutchinson's mother, Edith, had lived in No 6 since the 1970s, transferring it to Peter in 1990.

No 6 Mountain View
In the 1890s, Mary Jane Pepper had established an enviable reputation for Seatoller House as a destination for walkers and climbers. Her daughter, Mary Agnes (1871-1928), had married John Woodend (1865-1931) in 1895. He was a slate dresser from Kirkby Ireleth who, by 1893, was working at the Honister mine alongside her father, Moses.[34] By 1901, they were living in the new terrace of miners' cottages at Mountain View. By 1911, Mary Agnes and John were living at Seatoller House, and taking more responsibility for the running of the house, although her mother was listed in the census as *"lodging house keeper"* and no occupation was listed for Mary.

By 1911 Peter Longrigg (1873-1941) was living in Mountain View – in the census he described himself as '*traction engine driver, slate quarries, Honister to Keswick'*. He would have been one of the first drivers to use the new road bult by the Leconfield Estate. The mining company at Honister had been negotiating with the local authority to improve the road. They were using packhorses to transport the slate, up to twenty such journeys a day. By 1907, the estate had reached breaking point at the failure of their dealings with the council and decided to build their own road to the mine. It was completed by October

Fig 19: The Buttermere Green Slate Company's traction engine – Hodgson was a common Keswick name, and many were involved in motor engineering. This may be Albert Hodgson – see Fig 23

1907 at which point the company bought a traction engine, ten tons in weight and able to pull two trailers weighing eight tons. In 1926, the engine was Foden 6-tonner and the company were advertising for an experienced driver.[35]

From the pass, the new road followed what is now the Allerdale Way to the north of the modern B5289. Above Seatoller, it curved south and then west to go through the village in front of the New Cottages terrace. There are still two eight-foot posterns which identify the start of the road.

Peter Longrigg was a somewhat peripatetic worker, but he stuck to his trade: he was an engine driver in Lowther in 1901, again in Sunderland where his son, John was born in 1909; after Honister, he worked for a Huddersfield building firm, Wimpenny

& Co,[36] still an engine driver. In 1939, he was driving a steam roller in Penrith.

By 1913, Thomas Rigg (1862-) and his wife Agnes, née Riley had moved from Stonethwaite to No 6 Mountain View, living alongside their daughter Agnes Allison and husband, William, in No 4. Thomas was another migrant from Coniston while Agnes senior was from Whitehaven, probably from a family of farm workers. They had married in 1888. They had been living at Stonethwaite in 1911 where their daughter, Agnes, met and married William Allison in 1913. By that time, they had moved to No 6 Mountain View with their sons, with daughter Agnes next door, at No 4. Thomas and his sons were all slate quarrymen. But for the youngsters, such as Thomas's youngest, Ernest, and his friend Tom Bird, there was much to explore and fun to be had on the fells and at the tarns (Fig 20).

The Riggs were a tight-knit family, but in 1916 there was tragedy, the loss of the oldest brother and son, John, who was killed on the Somme in 1916. On 7th April 1915 John (1889-1916) enlisted and on 11th May, brother Thomas (1897-) followed. They both joined the Border Regiment but their brother, James (1894-1963) stayed with their parents. There must have been some tense family conversations as it is difficult to envisage that James did not also wish to enlist.

John was a private, regimental number 20166 in the 2nd Battalion. Another valley man, Edwin Boow, was in the same battalion. After training, they left for France on 17th December 1915.

The battalion went into action 1st July 1916, the first day of the Battle of the Somme. The battalion was positioned on the left-hand flank of the 20th Brigade for the assault on Mametz. To their left were the 8th Devons and to their right the 9th Devons. The plan was that these battalions would encircle the village to the

281

rowdale. He landed 12lb. of trout, one fish weighing 2¼lb. It is a common occurrence on Saturdays during summer to see schoolboys of Borrowdale setting off with their fishing rods. A casual observer would wonder what these young anglers were going to fish for, and where. With smiling faces they steer through Rosthwaite and turn to their right, making for Watendlath tarn to fish for perch and pike. It was last Saturday on one of these trips that Masters Tom Bird and Ernest Rigg, both about ten years old, living at Mountain View, were successful in catching two pike, one 5lbs. in weight and the other 2¼lbs. The manner in which the two fish were caught with the rod would have been no discredit to many older and experienced anglers. Only those who have fished this tarn know the difficulty in landing these fish, on account of the battle they make when coming to shore.

Fig 20: Cumberland and Westmorland Herald 28th June 1913

west in order that the 21st Division could press home an attack on Fricourt, a few kilometres to the north. The Borders had two mines detonated in their area at 7:28 am and made good progress. But, to their right, the 9th Devons were decimated by the Shrine machine gun emplacement just south of the village which the preliminary bombardment had failed to destroy. However, the 2nd Battalion of the Gordon Highlanders pressed on and teamed up

Fig 21: John William Rigg 1889-1916

with the remnants of the Devons and the Borders.

The Borders suffered over three hundred casualties that day, one of whom was Edwin Boow. John survived.[37] The Battalion was relieved on the night of 3rd July but was back in action on the night of 13th July in its position of deployment in Cater-pillar Wood by 1:15 am on 14th, the objective was Bazentin Le Grand wood. The attack attained its objective, but the war diary details the casualties: twenty-five dead, fifty-eight missing and over one hundred and thirty wounded. John Rigg was among these. There is no known grave, and he is commemorated on the Thiepval Memorial to the Missing of the Somme.

The next year saw the near loss of Thomas. On 16th December 1917, he was hit by shrapnel in his left thigh and was medically discharged.

In 1921, the family was still at No 6. The three surviving brothers were working at Honister with their father. On 14th September in the church of St John's in the Vale, Thomas married Anne Stanley (1896-1987), from Burns where her granddaughter, John Stanley, farmed and her father was a stonemason. The link with the valley was that she was the niece of Dinah Edmondson

Fig 22: The memorial to Keswick and Borrowdale soldiers of the First World War

née Stanley, who was married to John Edmondson at Seathwaite. Thomas worked as a foreman on the roads for the council, living in Graham Street in Penrith.

In 1922, his brother James married Jane Boyd and lived in No 4 Mountain View when his sister Agnes Allison moved to Yorkshire, with their parents, Thomas and Agnes. By then, the family had suffered another blow when the youngest son, Ernest Roberts Rigg, in 1928, died, aged twenty-seven.

The Riggs were followed in the house by the Plasketts. John (1901-1984) came from many generations of valley Plasketts, who had farmed or quarried. John's father, John (1877-1935) had married a collier's daughter, Mary Key (1879-1912) who had been in service in Rosthwaite. But Mary had died aged thirty-three, leaving John with a young son, John. John senior still enlisted in 1916. Initially he was in the King's Shropshires but when they became aware of his quarrying background,[38] he was transferred to the Royal Engineers as a sapper in the 323rd Quarrying Company. The unit landed at Le Havre 12th May 1917, consisting of two officers, two hundred and sixty-four men and two horses. They were stationed at the limestone quarries near Marquise and Rinxent, in the Pas-de-Calais. The work was non-combat but 24 hours a day and essential in maintaining lines of communication up to the front. One letter home from a sapper described daily routine,

.....we were split up into 3 parties for separate quarries and where I had to go was called the Happy Valley or Heureuse and was about 1 ¼ miles away but we have to rise at 5 and go to work at 5.45 and work till 5.30 with ½ hour for breakfast and 1 ¼ hours for dinner but you have so much work to do before you can give over for the day and for a company like ours we have to turn out 300 tons for the 24 hours work. So on the Monday morning May 20 we all began working in our quarry day and night shift. The quarry is called Beaulieu ...

For a Honister man, it must have seemed like home. John came home on leave for a fortnight in July 1917 to Thorneythwaite. He was also home in 1918 when he married a widow, Meggie O'Connor (1882-), née Bailiff. Meggie was the daughter of an innkeeper at the Hope and Anchor near Workington harbour but was widowed in 1911 and left with three young children. How she met John Plaskett remains a mystery although Meggie's sister, Hannah Bailiff, also married into the valley in 1921 when she wedded Maurice Slee at Grange.

From 1918, John junior and Meggie's daughter, Hannah

No Evidence of Recklessness, Says Coroner.

At a resumed inquest at Keswick, on Friday, on Albert Hodgson, aged 57, of Kerry's Head Yard, Keswick, and John Plaskett, also 57, of Stonethwaite Farm, Borrowdale, victims of the lorry crash on Honister Pass on April 29th, William Moore, the driver, said he had never driven a vehicle on the Pass before that day.

Fourteen men were on the lorry returning from work on the Buttermere side of the Pass when the crash occurred on the steep descent into Seatoller, at the head of Borrowdale.

Two of the men were killed outright and four were seriously injured, William Wren and James Nichol, both of Keswick, who are in Carlisle Infirmary with crushed limbs, and Thomas Deakin and Abe Cartmel, in Keswick Hospital.

Moore said that he was asked by the men in the morning to give them a ride down at night, and he told them it would be at their own risk.

He did not know how many men got on the lorry. At the bend he applied his brakes and changed down to second gear, then first. The brakes brought the lorry almost to a standstill and then failed to hold it.

He ran the lorry into the edge of the road to check its speed, but that did not stop it, and the lorry seemed to swerve over to the right and touched the bank and swung over to the left. He remembered nothing more.

The brakes were quite sound, he added.

Mr. Ashley Abraham, the climber, who was foreman of the jury, asked Moore how he could travel at 40 to 50 miles an hour in bottom gear, and he replied that he could not travel at 15 to 20 miles an hour when the accident happened.

Mr. Abraham: "Are you quite sure you didn't put the clutch out and let the lorry run free?"—"Yes, quite sure."

Inspector Bell said that when examined by the Ministry of Transport inspectors the brakes were found to be in good order and free from grease were jammed on hard.

When righted the lorry was in first gear.

"Accidentally killed" was returned, and the coroner said there was no evidence of any recklessness and the lorry could not have been travelling at a terrific speed, because it was in bottom gear.

Fig 23: Penrith Observer 14th May 1935

O'Connor (1905-1995), were brought up together on the farm. They married on April 23rd 1923[38] and continued to live on the farm until Mountain View became available in 1932, by which time they had already had six children. John had followed his father and was a rock hand at the Honister quarry. In 1935, the family suffered a tragedy when John senior was killed in a lorry crash on Honister Pass (Fig 23).

The men had left their bikes at Seatoller in the morning, walked up to the quarry and had hitched a ride down the hill. The road (which had been the old carriage road) had only recently been upgraded by the county council and it was the first descent that the driver had made. The press reports do not mention whether John had also been on that lorry. For a season, he was whip to a pack of otter hounds in Cockermouth but returned to Honister.

In the 1939 register, Hannah was filling in as the school caretaker. Alongside John and her in No 6 was her brother, John (1909-1981) who was a labourer for the council on the roads and later working at Yew Tree Farm. In 1953, the estate sold No 6 to Hilton and Emily Middleton. John Plaskett and Hannah moved two houses down and bought No 8 from the estate in November 1953.

Hilton Middleton (1887-1963) was a farmer's son. In 1916, he was the head horseman for Joseph Barnes at Barugh Syke, near Wigton. Barnes applied for Hilton's exemption from military call-up and there was a temporary exemption - Hilton already had three brothers in the army, one of whom, James was killed in 1918. Hilton was eventually conscripted in September 1916 with the 8th Battalion of the Yorkshire Regiment, known as the Green Howards. The battalion went to France in January 1917 and for two years, Hilton was in the front line. The battalion was involved in the battles of Messines, Menin Road, Polygon Wood

287

Military Medal Winner.

Private Hilton Middleton, Yorkshire Regiment, Main Street, Dearham, has been awarded the Military Medal. He showed great courage and determination in getting ammunition and rations up to the front line through a very heavy enemy barrage. He also took command of the party after the N.C.O. had been severely wounded, and by his energy and skill carried on this work as before. Private Middleton is a son of Mr. and Mrs. Hilton Middleton, Solway House, Kirkbride, who have four sons with the colours.

Fig 24: Wigton Advertiser 17th November 1917

and Passchendaele. During this time, Hilton was awarded the Military Medal for his courage.[39]

The battalion then went to Italy in November and again were on the front line in Montello in December 1917 and in action throughout 1918. At some point, Hilton was injured by a gunshot wound to his forearm and left ear – '*mild*' said the medical record.

After the war, Hilton went back to work for Joseph Barnes until retirement when they bought Mountain View from the Leconfield Estate in October 1953. This was not a random choice as the Middletons had links with Borrowdale and visited the valley for decades. Emily Middleton (1893-1970) née Lancaster was born in Dovenby and had an older sister, Annie (1892-1962). Annie was in service at Seatoller Farm in 1911, working for Daniel Jopson. In 1912, she married Walter Gaskell, a Honister quarryman, who was living at Longthwaite. By 1921, Annie and Walter were living in New Cottages and, nearly forty years later, were still in Seatoller, in Top Row. Jane, Emily's daughter, also worked in the valley for Tom Jackson at Seatoller Farm in the 1930s.

By 1978, the house was owned by Edith Constance Hutchinson. She transferred it to her son, Peter, in 1990. Peter moved next door to No 5 in 2010 and No 6 was bought by family until bought by the Chapmans.

No 7 Mountain View
One of the first tenants at No 7, Addison Pepper (1875-1945), was the fourteenth of fifteen children of Matthew Pepper (1819-1892) and Hannah (1828-) née Miller (see No 3 New Cottages). By 1896, Addison was already head of a company at Honister[40] working at Road End. In 1898, he married Isabella Armstrong (1876-1949), the daughter of a West Cumberland coal miner. Four years later, Addison's brother, George, married Isabella's sister, Mary.

Addison and Isabella were at Mountain View for a short time and then lived in Seathwaite and Grange, initially at Newton Place in 1921 and later in Grange. Addison worked at the quarry while Isabella ran a boarding house – in 1921, there were seven visitors including Thomas, the elder brother of John Snagge, the BBC sports commentator.[41] They let out lodgings and in 1925, Isabella was managing what were described as 'apartments' in Seatoller.

For a thousand years, there were no serious recorded crimes in Borrowdale, just illegal fishing and drunken quarrymen. But in 1928, Grange was the site of a notorious murder when Chung Wi Miao was convicted of killing his bride and leaving her body in Cumma Catta Wood near the village. Addison was a witness

289

at the trial as he saw the couple walking out together but then seeing the husband returning alone.[42]

Addison found himself back in court in 1942[43] when he testified against a Harrow schoolboy, Walter Bazley of Leathes Head, who convicted of maliciously wounding Addison's dog. Bazley was the son of a recently retired East India merchant, Robert Bazley, and was treated leniently as he was about to enlist in the Royal Navy. There was a link back to Mountain View as Annie Jenkinson, the Bazley's servant, lived at No 5.

After Addison and Isabella had left Mountain View, another Nuttall family moved in so that in 1911 there were three Nuttall families in the cottages: William in No 1, James in No 8 and James's son, William junior (1882-) in No7 with his wife, Edith Mary (1880-1959) née Randle and their young daughter, Beatrice. Edith was from Shropshire (where the couple married) but in 1901 had worked as a kitchen maid at Uppingham School. There is another mystery here as to how they met! William and Edith moved to Little Langdale, but they were back in No 2 and on the Borrowdale electoral roll until the 1960s.

The Cornishman, Hanson Tucker (1871-1947) and his wife, Annie (1878-1951) née Hetherington, who had been living in New Cottages, moved to Mountain View by 1921. By then a third child, Edward 1914, had arrived. Hanson and Annie were still in the house in 1939 with son Joseph, who worked as a joiner at the quarry. They had been in the cottage twenty-five years before Hanson died in 1947.

In 1960, Elizabeth Harrison was at No 7. She was the widow of Thomas Morley Harrison and they had lived at No 8 since the 1930s. In the late 1940s, Elizabeth had many family ties in the valley. Her sister, Jessie, lived at Bowderstone cottage with her husband, John Pepper. Jessie's son, Frank, was at Yew Tree in Seatoller. Elizabeth and Jessie had been brought up in

Fig 25: Billy Bland (on Ben Nevis in 1974)

Loweswater and Lorton. Their father Stephen was a general labourer. In 1939, their mother, Susannah Cowper (1861-1950) née Carson was living with Jessie. However, she moved in with Elizabeth and her address at her death in 1950 was No 8 Mountain View., Elizabeth's husband, Thomas, had died in 1949. In the 1950s, Elizabeth moved next door to No 7 where she lived for the next ten years.

Benjamin Pattinson (1898-1973), a farmer from Longthwaite, bought No 7 in March 1964 and applied in 1965 for planning permission for alterations and additions. His plan was to retire and live next door to his daughter and her husband. Margaret (Peggy) (1925-2015) and William Horsley (1917-1973). They lived at Peat Howe, close to Longthwaite Farm. Next door to the Horsleys was a Honister miner, Richard Wilson Richardson (1935-2016) and his wife, Evelyn Margaret née Dunwoodie. Benjamin's purchase allowed the Richardsons to move to Mountain View and for Benjamin and his wife, Elizabeth (1897-1976), née Dunwoodie, to move in at Peat Howe.

Also living at Peat Howe was Peggy's daughter, Ann Horsley (1949-). She was Benjamin Pattinson's granddaughter and her other grandfather, William Horsley, was a well-regarded Cumbrian wrestler and footballer for the Braithwaite team.[44] In 1970, Ann married a local man, the famed athlete, Billy Bland (1947-). Billy was brought up on Nook Farm in Rosthwaite, the son of Joe Bland and Ethel née Stuart. He was a fell runner (Fig. 25) and is unique as the only Borrowdale person to have a biography about his athletic exploits.[45]

For a time, Ann and Billy lived in the small Peat Howe cottage with her parents but Benjamin died in 1973 and his daughters, Dinah Lamb and Peggy Horsley, inherited the Mountain View house. It became available when Dickie Richardson secured the tenancy of Watendlath Farm from the National Trust.

Since 1973, it has been the home of Ann and Billy.

No 8 Mountain View

James Nuttall (1853-1927) and Ann née Birkett (1852- were the first tenants in No 8. They were the brother and sister of William and Elizabeth in No 1. James, the son of an iron ore miner from Dalton in Furness, Lancashire, was christened at Holy Trinity, Millom, in August 1853. The brothers had travelled to Langdale, to work in the quarries. James got married to Ann at St Oswald's in Grasmere in 1880.

Soon James was working in Honister – the name 'J Nuttall' was carved at the entrance to No 4 Low Nag Back level.[46] He was involved in the community life in the valley, as a member of the Mechanics Institute, centred on the Royal Oak in Rosthwaite. In spring, sports meetings were organised, often with walks around the valley, parades and church services and meals at the Royal Oak. The sports themselves were light-hearted with wheelbarrow races, potato races as well as three-legged races. The serious business was reserved for the wrestling, with the results in the press and decent prize money – despite this expenditure, the afternoon would raise money for the widows' and orphans' fund.[47]

There were regular concerts to raise money for the same fund. Often the performers were outsides but in 1895, the valley residents got their act together and did the bulk of the singing.[48] James sang '*Old Susannah White*', the lyrics of which have been lost but also '*Red, White and Blue*', an American patriotic song, popular in the mid-19th century. Fanny Simpson (1857-1926) from Hazel Bank accompanied him.

There were regular concerts to raise money for the same fund. Often the performers were outsides but in 1895, the valley residents got their act together and did the bulk of the singing.[49]

293

James sang '*Old Susannah White*', the lyrics of which have been lost but also '*Red, White and Blue*', an American patriotic song, popular in the mid-19th century. Fanny Simpson (1857-1926) from Hazel Bank accompanied him.

O Columbia! the gem of the ocean,
The home of the brave and the free,
The shrine of each patriot's devotion,
A world offers homage to thee;
Thy mandates make heroes assemble,
When Liberty's form stands in view;
Thy banners make tyranny tremble,
When borne by the red, white, and blue.
When borne by the red, white, and blue.
Thy banners make tyranny tremble,
When borne by the red, white and blue.

By 1911, the two Nuttall children had married and left home. Lodging with the Nuttalls was quarryman, John Cockbain (1883-1972) who would marry Annie Douglas (1887-1968) and would take over the tenancy of Seatoller House after the second World War.

In 1921, James and Ann were living in Fitz Cottages in Little Langdale - the Buttermere Green Slate Co had transferred James to their Elterwater quarries as a foreman. The Nuttall's daughter, Mary Birkett Nuttall (1885-1937) has taken over the tenancy from her father. She had worked at Seatoller House and then at Ormathwaite Hall before she married William Henry Brown ten years previously. He was from Parsonby, near Plumbland and worked at Rigg Head quarry. By 1939, the family was settled in Stonethwaite – by then, their daughter, Mary Birkett (1911-1981) had married James Bland, a Watendlath farmer.

By 1939, Thomas Morley Harrison (1875-1949), a

SEQUEL TO A KESWICK ELOPEMENT

At the Police Court on Wednesday, before Messrs J. Marshall and A. Mitchell-Dowson, *Elizabeth Harrison*, 22 years of age (wife of Thomas Morley Harrison, quarryman, Keswick), was brought up in custody in company with *Joseph Vickers*, 25 years of age, collier. The female prisoner was charged with stealing £7 15s in money together with a quantity of household goods the property of her husband; and the male prisoner with receiving the same, knowing them to have been stolen. Mr N. Robinson, solicitor, appeared to prosecute and asked for a remand in order to bring witnesses.—P.C. Lindsay deposed that he received the prisoners into custody at the county police station, Spennymoor, the previous afternoon, along with the goods produced. He read the warrant to the prisoners and cautioned them as to their replies. Vickers said, "I am not going to say anything." Mrs Harrison made no reply.—Thomas Morley Harrison identified the goods produced as his property.—Mr Broatch, magistrates' clerk, asked the prisoners if they had any objection to offer against a remand until Saturday noon.—Mrs Harrison said she wished to be tried that day, Vickers making no reply.—The Bench formally remanded the prisoners.—Inspector Logan, in answer to the Clerk, said he had no objection to the prisoners being liberated on substantial bail. He suggested two sureties for each of £20 and the prisoners in £40 each. They were removed to the cells and have not applied for bail.

Fig 26: English Lakes Visitor 20th August 1904

quarryman and iron miner, and his wife, Elizabeth (1881-) were living there. They had been married at St John's, Keswick in 1901. After the wedding, Thomas was staying at the barracks in Honister during the week, but Elizabeth was in Police Station Court in Keswick. The marriage was turbulent – after the birth of their daughter Florence in 1903, there was a scandal when Elizabeth ran off to Spennymoor with a Joseph Vickers. She had taken the housekeeping money and some household goods. Thomas pursued them through the courts, charging them with larceny.

However, they were reconciled, living in Egremont in 1921 where Thomas was an iron ore miner for the Beckermet Mining Company (taken over by United Steel in 1920). The couple had a further four children. Daughter, Nellie and her husband, Howard Bozie, a bus driver, were living with them in 1939.

Thomas died in 1949 and in November 1953, John Plaskett bought No 8 from the Leconfield estate and moved two houses down from No 6. Elizabeth Harrison moved next door to No 7 where she lived for the next ten years. John and Hannah would stay in No 8 until October 1978 when he sold the property to his son, James Jackson Plaskett and his wife, Veda.

From 1996, Michael and Sheena Chapman have lived in No 8 – until 2017, they also owned The Barn in Seatoller.

Glaramara
The Glaramara outdoor centre, just east of Seatoller is the most recent building in the upper valley,, opened in 1935 by the Co-operative Holiday Association (CHA).[50] The CHA was founded in Keswick around 1895. In the 1920s, a Lakeland mountain guide, J E B (Jeremiah Ernest Benjamin or Jerry) Wright (1898-1975), based himself at the Seatoller House, from where he ran rock climbing courses. Alongside him was George Starkey

(1900-1974) who assisted with these and led walking holidays, especially for the CHA.

Wright and Starkey became the moving forces to launch a new mountaineering club within the CHA and organised a meeting of interested members on 16th and 17th November 1929. That meeting agreed, subject to the approval of the CHA General Committee, to form the CHA Mountaineering Club, and this was ratified on 10th January 1930.[51]

The CHA planned to build a hostel in Seatoller, which was intended to be the Mountaineering Club's HQ but there was friction over a fatal accident and by 1933 the Club had broken away from the CHA, renamed itself the Tricouni Club and Seatoller House became its headquarters, meeting twice a year. The club was named after the nickname of the Swiss watchmaker who manufactured the toothed rock-climbing nail.

The CHA went ahead with their project and the hostel, named Glaramara after the nearby mountain, was built on an old field, named High Broad Dale in the 1842 Tithe map (Fig 2). It might well have been part of the ancient common field but by the 18th century, it had been enclosed and bought by the Fishers of Seatoller House. After Abraham Fisher's death in 1864, it passed to Henry Marshall and then onto the Leconfield estate. Leconfield sold the land to the CHA in 1934. It was a difficult time for farming in the early 1930s and perhaps the tenants at Seatoller Farm, Tom and Martha Jackson, received compensation for the loss of their field.

The building was designed by a Manchester architect, Ernest Newton, with beds for forty-six in two large dormitories. There was no electricity and hot water was provided by a coal-fired boiler in the cellar. It was formally opened on a Wednesday afternoon, 14th August 1935, by Lord Leconfield of Cockermouth Castle. Intriguingly he mentioned that there had been a hostel at

297

*Fig 27: One of the first CHA groups outside Glaramara in 1935
(Image by Countrywide Holiday Association)*

Seatoller for many years but was usually occupied by people who *'climbed the rocks and endeavoured to break their arms, legs and necks.'*[52]

In the years leading up to the Second World War, the centre was popular for those looking for strenuous walking holidays as opposed to CHA's more 'country house' centres such as Loughrigg Brow in Ambleside. In 1939, the centre was well staffed but there were no visitors. Emily Bellhouse (1880-1966) was the manager. She had worked in the Rochdale cotton industry but by 1921 was working for the CHA on the Isle of Man. With her were two cooks, Eleanor Denham (1901-1985), daughter of a Newcastle NER train driver and Winifred Kirkland (1909-1998) whose father worked for Edward Hughes pottery in Fenton, Stafford. There were two 'house helpers', Annie

Fig 28: Glaramara

Knowles (1901-1979) and Louisa Grahamslaw (1905-1989), from a Northumberland farming family. However the house was soon closed down for the duration.

After the war, Mary Alta (1911-2002) and Lilias Aspen were registered on the electoral roll. Mary was a long-time CHA employee who, in 1939, had been working at Abbey House in Whitby, set up in 1895 as the CHA's first holiday centre. Glaramara continued in spartan mode and as a 'strenuous mountain centre' until 1978 when a new bedroom wing was added and the dormitories in the existing building were converted to single rooms, with shared bathroom and toilet facilities. Glaramara was still focused on school parties and youth groups – there was a 'no alcohol' policy and a compulsory morning run before breakfast. But the CHA ran into financial problems in the 1980s. In 1998 it sold its remaining hostels to Shearings coach company. The company let the property stand empty and in the following year, David Oglethorpe, a Keswick accountant, bought the dilapidated building with his partners. They set about turning it initially into an outdoor activities centre. Within two years, foot and mouth brought trade to a standstill but better years followed. There are now fewer youth groups and from 2024, outdoor activities are no longer offered. Rooms and facilities have been improved over the past two decades so that Glaramara is now a fully fledged hotel.

Notes

[1] *Tyler I., (1994) Honister Slate 58*
[2] *CRO Carlisle SRDC/3/2/39*
[3] *Obituary, Penrith Observer 18th June 1889*
[4] *West Cumberland Times 1st December 1897*
[5] *CRO Carlisle DLEC/3/22/1/6*
[6] *Tyler I., (1994) 52; Millom Gazette 24th March 1894*
[7] *Penrith Observer 10th January 1933*
[8] *Penrith Observer 28th February 1950 for short obituary*
[9] *Tyler I., (1994) 72 for an account of the Easter Monday event which attracted participants from all over Cumberland.*
[10] *West Cumberland Times 18th May 1887 for a typical account*
[11] *English Lakes Visitor 27th May 1893 – John Simpson, solicitor, of Hazel Bank was the likeliest to have such influence*
[12] *Closely related to freemasonry, Mechanism started in 1757 as a schism of a couple masonic lodges in England. In that year the Independent United Order of Mechanics was founded in Lancaster; Harris H.,(2015) The Order of Mechanics CW3 183; Harris H.,(2019) A Cumbrian Friendly Society CW3 195*
[13] *West Cumberland Times 6th January 1894*
[14] *West Cumberland Times 1st January 1910 gives the name of the mission*
[15] *Lancashire Evening Post 1st April 1926*

[16] West Cumberland Times 6th July 1895
[17] West Cumberland Times 1st January 1910
[18] Penrith Observer 6th June 1947
[19] Tyler I., (1994) 57
[20] West Cumberland Times 8th December 1894, Carlisle Patriot 14th June 1895, English Lakes Visitor 20th March 1897
[21] Chepstow Weekly Advertiser 6th and 13th July 1907
[22] Lancashire Evening Post 8th July 1920
[23] While blacksmithing uses raw iron to make large and sometimes crude products, whitesmithing focuses on manipulating lighter metals such as tin and adding finishing touches through filing, polishing
[24] Lancashire Evening Post 9/8/1926
[25] Penrith Observer 24th December 1945
[26] Carlisle Patriot 27th June 1890
[27] Tyler I., (1994) 64
[28] This paragraph is based on the assumption that George was with the 1st Battalion - see thelonsdalebattalion.co.uk
[29] These details were found on a postcard from one of his comrades to Miss Hackett, Royal Oak, Rosthwaite - George had been writing to her.
[30] Leeds Mercury 27th June 1928
[31] This draws on www.mountain.rescue.org.uk/history/
[32] Chartres J 'Why They Climb Mountains' Manchester Evening News 3rd November 1949
[33] Tyler, I. (1994) Workforce appendix
[34] Tyler, I. (1994) Workforce appendix where he is referred to as John Woodend junior
[35] Lancashire Evening Post 15th July 1926
[36] In 2022 the company still exists, now managed by the fourth generation of the family
[37] thelonsdalebattalion.co.uk/wiki/2nd_Battalion_War_Diary_July_1916
[38] Keswick Reminder 28th April 2023 reprinted an account of their 40th wedding anniversary in 1963
[39] Supplement to the London Gazette 17th December 1917

[40] Tyler I., (1994) 58

[41] John Mordaunt Snagge, 1904-1996 broadcast his first sports commentary (Hull City versus Stoke City) in January 1927, after the BBC obtained the rights to cover major sporting events. He would later broadcast from the Normandy beaches and in 1949 announce that it was either Oxford or Cambridge in the lead in the Boat Race.

[42] Yorkshire Post 31st July 1928

[43] Penrith Observer 28th April 1942

[44] Penrith Observer 6th May 1924 – a benefit football match for the widow and children of William Horsley

[45] Chilton S., (2020) All or Nothing at all

[46] Tyler I., (1994) 51

[47] eg English Lakes Visitor 29th May 1886; West Cumberland Times 9th June 1888 (there were 50 on the club walk)

[48] Carlisle Examiner 28th February 1891 (dancing went on until 3am); West Cumberland Times 27th April 1895

[49] Carlisle Examiner 28th February 1891 (dancing went on until 3am); West Cumberland Times 27th April 1895

[50] Hope D, The democratisation of tourism in the English Lake District: the role of the Co-operative Holidays Association (2016) 8 Journal of Tourism History 105; the building is now privately owned but still run as an outdoor centre and hotel

[51] http://www.tricouniclub.org/origins.html

[52] Penrith Observer 20th August 1935- Leconfield may well have had High House in Seathwaite in mind which was the HQ of the Fell and Rock Climbing Club

13: Epilogue – Seatoller in modern times

The Honister slate workers had brought life to Seatoller for over a century but by the 1990s, demand for the mine's quality product had declined and the company closed down. When employment opportunities disappear, small villages can also easily vanish. The population dwindles, the pub and the post office close. The impact of such job losses could be seen across the country, whether it was slate in Cornwall or North Wales, coal in the Rhondda or iron and steel in Yorkshire. It is only too easy to find streets of derelict terraced houses, their communities blown apart by the free market policies of successive conservative administrations.

Nor were there other jobs in Borrowdale. Mechanisation meant that farm jobs had disappeared - the fastest period of decline was between the end of the 1940s and the early 1960s, during which time the agricultural workforce went from almost 900,000 to just over 400,000. Since then, the rate of decline has been slower. In 2010 the total workforce was 170,600. Fell farms are especially disadvantaged with their harsh climate, short growing seasons, relatively poor quality of soil and long winters. They often require state subsidy to survive, and governments have traditionally intervened heavily in the agricultural sector, probably more so than in any other productive sector of the economy. In January 2023, the UK government replaced the EU's common agricultural policy (CAP) with environmental land management schemes (ELMs). Unlike the

CAP, which provided farmers incentives based mainly on the acreage they farmed, the overhaul is meant to reward farmers for protecting nature and improving the environment. But Lake District hill farmers such as James Reebanks have warned that they would lose out to big arable farmers, with meagre pickings for small farmers in difficult environments, such as upland and moorland regions.[1] And rewilding projects, admirable in themselves, can mean the loss of traditional farms, such as Thorneythwaite.

These threats to rural communities and people's livelihoods were clearly visible in the closing decades of the 20th century, not that it meant that governments acted to protect the rural economy action or that the effects were in any way lessened. Other threats turn up out of the blue. Sometimes, as with the devastating floods following Storm Desmond in December 2015, the consequences are short-lived. And in the spring of 2020, the UK hospitality industry was closed down when the Covid pandemic struck. For nearly two years, the hotels, the boarding houses and self-catering cottages in Borrowdale lay empty or ran at reduced capacity.

And yet the village, the valley and its people survive, remarkably unchanged. The unique selling point is, of course, Wainwright's assessment that it is the '*most beautiful square mile in Lakeland*' which, shamelessly extrapolating, means that upper Borrowdale was also the most beautiful square mile in England. This meant that there are ample numbers of visitors, walking, climbing or just admiring. The threat here is the valley's very popularity – its single road clogged with traffic, narrow lanes impassable with poorly parked cars, the popular footpaths eroded, gates left open allowing sheep to wander, litter left on the fellside and the summer threat of fire from portable barbeques. It was ever thus? Such complaints often surface in the local newspapers from a century ago.

The Seatoller cottages no longer house the quarrymen. Instead, there is a mixture of those born and bred in the valley, retired incomers, family holiday homes as well as a flow of people staying just a week at a time. The latter form a transient population but provide a certain dynamism. Covid has had little lasting impact. The holiday lets and the two hotels flourish. Under the stewardship of the Lakes Trust, Seatoller House was cushioned from the worst effects. The Glaramara had been sold to the Oglethorpe family in 1999. The Oglethorpes were solicitors in Keswick where the firm's name can still be seen in St John's Street. For a time, the business model of the Co-op Holiday Association model was continued with holidays with basic accommodation and communal meals. Schools also took advantage of the hostel-style approach, with the Glaramara providing the children with an introduction to climbing, canoeing, ghyll-scrambling among other activities. But the last ten years has seen a focus on adult tourists and walkers and a shift towards a modern hotel. Government grants saw it through the Covid crisis.

The closure of the slate mine in the late 20th century was a blow to the village. Miners and their families had provided another dimension to village life for over a century. But in 2002, the Honister Slate Mine Ltd was incorporated under Mark Weir (1966-2011) (Fig 1).

Weir was a remarkable businessman. His two-pronged business plan relied first on exploiting a niche market for high quality slate and secondly on a public appetite for both industrial history and for extreme sports.

...he took his grandfather for a helicopter ride in 1985 over the Honister pass between Borrowdale, where he was born, and Buttermere. The old man looked sadly at the recently

Fig 1: Mark Weir 1966-2011

closed workings of the huge mine and quarry in the flank of Fleetwith Pike, where he had been employed as a river, or cutter, supplying slates to Buckingham Palace.

Peering down himself, Weir saw something different. The huddle of grey buildings, including a spartan youth hostel, had untapped tourist potential, a handy jumping-off point at 356m (1,167ft) for some of England's most famous mountain-tops. ...he set about turning it into one of the national park's leading attractions.

This took his talent for hustling and cheerful promotion to its peak, exasperating planners and sometimes alarming the Lake District's many conservationists. He won most of them over by skilfully linking the demands of modern tourism to Cumbria's industrial tradition...

Fig 2: Honister mine complex – the road to the left leads to Buttermere and that to the right to Seatoller (gpsroutes.co.uk)

While guidebooks rhapsodised about ancient characters such as Moses the quarryman, whose "trod" from Honister round Great Gable is a famous high-level path, Weir actually brought their jobs back to life. His 30 staff at Honister include waiters and shop assistants, but also excavator-drivers ... The beautiful Westmorland Green slate from the reopened mine is now used to fashion kitchen units, house nameplates and garden features[2]

The tours through the narrow, claustrophobic, tunnels opening out to vast caverns *'measureless to man'*, hollowed out inside the mountains, are extraordinary and attract schools as well as tourists.

Equally compelling is the via ferrata experience over ladders

Fig 3: Inside the Honister mine (Honister.com) – hard hats are essential, especially for tall people (gpsroutes.co.uk)

and wires stretched across the precipitous face of Honister crag.

Mark Weir died in a helicopter crash in 2011 but Honister.com kept going with his brother, Joe and his partner, Jan Wilkinson.

The acquisition of the mine also affected the village as Weir bought the Yew Tree and the barns facing it. The attempt to keep Yew Tree as a viable café and restaurant faltered but in 2022, Weir's son, Prentice Wilkinson-Weir, alongside a new generation of the family, took over and brought new energy into the project, with the Yew Tree scheduled to open as a licensed café in 2023.

The barn which housed the National Trust's information centre was transformed into accommodation. The staff accommodation behind the Yew Tree has also been renovated

Fig 4: The via ferrata experience on Honister crag

and now miners again live in the village. They drive to work rather than walk up the hill in clogs but their hours are long and they have the same mud and dust on their clothes in the evening as the Jacksons and Cockbains of previous eras.

There is a sharp contrast between the unchanging beauty of Borrowdale and the modern busy-ness of Honister, alongside its heaps of discarded slate, rusted rails and the adits of the old mine. Both contribute to keeping Seatoller alive. Both are, relatively, new. The constant and ancient activity in the valley since the Norsemen is farming.

After Nobel Bland, the farm was run by the Cubbys until 2005 when Steve and Christine Simpson moved to Seatoller from Patterdale. They worked the farm until 2019 when their son, Dan, and his wife Ruby, took over.

It remains first and foremost a sheep farm, with the ewes giving birth to several hundred lambs a year. But the need to protect the fells from over-grazing has meant that overall

Fig 5: Dan and Ruby Simpson at the opening of the craft shop on the farm in 2019 – it is now a farm shop for campers as well as drinks for exhausted coast-to-coasters

numbers have been cut. Auction prices in 2023 for prime lambs hover around £3.50 per but hill farms struggle to survive solely on the gross income from their lambs. Costs rise: even the income from wool does not meet the costs of shearing. Diversification is essential and more animals, such as fell ponies, can attract school groups. The intakes now have Jacobs sheep as well as the endearing Dartmoor long wool.

Campers are also a regular income stream, and the campsite now has been given a make-over and yurts are available for the less hardy (Fig 6).

A craft shop (Fig 5) was set up in the old 17th century barn and slowly morphed into a general shop, selling essentials for the campers and other visitors as well as providing coffee and ice cream for walkers - Seatoller is on the Wainwright coast-to-coast

Fig 6: Nichol Dub bridge over the Derwent leading from Seatoller Farm to Thorneythwaite – the yurts are in the field beyond

path and travellers often arrive exhausted after travelling through Ennerdale and over Honister. Another barn has also been converted into a weekend pizzeria (Fig 7).

By the time of the winter solstice, the rain has returned. The waterfalls at Taylor Force and Sour Milk are often in full spate. The tops of the higher fells will regularly be covered with snow but lower down it will settle much less often, even at the heads of the valleys. The B5289 over Honister is rarely closed. Flood remains a more potent threat: in December 2022, Seatoller Farm lost sixty of their breeding ewes when the river swept over the field, (known as Rash on the 1842 Tithe Map). Just across the

Fig 7: Farming's need to diversify - Seatoller Farm's weekend pizzeria

road, the houses at Mountain View were lucky. Seatoller village itself is safe, and at 390', is some sixty feet higher. In 2015 Storm Desmond brought some fourteen inches of rain in twenty-four hours. The road was awash, and its camber means that the rainwater flooded, yet again, through Seatoller House, but the farm and cottages remained dry.

By January, the House is on its customary mid-winter break and the village is quiet. The bus still runs several times a day but there are few passengers. The holiday lets are only occasionally occupied. The year's lambs and their mothers will be wintering away from the high fells. On the bird tables, the sparrows quarrel with each other, the tits peck at the fat balls gratefully and now and then nuthatches and woodpeckers appear. At the southern tip of Africa, the Seatoller swallows, martins and swifts feast on insects, preparing for their 13,600-kilometre journey back to Cumberland, via Zaire and the Congo. And suddenly in mid-April, the swallows, martins and swifts are darting back and forth, hunting insects in the Glaramara field. In the neighbouring field, newly born lambs are getting to know each other. The roadside verges are covered with yellow, first daffodils, then dandelions and buttercups. The 78 bus fills up with walkers and climbers and Seatoller is back in business.

Notes

[1] *The Guardian 26th January 2023*
[2] *Wainwright M., The Guardian 8th April 2011*

Select Bibliography

Abbreviation: CW1/2/3 – Transactions of the Cumberland and Westmorland Antiquarian and Archaeological Society Series 1/2/3 (Vol number corresponds with year – 2021=Vol 21

Alfonso I., (1991) Cistercians and Feudalism 133 Past and Present 3

Allan S., Folk Song in Cumbria: a distinctive regional repertoire (PhD thesis 2017) at https://www.village-music-project.org.uk/

Appleby A. B., (1973) Disease or Famine? Mortality in Cumberland and Westmorland 1580-1640 26 The Economic History Review 403

Asquith R., (2013) Buttermere Mill Lorton & Derwent Fells Local History Society Newsletter 52

Bailey J. and Culley G., (1794) General View of the Agriculture of the County of Cumberland

Baines, E., (1834) A Companion to the Lakes of Cumberland, Westmoreland, and Lancashire, In a Descriptive Account of a Family Tour, and Excursions on Horseback and on Foot

Barrow G. W. S., (1999) King David I, Earl Henry and Cumbria CW 2 117

Bishop of Barrow, (1905) On the Readers in the Chapelries of the Lake District CW2 89

Bott G., (2005 2nd ed) Keswick

Bouch C M L, (1949) Poor Law Documents of Great Salkeld CW2 142

Bouch C. M. L. and Jones G. P., (1961) The Lake Counties 1500-1830

Bradbury D., (2003) Senhora Small Fry: Mary Barker and the

Lake Poets

Brown G., (2009) Herdwicks

Brunskill, R. W., (1974) Vernacular Architecture of the Lake Counties

Bulmer's History and Directory of West Cumberland (1883)

Carter M., (2021) The Dissolution of Furness Abbey CW3 111

Caunce S. A., (2012) The Hiring Fairs of Northern England 1890-1930 217 Past and Present 213

Challands H., (1979) A Demographic Study of Crosthwaite Parish ch 3 (Durham University E-Theses)

Chilton S., (2020) All Or Nothing At All

Churches C., (1998) Women and Property in Early Modern England 23 Social History 165

Clarke J., A Survey of the Lakes of Cumberland (1787)

Clough T. H. McK., (1969) Bronze Age metalwork from Cumbria CW2 1

Cocker M., (2023) One Midsummer's Day

Collingwood W. G., (1928) The Keswick and Coniston Mines CW2 1 at 11

Cottam A., (1928) The Granges of Furness Abbey 80 Historic Society of Lancashire and Cheshire, 58

Crosthwaite J. Fisher, (1875-76) Old Borrowdale Transactions of the Cumberland Association for the Advancement of Literature and Science 1875-76 66

Crosthwaite J. Fisher, (1876) The Crosthwaite Registers CW1 225

Crosthwaite J. Fisher, (1883) The Colony of German Miners at Keswick CW1 344

Davies-Shiel M., (1972) A little-known Late Medieval Industry Pt 1 CW2 85

Davies-Shiel M., (1974) A little-known Late Medieval Industry Pt 2 CW2 33

Defoe D., (1724-27) A Tour Thro' the Whole Island of Great Britain

Denman D., (2014) Lord William Gordon and the picturesque occupation of Derwentwater in the 1780s CW3 207

Denman D., Materialising Cultural Value in the English Lakes 1735-1845 198ff (PhD thesis, University of Lancaster eprints.lancs.ac.uk/61596/1/Denman-ThesisEprint.pdf)

Dower R., and Trevelyan G., (1998) The Trevelyan Hunt: The First Hundred Years 1898-1998

Elliott G., (1959) The System of Cultivation and evidence of enclosure in the Cumberland open fields in the 16th century CW2 86

Elsas M., (1945) Deeds of the Parish of Crosthwaite CW2 40

Elton C., (1882) Custom and Tenant-Right

Fell, C. (1950) Early Settlement in the Lake Counties

Fielding K. J., (1986/87) Carlyle and the Speddings Carlyle Newsletter No 7 12 and No. 8 51

Fussell G. E., (1949) The English Rural Labourer

Fussell G. E. (1955) Crop Nutrition in Tudor and Stuart England Agricultural History Review 95

Geddes R. S., (1975) Burlington Blue-Grey

Gibbs S., Felony Forfeiture at the Manor of Worfield, C.1370-C.1600 (Cambridge Thesis Repository Orcid: 0000-0002-6832-7988)

Gillbanks J., (1906) John Crozier Manchester Quarterly January 1906 -

Gilchrist A. G., (1939) Some Old Lake Country Fiddlers 1 The

Journal of the Lakeland Dialect Society 16

Gilpin W., (1786) Observations, Relative Chiefly to Picturesque Beauty Vol. 1

Graham T. H. B., (1912) The Debatable Land CW 2 33

Graham T. H. B., (1913) The Debatable Land Pt 2 CW 2 132

Grainger F., (1909) Agriculture in Cumberland in Ancient Times CW2 120

Grant S., (2006) The Story of the Newlands Valley

Gray E., (2007) 100 Hunts: A Chronicle of the Trevelyan Manhunt 1898-2007

Gray T., (1769) Journal of his Visit to the Lake District

Green W., (1819) The Tourist's New Guide to the Lake District

Hall I., (2017) Thorneythwaite Farm, Borrowdale

Harris H., (2015) The Order of Mechanics CW3 183

Harris H., (2019) A Cumbrian Friendly Society CW3 195

Harrison P., (2021) Mountain Republic

Haverfield F. J., (1914) Report on the Exploration of the Roman Fort at Ambleside CW 2 433

Hindle B. P., (1984) Roads and Trackways of the Lake District

Holdsworth P., (2005) Manorial Administration in Westmorland 1589-1693 CW3 137

Hope D., (2016) The democratisation of tourism in the English Lake District: the role of the Co-operative Holidays Association 8 Journal of Tourism History 105

Hope W. H. St J., (1900) The Abbey of St Mary in Furness CW2 221

Hunt I. (2002) Lakeland Yesterday

Hutchinson W., History of Cumberland (1794)

Johnson S., (1981) Borrowdale, its land tenure and the records

317

of Lawson Manor CW2 63

Jones G. P., (1975) Some sources of Loans and Credit in Cumbria before the rise of banks CW2 275

Kaye W., (1966) Governor's House, Keswick CW2 340

Kipling C., (1961) A Salt Spring in Borrowdale CW2 57

Le Clerc P., (2018) The Isolated Tomb West Middlesex FHS Journal 8

Littledale R. P., Ennerdale CW2 156

Mansergh R., Windermere and Grasmere in the Great War

Marshall J. D., (1973) The Domestic Economy of the Lakeland Yeoman Transactions CW2 190

Matthiessen P. et al, (2015) A survey of longhouse structures in the Duddon Valley CW3, 117

McLaren D., (1974) The 1653 Marriage Act 28 Population Studies 319

McDonnell J., (1989) The role of transhumance in northern England 24 Northern History 1

Merriman M. H., (1968) The Assured Scots: Scottish Collaborators with England during the Rough Wooing 47 Scottish Historical Review 10

Millward R. and Robinson A., (1972) Cumbria in 'The Landscapes of Britain' 137

Morgan S. A., (2008) The Religious Dimensions of English Cistercian Privileges (PhD thesis UCL)

Morris J. E., (1902) Cumberland and Westmorland Military Levies in the time of Edward I. and Edward II CW2 306

Murray R. and C., (2022) The Old Mill

National Trust (2007): Borrowdale: Historic Landscape Survey

Neville C., (1994) Keeping the Peace on the Northern Marches in the Later Middle Ages 109 English Historical Review 1

Newman C. E., (2014) Mapping the Late Medieval and Post Medieval Landscape of Cumbria (PhD Thesis University of Newcastle) 159

Norman M., (2020) Telling the Bees and Other Customs: The Folklore of Rural Crafts

Parsons M., (1996) Troutbeck Chapel of Ease CW2 139

Pearsall W. H., and Pennington W., (eds) (1973) The Lake District: A Landscape History

Pease H., (1912) The Lord Wardens of the Marches

Penfold H., (1907) Superstitions connected with Illness, Burial, and Death in East Cumberland CW2 54

Prevost, W. A. J., (1968) The Death of Christie Armstrong, a Border Reiver CW2 57

Rohrbasser J-M., (2005) Counting the population. The multiplier method in the 17th and 18th centuries 409 Population and Societies 1

Rollinson W., (2nd ed 1987) Life and Tradition in the Lake District

Ross C., (2012) The Carvetii - a pro-Roman community? CW 3 55

Rowse A. L., (1953) The Coronation of Queen Elizabeth History Today 5th May 1953

Scott J. (1998) The Kendal Tenant Right Dispute CW2 169

Size N., The Secret Valley

Smith G., (1940) The Practice of Medicine in Tudor England 50 The Scientific Monthly 65

Sydney M., (2009) Bleeding, Blisters and Opium: Joshua Dixon and the Whitehaven Dispensary

Taube E., (1939) German Craftsmen in Tudor England Economic History Vol. 4 167

Thane P., (1999) Working Class and State Welfare in Gladstone D. Before Beveridge: Welfare Before the Welfare State

Toke L., (1913) Lay Brothers (in Herbermann, C (ed.) Catholic Encyclopedia)

Trevelyan G. M., (1904) England under the Stuarts

Tyler I., (1994) Honister Slate

Tyler I., (1995) Seathwaite Wad

Tyson B, (1995) Rebuilding the Medieval Court House at Keswick CW2 119

Uglow, S. (2015) Cornish Miners in Borrowdale (Cornwall FHS Journal)

Uglow S., (2021) Early Tourism in Borrowdale CW3 175

Vaux H., (2012) Anglo-Scottish Warfare CW3 123

Watson G., (1896) Aske's Rebellion CW1 335

West T., (1778) A Guide to the Lakes

White, John Pagen, (1873) Lays and Legends of the English Lake Country

Winchester A. J. L., (1987) Landscape and Society in Medieval Cumbria

Winchester A. J. L., (1997) Parish, Township and Tithing 27 The Local Historian Number 1 February

Winchester A. J. L., (2001) Personal Names and Local Identities in Early Modern Cumbria CW 3 29-49

Winchester A. J. L., (2017) Lake District Field Names

Wordsworth W., (1822) A Description of the Scenery of the Lakes in the North of England

Index

1902 guest book   *136ff*
Accidents, aircraft   *161*
Accidents, drowning   *34, 50*
Accidents, mining   *183, 202, 212, 215, 220-221, 236, 240, 271, 287*
Allonby, unexciting   *73-74*
Bland family   *161, 203, 292, 294, 309*
Borrowdale Parish Council   *118-121, 156, 251, 263*
Buses and tours   *153-157, 159, 160, 196*
Clark families   *189, 193, 206, 210, 227, 264*
Co-operative Housing Association   *160, 296ff*
Cockbain family   *107, 161, 164-171, 207-208, 260, 294*
Communications, roads   *119-120, 263, 279ff, 304*
Courts and justice   *81ff*
Death and disease   *85*
Death and disease, funerals   *102-104*
Dixon family   *174*
Domestic life   *193ff*
Drunkenness   *117, 123, 206, 216, 253, 257*
Education   *54, 61,63, 79-80, 120, 132, 148, 200-202, 212, 216, 248, 270, 286*
Electricity   *159-160*
Fell running   *208, 222, 254, 292*
Fisher family   *ch 8 passim*
Fisher, Abraham   *ch 9 passim*
Fisher, Abraham, European tour   *86-89*
Fisher, Isaac   *42-45, 47*
Flooding   *161, 170-171, 304, 311*

Gaskell family 211, 215, 238, 288
Glaramara 160, 188, 296ff
Grange 37-38
Hearths and heating 26-29, 157
Holme, Jane and Richard 107-112
Honey family 128, 137, 151, 157ff
Houses, 'Great Rebuilding' 15
Hunting 64-65
Jackson family 219-222, 236, 239ff
Jopson family 16, 22, 38, 49, 107, 111, 214, 224, 234, 238, 288
Land tenure 15
Leconfield Estate 107, 112, 125, 156, 185, 212, 215, 222, 237, 247-48, 255, 296-297
Lodore inn 68
Lyzzick Hall 51, 68
Marshall family 49, 50, 79, 102, 105-106, 124, 185-186, 247, 297
Mechanics, Free Independent and United Order of 79, 117, 192, 193, 202, 257, 293
Mining, Honister 39, 113-114, 181-186
Mining, wad 39, 53
Missionaries, domestic 117, 192, 255ff, 265
Mountain View ch 12 passim
Music, traditional 7-10
National Trust 18, 49, 107, 166, 292, 308
New Cottages ch 11 passim
Newby, George 54-55, 67
Nuttall family 251ff, 260ff, 267ff
Pepper family, other 117, 173, 213ff, 215ff, 226, 253, 264, 289, 290
Pepper family, Seatoller House 113ff, 184

Police 80-82, 85, 253
Politics in the valley   118
Post Office   153, 194, 212, 229-230, 272
Rechabites   114-115, 259
Religion, Borrowdale chapel 53-54
Religion, Crosthwaite   78-79, 126
Religion, dissenters   33, 116, 256, 265
Rescues, various   161, 165, 166-167, 165, 169, 208, 222, 224, 234, 276-278
Romantic poets   43, 76, 77
Seathwaite farm   16, 52, 667
Seatoller barn 48-49, 126, 296, 308
Seatoller House, building   11ff, 16-28, 29-30
Seatoller House, guest house ch 9 passim
Seatoller House, library and furnishings   91-96
Seatoller, farm 49
Shopping   142, 193ff
Spedding family   74ff, 83
Sport   63ff, 132, 148, 202-206, 257, 269, 293
Stanger family 75ff, 83, 86-89
Stephenson family   77
Temperance movements   115-117, 192, 259
Thorneythwaite farm 49-50, 67
Top Row   233ff
Tourism   ch 10 passim, 296ff
Trade unions 191-193
Trevelyan family   107, 127-128, 132ff, 140, 146, 162, 166, 170, 172-173
Tricouni Club 160, 171, 297
Trinity Hunts 107, 127, 132ff, 166
Water supplies, hot and cold   13-14, 131, 157, 186ff, 197, 212,

323

238, 250, 297
Weir family 208, 305ff
Wills and inventories 30, 34, 35-36, 40, 49, 101
Woodend family 128, 148ff, 150, 151, 152-154, 157, 203, 279
Yew Tree, building 16